Dorothy G. Maclean

Memoirs of an Ordinary Mystic

Also by Dorothy Maclean

The Living Silence

Wisdoms

To Hear the Angels Sing

The Soul of Canada

To Honor the Earth

Choices of Love

Call of the Trees

Seeds of Inspiration:
Deva Flower Messages

Come Closer:
Messages from the God Within

Foreign language editions for selected books include Spanish, Portugese, French, Japanese, and German.

Memoirs of an Ordinary Mystic

Cover Photograph by Geoff Dalglish
Frontispiece Portrait by Ron Rabin
Edited by Catherine MacCoun

ISBN 10: 0-936878-31-2
ISBN 13: 978-0-936878-31-7

Maclean, Dorothy
Memoirs of an Ordinary Mystic/Dorothy Maclean

Library of Congress Control Number: 2010934447

First Edition: July 2010

Printed in the United States of America

0 9 8 7 6 5 4 3 2 1

Published by LorianPress
2204 E Grand Ave
Everett, WA 98201

www.lorian.org

Dedication

I dedicate these Memoirs to my parents, as they were not only responsible for my entry into the world, but for surrounding me with a love so powerful and constant, that it overcame all my inborn hostilities against life.

Acknowledgments

First and foremost, to Judy McAllister for spending countless hours at Kinkos making readable copies of my early messages that she found wilting in forgotten files, and then urging me to carry on writing my memoirs. That done, Hiro Boga gave me helpful suggestions and support. Julie Spangler and Judy McAllister spent endless hours at the computer with me, refining and expanding the content. Editor Catherine MacCoun took a story told sequentially and turned it into a story told very differently. Jeremy Berg and Freya Secrest, through Lorian Press, have laboured lovingly to bring this book to print. Finally, to the friends and associates who have supported and encouraged me to write my story. You all know who you are!!!

Another person I want to acknowledge is my younger brother Donald. His wonderfully wise action in initiating a legacy which ensured that I always had enough money to cover my expenses throughout the years was a great boon! I doubt that Donald knew much of my appreciation; he died a young man. Maybe acknowledging him here will inspire readers to help others in similar ways.

Contents

Chapter 1

If we choose our parents and our birthplace—which I believe we do—then I chose well. As the middle child of three, and the only daughter of Marjorie Chambers and Gordon Ball Maclean, I grew up in an atmosphere of love. My father, a banker, was quiet with a dry sense of humor. He was the sort of person others turned to when they were in trouble. I adored him and he adored me back. Mother was the active core of our household. When she died, I remember an aunt saying that my uncles had lost the favorite of their five sisters. "Everyone always felt better when your mother entered the room." I suppose all small children think their parents are the most marvelous people in the world. A great blessing of my life is that as I got older, I continued to admire them, and to find that others admired them too.

At my mother's urging, my father chose to forego advancement in order to stay in our hometown of Guelph, 60 miles west of Toronto, Canada. That meant that we could remain in the lovely Victorian home where he had grown up. It also meant that we didn't have a lot of money. I am thankful my parents made that choice, for it afforded me a stable, small town upbringing, close to nature. The grounds surrounding our house were extensive, and I could roam the adjoining woods whenever I liked. I considered these woods my own, not only because I was the only person who ever seemed to walk in them, but because I knew and loved all the wildflowers and trees that grew there.

I cannot remember ever eating out in all the twenty years I lived in Guelph. It was an era when people lived a home-centered life: provincial, but very secure and supportive. The days and weeks unfolded with a predictable rhythm. My school was a mile and a quarter from home: a distance I walked—or, more often, ran—four times a day, as everyone went home for dinner at noon. I was also allowed to walk to the town library on my own, and did so nearly every day. In the evenings, we gathered in the back parlor with the portrait of my great-great uncle (George Brown, father of the confederation, leader of the Liberal Party, owner of the *Toronto Globe*) gazing down at us from over the fireplace. Charlie McCarthy, George Burns and Gracie Allen entertained us over the radio while my brothers and I did our homework and my mother sat mending. On Sundays, the cinema

1

and all the stores were closed. We got dressed up to attend the service at the Presbyterian church where my father was treasurer, followed by an afternoon of Sunday school and a casual family supper in the back parlor instead of the dining room, a variation on the weekly routine that I especially loved.

The seasons, too, offered predictable delights. In the fall we would rake the leaves into great piles and jump into them, then burn them. The fragrance of burning leaves is something I miss now that bonfires are banned. In the winter, my father would pour water on our terraces and we would skid noisily along the ice on tin trays. As our house was built on a hill, we could ski or toboggan without leaving our property, and the whole family would go ice-skating on the nearby river. Snowdrops were the first heralds of spring, followed by a succession of wildflowers that reappeared each year like long lost friends. Summers were hot, and wonderful. In July we sometimes rented a cottage on Lake Huron. I adored the sun and spent hours lying blissfully on the sand dunes.

I have often been asked if I had any spiritual experiences in my youth. No, I was excessively ordinary. Once, while sucking my thumb, I saw a figure that I took to be Jesus, floating on our front lawn. When I mentioned this to a friend at kindergarten, she told me it meant that I would die within seven years. Not until the seven years were up did I feel free of the threat. That was enough to put me off visions.

What I did have, from an early age, was one abiding question: "what is the purpose of life?" This question was always in my mind.

Though I have many happy memories of growing up, inwardly I sometimes felt at odds with the world. I can trace this feeling back to another distressing experience in kindergarten. Our teacher announced that, on one particular day, we were to come to school in the afternoon instead of the morning. I was so excited by the novelty of this that I counted the days and could think of little else. In due course, I showed up at my usual classroom in the afternoon, only to find it filled with different children and headed by a different teacher. I had come on the wrong day. The teacher looked at me pityingly and, in front of the whole class kissed me, saying, "Poor little girl, you forgot." Forgot! I had been obsessed with the idea. I couldn't get the words out to explain myself. When I realized I was misunderstood by that teacher, I concluded that I was misunderstood by the entire world, and that the entire world was somehow against me.

2

In itself it's a trivial incident, but I believe we all are born with certain issues or tendencies carried over from previous lives. Reacting out of all proportion to some minor upset when we are small often signals the re-emergence of one of those issues. For me, it was a tendency to feel isolated, misunderstood, unsupported and guilty. From that afternoon on, I was self-conscious and shy, and perpetually expected the worst. I set up a protective barrier between myself and the world, and did not allow myself to feel loved. Had I not been brought up in an atmosphere of affection and constant support, that barrier might have proved impenetrable. As I say, I chose well when I chose my parents. Their love got through to me.

In my shyness, I sought solace in the company of nature, my daydreams, or a good book. I was fascinated by Egypt from the age of eight, and later devoured the writings of Egyptologists J. H. Breasted and Sir Alan Gardiner. I also read volumes of Grolier's *Child's Book of Knowledge*, attracted mostly to the first category (the universe) and the last category (fairy tales)—a strange combination. Since I loved to stay up and read long past the time my parents had set for "lights out," I came up with a way to fool them. The grandfather clock on the landing near my room clicked loudly exactly 62 seconds before chiming the hour. I would listen for the click, then count the seconds and flip my light switch at the exact moment the clock struck. My parents would hear nothing except the chime. I can still count seconds with uncommon accuracy.

In high school, my shyness got worse, for I suffered from acne and believed that no boy would ever like me. My parents' social circle organized dances at which the boys would line up on one side of the room, sizing up the girls in long gowns lined up on the opposite side and trying to summon up the courage to ask for a dance. I never expected to be asked, and seldom was. Once again, I escaped into books and a vivid and elaborate fantasy life.

My older brother went to the University of Toronto, and it was understood that my younger brother would also attend university. Not wishing to add to my parents' financial burden, I resigned myself to attending a technical school instead. My maiden Aunt Ina came to my rescue, offering to give me the money she had been intending to leave me in her will so that I could apply it to college tuition. In those days, I approached decisions pragmatically, so I researched all the college programs I could afford, and made a list of pros and cons. I figured that with a B.A. in Secretarial Science from the University of Western Ontario (the best program of its kind in Canada), I would always be able to get a good job, no matter where I traveled. That proved true—and abundantly useful, given the unconventional turn my life was later to take—yet my heart was never really in it. What I really wanted to be was an artist, but I doubted that I was talented enough to earn a living at it. Later I would discover that I was actually pretty good at drawing and painting—and pretty awful at typing and shorthand. Passing those two courses proved quite a struggle. Nevertheless, by cramming during the summers, I managed to complete the four-year program in three years.

Going to a university where no one knew me—or my background as a wall flower—was liberating. I was invited to join the sorority of my choice, Kappa Alpha Theta, and lived at their house. At Western I went in for sports, and ultimately became captain of the badminton team. We traveled to meet other university teams, but I always went to pieces when playing in public. The same pattern also came to the fore in public speaking. The first time I spoke in front of a university class, I suffered such stage fright that I was literally petrified and had to be carried off the stage. After that I vowed never to make another public speech. But of course, never is a long time: I have since broken that vow a thousand times over.

At Western I managed to acquire my first boyfriend, an excellent badminton player. We went to most events together, as I relished all the extracurricular activities that university life had to offer. I loved going to the large dance hall at Port Stanley, where the big bands played. There I enjoyed the Dorseys, Duke Ellington, Benny Goodman, and Benny Carter.

Like most university students, we indulged in searching late night discussions about the meaning of life. In my early teens I had read a book about an Indian guru which had made a big impression on me. I didn't know why it was significant then, and can't remember the book now, but it led me to questions to which I wanted answers. My conventional Protestant upbringing had not explained to my satisfaction what life was really about. I didn't make much headway with this question while in college. In Canada during the 1930's, books on spiritual subjects, especially on "foreign" religions or unorthodox views, were hard to come by and rarely mentioned. With the all-knowingness of youth, my fellow students and I concluded that no

4

one had ever really found any answers.

World War II broke out during my final year at Western, and changed the lives of my generation, dispersing us all over the world. On the day Canada declared war, my older brother joined the Signals, choosing it, as he told me many years later, because he didn't want to kill anyone. He came through the Dieppe raid (a trial attack on the German-held French coast before the actual invasion, mostly by Canadian soldiers) physically intact but deeply critical of an exercise in which so many Canadians had been slaughtered. My boyfriend Jim joined up, and was eventually killed in Holland.

During that period, many young Canadian women were being hired by Great Britain for wartime jobs in the U.S., because we were part of the British Commonwealth, and because it was difficult to bring office staff from Britain across the submarine-infested Atlantic. An employment agency sent me on an interview for such a job, and I landed it. The exact nature of the position was unclear. I was told only that I would be employed by British Security Coordination in New York, doing some sort of war work. Because of this vagueness, some mothers feared that their daughters were being recruited as white slaves and refused to let them go. My parents had no such objection, as they knew the family of my interviewer for the job, although they and all my other friends and relatives—especially Aunt Ina, who had lived in New York—worried that I would feel lonely and overwhelmed in the city.

I dithered for a while, attracted by the adventure but reluctant to oppose my family and friends. Finally I resolved to accept the job— only to hit an unexpected snag. When they learned that I was only twenty-one, the people at the employment agency felt that I was too young. By then I was determined to go, and refused to take no for an answer. My tenacity paid off, but as a concession to my age it was arranged that I would travel to New York with a chaperone. This was Sheena Govan, whose influence would forever alter the course of my life. Later I learned that Sheena's home in Canada was a duplex shared by my grandmother—it seemed that Sheena and I were definitely meant to meet.

Looking back on these and other events, I've come to the conclusion that early on in life, our soul guides us toward a destiny that we will someday choose freely, but haven't chosen yet. Our conscious decision-making process has little to do with it. In that sense, our will is not entirely free when we are young. I believe that I was meant to go to New York, and that if I had allowed myself to be talked out of it, something else would have happened to steer me there. In youth, we are recapitulating past life learning —positive or negative— and being steered toward the future in a mostly unconscious way. We only come into full freedom around the age of twenty-eight or so, when the steering stops and we have real choices to make, based on self-awareness.

So I left my native land to see the world, still not suspecting how much of it I was going to see. On my departure, my father said to me, "Daughter, we have brought you up, we've done the best we could for you. Now you are on your own and we trust you. You won't get any money from us because we haven't got any. But here is some advice: never drink more than six double whiskies in a row."

Sheena, my designated chaperone, met me at Union Station in Toronto. A beautiful and cultured Scot, she was seven years my senior. During the train ride, I worried about how much to tip the porter, but Sheena knew all about that sort of thing. We had been booked in at the Beekman Towers, and together took a suite there. Then we presented ourselves to our office high up in Rockefeller Center, where we were asked to sign the Official Secrets Act and swear to stay silent about our work. We had just joined the British Secret Intelligence Service! I walked the streets of New York in a daze. I was a spy! What fun!

The work turned out to be mainly secretarial, although the men we worked for seemed glamorous, at least to this backwoods Canadian. Some were famous, like Eric Maschwitz, the writer of *The Nightingale Sang in Berkeley Square* and *At the Balalaika*. Many of them were highly educated Oxford and Cambridge dons, with what seemed to me snobbish British accents—accents that I later came to like very much—and most were widely traveled. It was a different world for us provincials. A number of us got very excited when we learned that a real lord was coming to join us. When he appeared, all our fantasies collapsed, for what we saw was a short little fellow with glasses who did not look at all like my imagined knight on a white charger. We had a lot of illusions to be dispelled.

Sheena and I eventually made our own friends. Hers were from the world of music. (I learned later that she could have been a concert pianist.) With Betty Judd, a friend who shared my enjoyment of badminton, I took a tiny apartment in the Beaux Arts complex. We were fascinated by the Murphy bed that folded up into the wall. Together we explored Manhattan, read *The New Yorker* and *Downbeat* and felt quite cosmopolitan. We went to Radio City Music Hall so frequently that the doorman eventually came to recognize us and would wave us through for free. Sheena and I stayed in touch, and occasionally would dine out together. That was most embarrassing to me: I somehow had the idea that women should be accompanied by men when dining out. I loved being with the beautiful and refined Sheena, except when a migraine headache made her dejected and miserable. Then, I regret to say, I was ashamed to be seen with her because she looked so wretched. She tried to educate me musically, giving me records like the Romeo and Juliet Overture by Tchaikovsky, while I, who loved blues and jazz, tried to interest her in Billie Holiday's rendition of "Strange Fruit".

The New York office in which I worked coordinated British security intelligence and special operations for both North and South America. It was headed by William Stephenson, whose life has been chronicled in *The Quiet Canadian* (or *Room 3603*) by H. Montgomery Hyde, and in the more sensational but sometimes inaccurate *A Man Called Intrepid*. As clericals, we only glimpsed snippets of Stephenson's work, which included obtaining essential supplies for Britain, investigating enemy activities, taking measures against sabotage to British shipping and property, and mobilizing American public opinion in support of Britain's war effort. Years later, I saw on TV the tail end of a program called "Intrepid's Girls," in which two eighty-year old women were being interviewed about their World War II work. I didn't recognize them, but was struck by how little they appeared to know about what was going on in other countries in those days. Because of my subsequent moves from New York to other intelligence stations in the world, I had gained a broader view, though my glimpses of the world of intrigue were still somewhat limited. Staff members in the British Secret Service were designated numbers that were changed as we changed countries, but I was never 006!

Coming from Canada, I had not realized the extent of pro-German and anti-British sentiment in the U. S. It led Franklin Roosevelt, who was pro-British and anti-Nazi in spite of the defeatist reports of his Ambassador to Britain, Joseph Kennedy, to be very careful, politically. In the United States there were many dummy corporations operated by the vast German industrial cartel of I.G. Farben, so there were economic reasons to keep the U.S. out of the war. There were also ideologues like the isolationists, whose slogan was "America First," and who were a dominant force in keeping the U.S. out of the war.

American public opinion was shaken and re-formed by the bombing of Pearl Harbor. I vividly remember that day in New York, when white-faced Americans stopped in the street, utterly unnerved and incredulous. In contrast, we in the office were jubilant to realize that the Commonwealth would no longer be alone in fighting the Nazis. They had conquered country after country in Europe, leaving only Britain and Russia to fight them. At the time, the U. S. did not have a coordinated intelligence service, so the Americans came to Stephenson for direction. With the help of the SIS, the American Office of Strategic Services (OSS) which later became the CIA, was formed. In our office we met its founder, "Wild Bill" Donovan, and other Americans. The British had already been collaborating with the FBI.

We Canadians, who constituted most of the female staff, had good working relationships with our British bosses who, I think, liked our free-speaking manner. Though I knew my work was connected to something very important, it was sometimes boring, and after about nine months, I began to feel restless. One day I complained of this to my boss. His roommate, whose area of jurisdiction was Panama, said, "You're not happy? Go to Panama. They need secretaries there." I didn't think much of the idea at first, but when I shared it with Betty, she said, "Why not?"

Indeed, why not? When we questioned others in the office who had been in Latin America, they all encouraged us to go, saying that we would have a whale of a time. Betty and I volunteered formally for the post, and began reading up on the area. Just for the fun of it, we dug up as many negative aspects of Panama as we could find, such as the tropical climate, the excessive rainfall, the poisonous snakes (particularly the coral snake), and the distance from home. These we listed, and as compensation for enduring such tribulations, claimed that we would require a diplomatic passport, a doubling of our salary, and a visit home before our departure for Panama. As a joke, I presented this document to my boss. To our extreme embarrassment, we were summoned to the office of Stephenson himself. He told us that although we were accepted for the posting, it was not possible to accede to all our requests. He said this with an expressionless face, and we never did find out whether or not he had realized that our document was a lark. We backed out of his office as soon as we could, feeling mightily chagrined. Betty and I became the first of many volunteers from the New York office to leave for Central and South America.

We did get to visit home before we left, but we couldn't tell family or friends anything about our work or where we were going. My doctor, an old family friend, knew I was going to the tropics because of the various injections he was asked to give me. It was fun being mysterious, and my family accepted that I was doing some sort of war work.

Traveling to Panama was a great adventure. In those days there was no night flying by our DC3s, and we stopped several times overnight at various points en route. During one stop in Houston, we were so fascinated by the Southern accents that we followed people around just to listen to them talk. Another stop was in Brownsville, Texas, where we walked across the Mexican border and back. With great glee we picked and bit into our first oranges from real trees, only to find, to our shock, that they were the bitter kind. In Mexico City, we were warned not to eat the spicy Mexican food. The next day we were glad that we had heeded this advice as many of our fellow passengers—mainly American men going to work in the Canal Zone—were experiencing the dire consequences of ignoring it.

Flying into San José, Costa Rica, we prayed that something would go wrong with the plane so we could have extra time in the place. To our delight, it seemed that our prayer was answered. One of the aircraft's engines was faulty, and we had to remain in San José for a couple of days. We checked into a good hotel and then wandered out into the streets. The day was Holy Thursday, followed by Good Friday, the most interesting days of the year for tourists because of the great Passion processions. In one, a man playing Judas was jeered and hissed and pelted with rotten eggs and tomatoes. There were lots of begging urchins in the streets, and we let ourselves be adopted by a small boy who became our guide. In the evenings we joined the local populace as they paraded around the central square of the city. In those days the senoritas were allowed to walk out only when accompanied by a duenna, all very solemn and generally dressed in black. Eventually our airplane's engine was repaired and we were off again at four in the morning. Pan Am always departed at that very early hour. We seemed to sit for ages as the plane tried out all its engines in a furious rickety dance until it achieved enough momentum to take off.

I arrived in the humid heat of Panama in my new wool suit, and quickly learned to wear lighter clothing. The vegetation grew so quickly in that heat that we could almost see it coming up. At our living quarters we had to choose between having netting on our windows to keep out insects—which made the room even hotter and stuffier—or being eaten alive by mosquitoes. We tried to adapt to the local custom of having a siesta after lunch, but the nap made us so groggy that we decided to swim at a local pool instead. The ocean was too hot to swim in. The only time I was ever cool was after an energetic and sweaty game of badminton, when, for a few moments after a shower, I felt normal.

Our office, where we lived and worked, was a separate building under the cover of the Economic Attaché of the British Legation to the Republic of Panama. It was located in the Republic and not in the Canal Zone where the Americans lived. We were a small and intimate group of about a dozen, mostly British, although we did have an exiled Russian countess. Peter Wood, our charming Head of Station, served us pink gins at eleven o'clock each morning. When I complained that I hadn't yet seen a scorpion, my helpful co-workers thoughtfully arranged one next to my food in the refrigerator.

The work was interesting, and we saw more aspects of it than we had in the huge New York office. I would sometimes be sent to the U. S. letter censorship authorities, where I poured over all incoming and outgoing mail in Panama to extract anything that might be of interest to our office: perhaps a letter that made mention of a known Axis sympathizer, or one that didn't make sense and might therefore be written in code. Our office had sub-stations in the region, which sent in intelligence reports of Axis activity and political incidents in their particular countries, which we then had to evaluate and report to HQ.

One of the staff was a courier named Robert who made regular trips to northern South America to pick up intelligence reports. Robert was slightly dyslexic and would put numbers in the wrong order. As all our codes used numbers, chaos would result. We named this malady "Robertitus." However, he was a wonderfully kind man and would return from Venezuela laden with exotic orchids for us. I enjoyed sitting and typing in the office wearing these unusual and beautiful flowers. That was something to write home about.

My weekly letter home was often difficult to write, because I couldn't talk about the all-consuming work. Instead I filled it with chatter about my social life. In the American Canal Zone there was said to be a ratio of five hundred English-speaking men to one woman, owing to the many hundreds of U. S. personnel who had been sent to guard the Canal. Betty and I had more requests for dates than we could ever have wished for. As a former wallflower, I relished my newfound popularity. We joined the Patriettes, a group that arranged dances at various U. S. military camps in the Zone, and excursions into the jungle. One evening, our Russian countess, Ariadne, gave a party and served various kinds of caviar. I had expected that caviar would be the most delicious gourmet food one could ever experience. Instead I got fishy eggs. What a disillusionment!

Betty and I were very happy that we had chosen to travel, and wanted to do even more of it. I applied for posts offered in Guatemala and British Honduras (now Belize). I particularly fancied the latter, as I was told that the office there, run by zoologist Ivan T. Sanderson, was on a yacht situated by the coral reefs off Belize. But I must have over-reached myself, for I received from New York a telegram that, when decoded, read: "This is not, repeat not, a travel agency."

Chapter 2

The female staff in our office often talked about an absent member of our staff, an officer who was undergoing instruction near Toronto at Camp X, the British training center for secret agents. They said he would make a good boyfriend for Betty or me. He was a mysterious figure, of unknown nationality, described as being brilliant but eccentric. For instance, he had been seen sitting Buddha style, something I had never encountered in my Canadian upbringing, for long periods under a tree. I was so intrigued by those stories that I found myself writing my name as though I were his wife: Mrs. John Wood.

When he finally arrived back in Panama, I went on being intrigued. He was an untidy redhead who seemed very English, yet led people to believe that he was Norwegian. He was clearly very intelligent, but revealed little of himself. I dated him at times, along with many others. We talked of spiritual matters, and he was the first person to give me answers about the meaning of life that satisfied me. When John introduced me to the idea of reincarnation, my search about the purpose of life began to get answers; of course many lives were needed. I was delighted to come across clues to my constant searching. He spoke of the lost continent of Atlantis as if it were a vital part of the history of our planet. I'd never had conversations like this before, yet recognized them as something that my soul had been craving.

One day John asked me to marry him. Although I was pleased that he had asked, I was having far too much fun to want to settle down. Besides, he was definitely odd. Despite my initial refusal, he went on saying, "When are you going to marry me?" as if he took it for granted that eventually I would and it was only a question of when. Betty, though, was adamantly against the match. "Don't do it," she warned.

When John arrived at my desk one day to show me a telegram transferring him to Buenos Aires, I instantly knew that I had to marry him. This was the first deep intuition I had ever had, and it was so strong and persuasive that there was nothing to do but follow it. After a hasty search for a long white gown —for, to my surprise, this unorthodox fellow wanted a traditional white wedding—we were married by the Anglican Bishop of the Canal Zone. When I phoned my family in Canada to give them the news, they expressed surprise and delight, but I could tell that they were disappointed to have missed the wedding. My mother had always dreamed of seeing me married on the family homestead. Wars do tend to disturb plans.

After the wedding we flew south. It was only when he produced a British passport at the airport that I learned that my new husband was not, after all, a Norwegian. We stayed overnight in capital cities like Lima and Santiago, and loved seeing the dry west coast of South America, and sampling local food in the cities. Flying over the Andes from Santiago was exciting. As DC3s could only attain a modest altitude, we seemed to almost touch the sides of the mountains. Yet we flew high enough that we all had to use oxygen masks, for this was back in the days of unpressurized cabins.

In Buenos Aires, we lived in a small hotel, ate our meals in the many wonderful restaurants, and learned to drink wine noon and night as the locals did. Our work was in the secret intelligence section of the British Embassy. We were well off financially. I continued to receive the equivalent of my New York salary, which was lavish by Argentine standards, so we lived on my earnings, while John put his own in the bank. We were made honorary members of the Hurlingham Club, which was so British, snobbish and Colonel Blimpish (it seemed Argentineans weren't allowed there as they might have polluted the swimming pool!) that we joined the Norwegian Rowing Club instead. John, who had a degree in Modern Languages from Cambridge, spoke Norwegian so perfectly that the Norwegians there, mostly Captains and crew of whaling ships, accepted him as one of their countrymen. On Sundays off we rowed in the many inlets of the River Tigre, seldom having to repeat our route. It was strange seeing our "enemies" out rowing as well. One could recognize the Japanese by the rising sun on their oars. We met few Argentineans, however, for the secret nature of our work tended to isolate us socially.

We were in Argentina during the revolution which brought Farrell into the presidency, the one before Peron came into power. I was excited by this turn of events, and upset that I, as a woman, was not allowed out into the crowded streets on my own to witness what was happening firsthand. Later in the day I did get outside with John. The revolution was not bloody; merely a march from military barracks to the Casa Rosada (the Pink House, equivalent to the White House), but young ruffians took advantage of the general confusion to wreak havoc in the streets. Amid all the agitated milling around, what I remember most distinctly were the youths who put out their hands to stop the streetcars, ordered everyone out, toppled the cars over, and then set them on fire. After I had watched one boy do this, I looked him straight in the eye as his mother might have done. He had the grace to look ashamed and turn away.

Although John had what seemed to me sensible ideas and answers about the meaning of life—simple truths like "No one can be human and not make a mistake,"—he would not tell me what his background was, or where or how he had acquired his unusual knowledge. The more I questioned him, the more he clammed up. Eventually I stopped asking. Once I found him sitting cross-legged on the floor of our sitting room in the middle of the night. I had no idea what he was doing and he explained nothing. I felt frustrated and upset that he would not share with me what was obviously of primary importance in his life. But what could I do? As I had known that I had to marry him and continued to trust that intuition, I felt I had to put up with the consequences.

We went on a Brazilian holiday via coffee-scented Santos and the huge city of Saõ Paulo, then by train to Rio de Janeiro. There John left me for hours in a park while he went to visit friends on his own. When the friends discovered that he had his wife with him, they insisted he bring me to visit them. The next day John took me to their suburban home. The doorway was topped by a symbol of a winged heart, and a Service of Universal Worship was being held inside. During the service, a candle was lit in honor of each of the six main world religions, and the group shared readings from various sacred books. It was a simple but impressive ceremony. I had always believed that all religions lead to the same God, so when the leader, Shabaz Best, asked if I would like to join their group, I said yes. I was told that they were Sufis, following the Indian Master Hazrat Inayat Khan, who had come to the West in 1910 and died in 1927. Shabaz showed me a picture of Inayat Khan and said, "Of course, you know who this is."

When I said I didn't know, he flashed John a disapproving look and explained that Inayat Khan was the greatest man since Jesus. I didn't believe that for a moment. Though I thought I had discarded my Christian background, I still felt that no one was the equal of Jesus, the Son of God. In fact I spent the next four years trying to make nonsense of Shabaz's assertion, mainly by bringing up the subject of Inayat Khan to people who had met him. At the very mention of his name, these older people's expressions would invariably soften, and they would become more loving and tell me something favorable about him. I learned of some of his personal quirks, such as liking to eat peanuts while riding on trains, but I never came across anything negative about him. After four years I had to surrender my bias and recognize that Inayat Khan, like Jesus, was a man of vast spiritual stature.

Shabaz initiated me into the esoteric Sufi order (I didn't know then what esoteric meant) and gave me Sufi teachings to study, as well as a morning breathing exercise. Some dictionaries state that Sufis are Moslems, but Hazrat Inayat Khan (commonly called Murshid, which means Master) taught that Sufis were the mystics of all religions, and that all religions were deserving of respect. I began to appreciate the many different approaches to spirituality, and was happy to be coming to understand and share some of my husband's interests. To this day, I still love and respect Inayat's simple and direct teachings, though I have not remained active in the Sufi Order.

In pro-Axis Argentina there were many Germans and lots of scope for intelligence gathering. We worked long hours there, and life was bounded by the office and rowing on the Tigre. After nine months, we were moved across the River Plate to Montevideo, capital of pro-Allied Uruguay, a smaller country with few Germans. Flying over the very wide river we could see the remains of the German battleship, the Graf Spee, its hulk still protruding prominently out of the water. Later, I heard its remarkable story. In 1939, during the Battle of the River Plate, there had been an exchange of fire between the Graf Spee and three small British ships, in which all were damaged. The Graf Spee headed for Montevideo harbor, while two remaining British ships, the cruisers Ajax and Achilles, followed; all these ships continued to exchange shots and incur more damage. International law permits refuge in harbor for only forty-eight hours. The Graf Spee requested and received an extension on this limit. After that, the German captain, who had been very well known and liked in Montevideo and Buenos Aires before the war, sent his crew ashore in lifeboats and scuttled the ship. Shortly after he committed suicide in a hotel room in Montevideo.

John and I were part of a small group of seven people working under the cover of Ferrocarril Central del Uruguay (Central Uruguayan

Railway) headed by its British boss, Hugh Grindley. At that time the railways in most South American countries, including Argentina and Uruguay, were run by the British. Hugh Grindley was very influential—I heard him called "El Dictador Ingles"—and worked in an enormous office guarded by a huge Great Dane. We and the Anglo-Uruguayan staff were his meek subjects. I remember the Grindleys inviting us to dinner, a meal made memorable to me chiefly because we ate a strange new vegetable called avocado, served with tomato sauce.

We lived in a delightful house in the suburb of Colón where we enjoyed the trees and gardens after the big city environment of Buenos Aires. Again, we were very much on our own. We had an illiterate Guarani Indian servant, whom we called Faustina after her black husband, Faust, who was our gardener. John spoke Spanish with them but, being hopeless at languages myself, I had to rely on other means of communication. It was Faustina's outstanding intelligence that made this possible. She would notice how I did things, or what I cooked, and would replicate what she observed. A favorite dessert of mine was Brown Betty, and she produced this almost every other day. Their daughter Celeste would write down, from her mother's intricate memory, the daily transactions in buying food and other household necessities.

John and I would swim in the ocean, but not before a priest had blessed the waters to open the official swimming season. John was once severely reprimanded by a policeman on the beach because he was not wearing a bathing suit top, which was illegal even for men. We bussed to and from the office, ate at the office dining room and at home in the evening. I recall that both Argentineans and Uruguayans seldom ate anything but meat. Vegetables or salads might be served, but were normally left untouched.

As usual, my job consisted of taking dictation and typing letters or reports based on the intelligence gathered about the country. Argentina, being neutral but pro-Axis, was full of spies of all nationalities. In friendlier Uruguay, John and others were concerned with intercepting and monitoring radio messages from German ships, for the area was an important source of food for the Allies, now threatened by the submarines that were lying in wait to destroy cargo ships. We ran double agents, people who ostensibly worked for the enemy. When I visited Montevideo fifty years later, I found I remembered nothing of the city, unlike the vivid memories I have of many places in Buenos Aires, with its beautiful French-style architecture. Looking back, I realized that we were deliberately kept from mixing with people, for how could I have explained that I was working in Uruguay in a business of which I knew nothing and where I didn't speak a word of the language?

While we were in Uruguay I became pregnant. John immediately said that he would leave me if I had a baby. He seemed to fear having that responsibility. I did not have any particular desire for children, and was afraid of having to bring up a child alone in a foreign country. So we found a clinic and I had an abortion. Though I disliked the process, I have never regretted that decision, and believe it was the right one for me. It was in Uruguay that an office member told me that John was the most selfish person she had ever met. At that time I didn't agree with her. Anyway, I had known I must marry him and that was that.

Chapter 3

As the war raged on in Europe, John and I longed to be in the thick of things. We decided to leave Montevideo, and traveled to Britain on the *Rippingham Grange*, which was the largest refrigeration unit afloat at the time, built to carry Argentine meat. We raced across the Atlantic to Freetown, Sierra Leone, where we would join a convoy of assorted ships. I hoped to go ashore there, as I had never been in Africa, and was annoyed that John was permitted to do so while I was required to stay aboard the ship. To appease me, he brought back some African earth, which I spread on the deck and walked on, thus enabling me to say I had walked on African soil!

The ship, which normally would have held ten passengers, now had twenty, consisting mainly of Anglo-Argentineans, Anglo-Chileans and four of us British Security Coordination members, all volunteering for war work. We were a happy group, organizing ourselves to prepare for the future. We would get up early to exercise, arranged useful classes such as Morse code, taught by John, and games to be enjoyed by ourselves as well as the crew.

Our convoy included a submarine and several destroyers and cruisers, our protectors. Among the many vessels was an aircraft carrier, whose planes used to dip down to peek at us, for our ship was the only one that carried women. We were on the fast Commodore ship, but all vessels in the convoy had to keep to the speed of its slowest member, which was the eight knots of one little boat generating clouds of black smoke in its efforts to keep up. The route that we took along that part of Africa to Britain was the target of Nazi U-boats, and during the previous year only one out of eight ships had arrived safely. Despite this, I had no sense of danger. It was all a great adventure, and I enjoyed the trip tremendously.

From the Mediterranean another convoy steamed out to join us for the voyage to Britain. Instead of landing at the usual English southern ports like Southampton or Liverpool, we went around Ireland and docked at Oban in Scotland. I took this event personally, for the first part of the Old World that I saw was the Maclean island of Mull. That cost me drinks all around! After the expanses of the Americas, Oban and its environs looked doll-sized. Immediately we were plunged into the shortages of a wartime country, but being on official business, we had no difficulty in obtaining tickets on the crowded train going south.

On approaching London we heard a loud explosion, and learned what had been so carefully hidden in broadcasts from Britain: London was being besieged by flying bombs, V-1 rockets. We eventually got used to these and, like others in London, would listen to the engine overhead and hope the noise would continue. As I recall, it took twenty-six seconds of ominous silence after the engine cut out for the V-1 to hit the ground and explode. Later, the V-2s gave no such warning.

We were both taken on at the Counter-Espionage Section of Britain's Secret Intelligence Service, and settled down in blacked-out, bomb-besieged London. I loved the city, even in its shabby, unpainted, wartime garb. To me it was a thrill to see places made familiar by books—Harley Street, Wimpole Street, Baker Street, Piccadilly Circus—and to travel on the extensive underground. The eccentricity of the English was a surprise to me. On London streets, I would sometimes see Africans in headdresses six feet high, and aristocrats decked out like tramps. No one paid them the slightest attention. This was very different from North America, where people tended to dress alike in the current fashion. Though I was glad to have grown up in the general freedom and access to sports that Canada offered, as an adult I was coming to prefer the tolerance and sophistication of the British. They seemed more civilized somehow.

In spite of the shortages and meager rations, the constant bombing, the worrying news of battles, the death and destruction all around, the British people shone. The whole nation shone. I am sometimes asked how I, a spiritual person, could have taken part in a war. In my experience, the war brought out the best in everyone. People accepted what came up and coped, generally cheerfully. In wartime London, people were united in working for the common good and gave up their personal agendas, making the spirit of the place wonderful, purer and higher than I have ever come across anywhere, before or since.

One of the first things we did in London was look up the Sufis. On our way to one of their meetings in suburban Bromley, a V-bomb exploded behind us just as our train was entering Penge tunnel. We were in the last car, which got the worst of it. John was later upset that his intuition had not warned him to take a car further along in the train. All the glass shattered, including the lights, and for three minutes in complete darkness we could feel blood trickling down our faces from where the flying glass had hit us. When the train pulled up at the end of the tunnel, doctors and nurses were already waiting to look after us. That incredibly fast response demonstrated how marvelously London and its outlying districts were organized to deal with such incidents. We turned up late at the Sufi meeting with our heads turbaned in bandages, looking very outlandish.

I was in my husband's country—even though he hated to admit being English—and often we spent the weekend with his parents at Waggoners Wells Cottage in Hampshire, over an hour's journey from London. The word cottage was a misnomer, for it was quite a large house. Because of gasoline rationing there were few private cars, and we could do little sightseeing, though I do remember being amazed to see Silbury Hill, an enormous pyramid-shaped artificial hill of unknown origin. Brought up as I was in a country that had no ancient architectural past, Silbury Hill seemed incredible to me, but in England it was just taken for granted, as was nearby Stonehenge. I loved the beauty of the many Gothic cathedrals, particularly Wells, with its inverted arch and moat.

I liked and admired my in-laws, but always felt uncultured in comparison to them. My father-in-law was the most erudite person I had ever met. He had traveled the world, and was interested in many subjects. One of his hobbies was growing orchids. He had had to cut back severely on the number of plants he grew because the coal ration gave him little heat for his greenhouses. Still, to have orchids in a land of so many privations seemed a great luxury. I used to try to make myself useful by clipping the grass around rocks and borders at Waggoners Wells, something I had often done at home in Guelph, but in the wet climate of Britain the grass grew so prodigiously that I gave up after a while. My mother-in-law was unfailingly cordial, but I couldn't tell what she really thought of me. I lacked confidence and was always trying to figure out how to ingratiate myself.

During these visits I learned a few things about John that he had never mentioned: that he was an only child, that he had refused to go to school at Winchester, where his parents had enrolled him, and that he had a substantial private income. This came as a shock to me, since in Argentina he had pleaded the need to save money by living on my earnings alone. By then, I had come to recognize how secretive my husband was. This wasn't obvious in the beginning—not even when I learned on our honeymoon that he was English and not, as I had believed, Norwegian. I was accustomed to not really knowing what was going on and to assuming that nothing was quite as it seemed, for I was working among spies in war time, in countries where I didn't speak the language. In that context, John's enigmatic quality had at first been part of his glamour. But as our marriage grew longer without seeming to grow any more intimate, I gradually realized that withholding information was more than a professional necessity with him. It was part of his character.

In the London office I met Sheena again. While I was in South America, she had been entertaining troops overseas with ENSA (Entertainments National Service Association), as an actress. We resumed our friendship, and now it acquired a new dimension, for I discovered she had a deep interest in spiritual matters. Brought up by religious parents who had founded the Faith Mission in Scotland, she had, even as a small child, been passionate to do what she called "God's will." She had had unusual inner experiences, not talked about in Christian circles. John, with his extensive esoteric and occult knowledge, helped her to frame these experiences in the larger context of spiritual and mystical development throughout the world. She had a flat in Pimlico, which at one point she lent us, until we found our own apartment on Chelsea Embankment. We would be close for a period, and then go for months without seeing each other.

Sheena was attuned to the spiritual energies of Britain and for a while lived in a trailer in Glastonbury. Occasionally we went there, at one time looking for the Chalice Well, which we finally discovered under a lot of overgrowth. This was before Wellesley Tudor Pole set up the Chalice Well Trust and the area became popular again. John and I, with our friends the Bathams, also tried to find the center of the Somerset Zodiac, an area ten miles across whose physical features, according to some, resembled the zodiac when viewed from the air. We ended up amid a huge crop of healthy nettles and brambles, and concluded that the zodiac center was one of negative energy!

Years later I stayed at the Chalice Well Trust house and met Tudor Pole. He was over ninety then, still active and definitely a Master. He was the person who, during the war, suggested that people in Britain pray for peace when Big Ben struck nine each night. Many people collaborated in this prayer. After the war, Nazi archives revealed that they had suspected some sort of powerful enemy action was being taken against them at nine each night, but had never determined exactly what it was. This to me was a good example of how inner work brings results on outer levels.

London offered us access to many groups interested in spirituality. We attended meetings of the Order of the Cross, the Marylebone Spiritualist Society, and White Eagle Lodge, where Grace Cooke channeled the very fine teachings of White Eagle. We also met local Sufis, including Vilayat, the eldest son of Hazrat Inayat Khan. At the time Vilayat was an officer in the Royal Navy, and he and John often held services of Universal Worship in our flat. All this was fascinating to me as a newcomer to spiritual endeavors. Books by Ouspensky, Gurdjieff, Steiner, Krishnamurti and Alice Bailey awakened me to different perspectives and surprising new ideas. The novels of Joan Grant rekindled my childhood interest in Egypt. I loved her book, *Winged Pharaoh*, so much that I forced it on my friends. Because of her books I viewed the First and Twelfth Dynasties as expressions of spirituality, something that was lost during other eras in Egypt. These explorations enlarged my knowledge of and belief in spirit, giving me a broad background which helped me to discriminate better between spirituality and psychic phenomena, and to accept the reality of other dimensions.

I lived in London for eight years, initially continuing to work for the SIS in the same building as Kim Philby, later famous for being a spy for Russia. At one time my boss was Colonel Philip Rea, who was in charge of propaganda and was concerned about the growing influence of Communism in the Arab world. When I mentioned this issue to John, he and his friend, Allan Batham, wrote an excellent paper entitled "An Ideological Answer to Communism". It analyzed the problem, and suggested a positive alternative, giving basic principles and vehicles for publicizing a new ideology of traditional spiritual principles stated in current laymen's language. I submitted this document to my boss, who was so impressed that he distributed it. It was even read by the Chiefs of Staff. As a result, I received an offer of promotion from secretary to officer: an offer that I declined, since I had had nothing to do with the actual writing of the paper. In another branch of the SIS, under another boss, I had been told that my work was "quite good." Unaware back then of the English penchant for understatement, I felt as if I were being damned by faint praise. The remark rankled for years.

Toward the end of the war, I left Britain for several months to work in Finland. John wanted to be in Scandinavia, particularly Norway, and when the Finnish appointment was offered to me, we thought it a good opportunity for me to go there first. In Finland, which had been defeated by its hereditary enemy Russia, my boss Rex and I were the only two SIS people, ostensibly part of the British Military Mission in Helsinki.. Although at the time the Russians were still our allies, we had a lot of difficulty liaising with them, and heard nasty stories about privileged groups running the country—not the equality that Communism preached. The Helsinki airport was under Russian control, and we were never told when planes were due to arrive or depart. The Russians might give us an hour's notice of when a plane would be leaving for Britain, and then we would rush madly to get our reports and letters into the diplomatic bag in time.

Finland was in desperate straits due to its war efforts, and everything, including water, was very strictly rationed. I remember going to Stockman's, one of the largest department stores in Europe, and finding staff manning miles of empty counters. Practically everything for sale was made of wood. I bought wooden shoes, which had cuts in the soles where the foot bent; mine did not last long as part of the sole soon flew off.

With other British Legation female staff I moved to an island home belonging to a Swedish family, and traveled back and forth to Helsinki by boat. We enjoyed swimming and kayaking in the Gulf of Finland, but I didn't enjoy having every day to eat yogurt, a new food for me. When VE day arrived, it was hard to celebrate in a country where people had a pathological hatred of our Russian ally and were mourning the victory.

I fought another kind of war in Finland. My boss, Rex, was married to a beautiful, exiled Russian who was living in Sweden as it was not diplomatic for her to go to Finland. So on social occasions I acted as Rex's hostess, and came to consider the officers my friends. The other women in the British Mission were secretaries who socialized only with enlisted men, and I went to their parties also. By associating with these two inimical groups, I tried to beat the class system. Quite apart from being brought up in Canada, a society less class-ridden than England, I had a natural antipathy to putting people into rigid compartments or to being categorized myself. When I found that both groups were uncomfortable because of my actions, I became miserable, and in 1946 decided to return to Britain.

John had remained in England, probably enjoying the freedom of being a bachelor again. It seemed to me that he did not truly welcome my return, that I was interrupting habits he had formed of going out with his men friends. I felt hurt, but accepted this as something that came with marriage.

He was contributing to our household expenses by then, so at least there was no shortage of money. Now that the war in Europe was over, we could travel freely, enjoying delightful skiing holidays in Norway with a Norwegian friend John had met at Cambridge. About a year after VE day we attended a Young Sufi gathering in Holland and met members of Hazrat Inayat Khan's family, many of whom lived in Holland. I have a clear memory of listening to the sitar being played by Musharaff, Hazrat's brother, and being pierced in the heart by the beauty of it. Much later in my life when I met Zia, Vilayat's son and leader of the Sufis, he discovered that I had met more members of his family than he had.

From my experience in Holland I understood a little better just what Nazi-occupied Europe had endured. The Dutch were still struggling to recover from the skeletons they had become during the war. Although we were there for over a week, the only dinner they were able to offer us each day was mashed potatoes and gravy.

When Japan surrendered and the war ended, I had an acute attack of homesickness, since I hadn't been home for over five years. I managed to get leave and my fare, and with John visited my beloved parents at my home in Guelph. John, whom my parents simply treated as one of the family, said they were the most wonderful people he had ever met —high praise indeed from someone not given to praising anyone.

I left SIS shortly after the end of the war, when most people went back to their peacetime jobs. The wonderfully united spirit at the office dissipated when there was no longer any need for intelligence and secret operations against an enemy. I wanted to do worthwhile work, but what would that be? And where? I explored various openings. One organization, called Moral Welfare, appealed to me, as I thought of morals in Sufi terms: "There is one Moral Principle, the love which springs forth from self-denial, and blooms in deeds of beneficence."

I discovered, though, that what this Church of England group meant by morals applied only to sex.

Instead I went to work for the Quakers at Friends House near Euston. It was during this period that J. Krishnamurti gave his annual lecture series there. I was immediately struck by how good-looking he was. He seemed to offer a sparse approach to spirituality, a taking away of beliefs without giving anything to put in their place. I would never have dared to ask him a question because he came down so hard on some of those who did. His friend Rajagopal was more approachable, and he and I became good friends.

I admired the Quakers and the work they were doing, but eventually concluded that even Quakers shouldn't be trying to tell people in other countries what they ought to do. Thus ended my do-good period. I changed course and went back to normal secretarial work in the commercial world, in a company called Thorne Electrical. I found it interesting that the founder of this company, an Austrian immigrant by the name of Jules Thorne, had made many of his innovations and decisions based on his dreams. Against all odds, he was successfully competing with the all-powerful monopoly in electrical equipment, GEC. Dinah Brook, the wife of my boss there, became a good friend.

At one point, following a deeply rooted desire, I enlisted as a day student for some months in the art school of Regent Street Polytechnic, where I happily drew and painted. I had always enjoyed doing artwork, but had not fully realized the extent of my talent for portraiture and sculpture until it was reflected back to me by my teachers. They told me that I was their most talented student. I might have really concentrated on art, if developments in my personal life had not intervened.

In post-war London, our friends were mostly people who shared our interest in spiritual matters. Sheena was very much part of this circle and was becoming more overtly a teacher. She wrote a paper, which seemed to me very profound, likening Jesus' life experiences to a pattern that every human soul went through: the birth of the Christ child within, being wrapped in swaddling clothes for protection, the flight into Egypt away from the intellect, and so on. She also began sharing with a small group of us what she received from her attunement to the God within. I would take down her talks in shorthand and type them out afterwards. To my regret, all these papers were subsequently

25

destroyed, so I have no written record of the teachings Sheena gave us in those years.

Her most potent teaching came about through everyday contact. Instead of discussing abstract philosophical principles, she would teach by responding to what I did, pointing out where I was acting splendidly and where I was messing up. For example, because her health was poor, I offered to help her by dusting her flat. I'd always disliked that particular chore, for my mother, a scrupulous housekeeper, used to insist on a thorough weekly dusting of rooms where there was no visible dirt. To me, that seemed pointless. Dutifully I dusted Sheena's flat now and then, keeping my negative feelings to myself. One day Sheena quietly and lovingly asked me to stop and leave, because my thoughts and feelings were so upsetting to her. I had thought I was being so noble and helpful! I didn't see her for months after that, and learned that the attitude with which one approaches a job is more important than simply doing it.

Another remark of hers that was very helpful to me was that being worthy or unworthy had nothing to do with our deeds, that God loved us no matter what we did. Sometimes, though, she gave me advice that I felt uncomfortable following. For instance, she recommended that I stay home from work on the first day of my menstrual cycle. I hated that the regular monthly intervals of these absences would make the reason for them obvious to my boss. To me, such matters were meant to be private. Nevertheless, I followed her advice.

In those days I was a smoker, trying to give up the habit. I would manage to quit for a few days, and then succumb to my craving and feel very annoyed with myself. For as long as I had known Sheena she had been afflicted with migraine headaches. She phoned me one day to say that she had a headache that was somehow connected to me; could I account for that? What had I been doing? I could think of nothing. Some time later the same thing happened: another migraine with some link to me. After yet another such phone call I realized that on each of the occasions I had been smoking again. I concluded that somehow my smoking was bringing on Sheena's headaches. I realize that it wasn't the smoking itself— it was my guilty feelings that affected her. In any event, the link between my habit and her migraines was a powerful incentive to quit, and once I was motivated, I managed it easily.

I would not like to give the impression that Sheena was forever admonishing me, for at other times, she was a joyous, delightful, dancing sprite. I remember her leaping up onto chairs and tables in her flat on a spontaneous impulse to dance. On one occasion, we went on a train ride together. Sheena bought the tickets. I kept pestering her to tell me where we were going and she refused to answer. We finally arrived at Richmond Hill, and I (the unmusical one) tried singing to her all the words of the "Lass of Richmond Hill". Not knowing where we were going made an ordinary trip great fun. I also remember going to a flea circus with her, where the tiny fleas were made visible by having a bit of feather attached to them. They were being forced to race one another, and I was amazed at Sheena's deep concern for them while they were being pushed. To me, they were mere insects. I would never have considered worrying about how they felt. Sheena loved all creatures.

Through Sheena I became acquainted with Peter Caddy, a Squadron Leader in the cookery division of the Royal Air Force. Peter and Sheena had met each other on the train when Peter was returning to London after visiting his wife Nora in Christchurch. I remember thinking how handsome he was in his uniform, but I was not drawn to him in any way. He and Sheena became close, and eventually he divorced Nora and married her. This surprised me greatly, for to me Sheena was vastly more spiritually developed than Peter. She told me that she wished she could marry all of her male disciples, for there was no better way to influence anyone than through the close relationship of a marriage. Peter accepted her spiritual authority without question. To my knowledge she was the only woman from whom he willingly accepted instruction.

Chapter 4

Gradually I had been coming to realize that I wasn't happy in my marriage. John treated me more like a sister than a wife. There just wasn't the closeness and sharing I had hoped to find with a spouse. I was still in love with him yet, unable to tell whether he loved me back, I felt diminished. Divorce was an option I never considered as I continued to trust the inner knowing that had told me to marry John. No matter how unhappy I felt, I never called that intuition into question. I was stuck.

It was Sheena who helped me to get unstuck. Fond of both of us, she at first tried to counsel me on how to improve our marriage. I remember one bit of advice she gave was to pay more attention to things like grooming my fingernails. But the relationship was too far gone to be helped by anything so simple as a manicure! Nothing changed. Then Sheena received some guidance for me from the inner planes. The guidance had suggested that John might be better off without me. Could I accept that?

On hearing this, I immediately realized how much I depended on John, how I clung to him and relied on him for most decisions, how I wanted him all for myself and depended on him in all matters. In my persistent search to the answers to the purpose of life, I had sought to identify the people who had been most influential in the life of the planet, who turned out to be the founders of the various religions. They all basically agreed that love was the most important ingredient. That became my belief. But it was only a belief; I didn't know it. Did I believe it enough to put John's welfare before my own? Was I willing to divorce him? For me it was a real test of love. I didn't think I had the courage to go through with a divorce.

It was 1948, and John had just been sent to Berlin to continue his SIS work. This was the time of the Berlin Airlift. The city was divided into four sectors, the French, American and British sectors with the Soviets occupying the Eastern part. In order to force the western nations to leave the western sectors, the Soviet Union imposed a blockade, cutting them off from supplies of food and fuel. British and American planes did an incredible job of delivering millions of tons of supplies, landing day and night for fifteen months. On the record day of Easter 1949, flights came in at the rate of one per minute. Seventy-five U.S. and British airmen died while executing the rescue, and over two million Berliners were saved from starvation.

In London, I was living alone for the first time. Every day when I returned from the art school, I would read and study whatever I could find about being loving. I kept trying to face the reality of a divorce. I didn't think I could do it, yet felt I had to. I was committed, and all my energy went into trying to be filled with love for John's sake. For months I kept on, telling no one, determined to find the courage to go through with it, to prove the power and rightness of love. One day when I was sitting alone in my flat, sipping milky coffee and trying to grapple with the situation, I had the extraordinary cosmic experience of knowing that God was within me. God was no longer a belief but a reality, and I was a part of that reality. I experienced myself as divine. I was no longer a lonely misfit, but part of a wonderful, joyous, loving universe. This experience probably lasted only a few seconds, but my life was forever changed by it. I felt reborn and able to cope with anything. At art school the next day friends remarked that I was different , even my voice was different. They asked me what had happened. I couldn't answer them; I could only smile. Years later, when I returned to Canada, old friends also remarked on the change in my voice.

My immediate problem was how to act on this revelation, which gave me the strength to deal with the situation with John. I composed what I considered to be a superlative letter to John, putting all my heart and soul into it. This is probably the most important letter I have ever written. Here it is:

Most beloved John,

Since I last saw you life has been good to me, and I have had the opportunity to realize that my way of life has not been what it should be. Love has shown me many things, the most important being that I love you far more than I thought myself capable of.

I cannot really tell you how I feel towards you, as it is impossible to analyze love. But there are some things I must say. Now I can recognize love as the greatest force in the world, above other powers. Murshid says: "Is love pleasure, is love merriment? No." To my understanding, love is certainly all that, and above all it must be practiced. I believe that such a close relationship as marriage is a magnificent opportunity to practice love; in fact, it is one of the greatest privileges that can be given to us. And it can be practiced in so many ways, but the best way is in service. That means thinking of the other before oneself, seeking all the time to help the other, to make them happy, to share their sorrows and joys. In everyday little things it would be expressed, for the love is there and seeks expression, and nothing is beneath love. It knows no limits, it keeps back nothing. It involves self-sacrifice but it isn't known for that, for it is so willing. It makes one feel most humble and yet in any situation it can help, for love sees truth and helps just by existing. It does not alter by alteration, for it is there and wants the other to be there, just as they are. It makes one faithful, as one would not wish to be anything else. In marriage, the helping and sharing covers most things, and a most beautiful relationship, a true marriage, would exist.

Such marriages do exist, but I think you will agree that ours is not an example—I, at least, have usually failed. But now the time comes when I must be true to myself. I cannot continue in the old way. Of course the new way will be difficult, as we are only human and 'forget' through circumstances, but with love and an ideal one cannot go wrong for long. I would like nothing better than to have the opportunity to build such a marriage.

In a true marriage, real love must be felt on both sides. And you, darling, may not feel that love for me.

In this situation, there is one thing for me to do, and that is to give you absolute freedom of choice. The decision is up to you, and the only thing that must influence you is whether you have that love for me. In the past you may have been influenced by a sense of duty towards me; now this letter breaks that bond. I know how difficult it would be for you to tell such people as my parents, or Shabaz, if you decide no, but that has nothing to do with it. Don't be afraid to tell me if you don't wish us to continue together. I have faced such a decision and would rather have the truth, however unpleasant it may be. For the sake of the Message you must be truthful, and the way to help the Message is to live it.

It is how you feel that matters, but would it help at all to ask yourself why you married me? Only true love doesn't grow less, and other reasons are not valid unless they lead to true love.

To give you a chance to decide on our own, I'm taking action! On 11th December I sail from Liverpool on the 'Media' for New York.

There I shall stay a few days with Ken and Joan, and the three of us are going to Guelph for Christmas. They are all hoping you will come too, and you know how very welcome you would be. I've told them you may or may not get off.

Knowing your capacity for not answering letters, I'll make the position clear now. I don't intend to remain a grass widow indefinitely, so if I hear nothing from you, I will take steps for a divorce within a reasonable time.

I've told nobody about this except one person. If you care enough to hear my side of it, that person will tell you. To others I have said that I'm going home for Christmas, that I shall probably stay there until I can join you (!) and that I have no idea what my plans are. The flat will be occupied for at least some weeks by five people: Hidayat and family, who have nowhere to go. I'm taking as much as possible with me and have asked Joyce to keep an eye on other things. If you are caught in ignorance of my plans, it can be explained by letters going astray.

So, dearest John, it's up to you, and you will find the answer in your heart. How I wish I could convey how strongly I feel that we must face reality, that we must live the life and bring love into every act. One can't succeed all the time, but how we must try! We must try all the time, not by an effort of will but by loving, and we need to help and get help from all creation.

May God be with you.

My love,
Dorothy

John was due to arrive on 12th of December, 1948. I had intended for him to find the letter upon his return, after I had already left. To my consternation, he arrived a day early. All I could do was to hand him the letter in person. When he read it, he immediately said, "Of course I want that sort of marriage."

I was bewildered and perplexed. Did he or did he not mean it? I saw no signs of a change in him. The moment I could be alone, I prayed as I had never prayed before, desperately asking to be shown the truth, even if I didn't like it. I just needed to know the truth, no matter what it was. I needed to be shown what to do. What came into my mind then, very clearly, was the name of the ship: Media. I knew then that I must board it. In that moment I also learned that if we honestly ask for help, open to receiving guidance whether we like what it says or not, we get that help.

The next day, as planned, I boarded the *Media* and sailed for New York. I felt a great sense of freedom and ease, a comfort in the knowledge that my action was guided from within. I didn't worry about what the outcome might be— didn't even think about it— for I trusted now that the situation would unfold according to its own timing. The five-day voyage was wonderful. I relaxed completely, enjoyed the delicious food and, despite some rough weather, did not become the least bit seasick.

John flew to New York and met me as the ship docked. I greeted him distantly, for I didn't feel I could trust him, and I wanted him to know that I meant what I had said in the letter. As far as I can recall, he didn't ask me any questions or refer directly to the possibility of divorce. He had never been one to talk about our relationship, and he wasn't about to start now. I still hoped that our marriage might resume at some time, but for the present I was content to let matters take their course, whatever that might be. We spent a few days with my brother Ken and his wife in New Jersey before going to Guelph. John couldn't stay long, as he had to return to his job, but I remained in Guelph for several months. I painted oil portraits of my parents. My father was so proud of his likeness that he showed it to all his friends. Local people began to ask me to paint them, and it was nice to know that I could have made a living there as a portrait painter. But my focus at that time was on my spiritual life, and I knew I had to follow through with whatever happened with John.

From Canada, I went to California to stay with Erica Hathaway, a German whom John had met in Cambridge. He had introduced me to her in London and she had invited me to visit her. En route, I lived in Hollywood for some months with Erica's friend, Renée Taylor, who then ran the Blue Pencil Manuscript Service. As the manuscripts were either essays or scripts that were needed the following day, if not yesterday, she and I often typed through the night. Though being in Hollywood was an interesting experience, I was glad to leave the place, if only because I no longer would have to share Renée's meals of cream cheese, which I hated.

Erica lived near San Marcos in what was then a wild area of

sagebrush adjoining orange orchards. She was divorced and lived with her two boys, Michael and Daniel, aged six and seven, supporting them, marginally, with a small printing business. Ben, an older Australian who ran her offset litho printing press, was part of the household. Erica was the most exuberant person I had ever met. I found her wonderful company, the more so because she shared my interest in the spiritual life. She had little money, and the boys' clothing came through faith, not purchase. Just as their clothes wore out, a gift parcel would arrive out of the blue. Erica's faith was tremendous. After I left and she could no longer rely on the small amount of money I had contributed, her faith wavered. She went through a very difficult and frugal time until she realized why and began to depend on God again. Then again her needs were met.

Erica had moved to San Marcos in order to be close to Vitvan, a spiritual teacher. Born in Kansas, his birth name was Ralph Moriarty DeBit. He had been trained and initiated into Shakti Yoga by an Indian teacher, Mozumdar, who had come to the United States with the sole object of finding and training Vitvan. The group of devotees that had formed around him in San Marcos was called the School of the Natural Order. The compound had extensive gardens and large compost heaps. (The latter led a friend to dub it the "School of the Natural Odor.") Erica and I helped in the garden one day a week, and in return we received all the vegetables we needed.

After coming to the conclusion that Eastern exercises were not suitable for Western bodies, Vitvan had started to blend his Eastern knowledge with that of Western science, in particular the findings of Einstein and the work of the semanticist Korzybski, who emphasized precision in the use of words. Erica and I were irritated by the fanatical verbal exactitude of his disciples. If I said "The sun is setting", they would point out that it was the earth that was moving, not the sun.

Early each morning we trudged over a hill to listen to Vitvan's 6 a.m. lecture. I learned a great deal from him. Some of his teachings were homey and practical, and I continue to apply them to this day. His phrase "Act, don't react" has been invaluable, though it took me years to understand what he meant, and even more years to put it into practice. When I find I am upset or deeply affected by a situation, I know that there is always something to look at within myself—usually something I need to change. Then I have the choice to act from my center, to choose what kind of energy I truly wish to express. Another of his teachings which I have found reliably helpful is to avoid blaming others. As he put it, when we point a finger at someone, three fingers are pointing back at us. I am glad I caught on to that in my early thirties, for it instilled a lifelong habit of not feeling put upon. I also shared Vitvan's distaste for the attitude which he called "ungrounded sweetness and light."

Other teachings were more esoteric. He talked about how the senses interpret other dimensions, and described how we register frequencies on different levels. He taught me a different way to look at Christ: as a dynamic energy, a higher state of consciousness that Jesus embodied and that all human beings can aspire to.

Often he went over my head. He wanted us to perceive the cosmos as a Conscious Light-Energy-Living-Matter organism, self-governed as if by a Supreme Intelligence in which we are integrated. When he talked of Einstein's Theory of Relativity, Erica and I were lost. One notable day, we both found ourselves nodding happily through his lecture, confident that at last we understood. But as soon as we left his presence, our comprehension vanished. I believe this is why some people become so enamored with being in the presence of aware people like Sai Baba or Mother Meera. In the aura of such teachers, our understanding is often expanded.

I was rather intimidated by Vitvan, though he behaved like any normal person, drove tractors and was very approachable. Buoyant, lively Erica was made of sterner stuff and talked to him often. Neither of us became adoring disciples like the rest of his group—both because it was not our natures to be devotees and because Vitvan had a tittery laugh that annoyed us. Erica complained to him about the laugh. He apologized, explaining that it happened at times when he came down from spiritual into material realms. He promised to try rubbing his nose instead, and often did—with a glance at us.

In one of his talks, he said that the primary colors were red, green and violet. That time I was emboldened to speak up, for from my experience as a painter, I knew the primaries as red, yellow and blue. Vitvan said he couldn't explain why his primary colors were different, but suggested I shine light through green and red cellophane. I did this and to my great surprise got yellow. He had been right. This still puzzled me, and reading up on color theory left me none the wiser. Years later, my brother Ken, a scientist, explained to me the difference between direct and reflected light.

As part of Vitvan's "Eastern" teaching, we practiced raising our life force, the kundalini, up the spine through the crown charka. Though I was able to do it, I have not made a practice of it. Somehow life has led me to deal with it more directly—which is the Sufi approach as I understand it, and is more natural to me. Living a loving and balanced life, I believe, automatically adjusts the forces in our chakras. In one situation, though, I found the kundalini system helpful. I was having an argument with a powerful friend, who became so angry at me that I felt as if I were literally being hit in the solar plexus and was about to vomit. Hastily I went into the bathroom, raised my forces out of my stomach area, felt fine and could deal with the situation without being physically affected.

I was with Erica in California for almost a year. In all that time, no loving letter—in fact, no letters at all—came from John. I heard through the grapevine that he had a girlfriend in Berlin. I was not especially surprised by that. Learning of it was a great sorrow, but also a relief in a way, for I now knew where I stood and knew that I had to take action.

Setting out to find legal grounds for a divorce, I went to Berlin on my own. This took all my courage, for I knew no one there and spoke no German. Erica gave me the name of friends of hers in Berlin, and I connected with them, not with John. I wanted to get evidence for a divorce without his knowledge. Much to my dismay, Erica's friends contacted him. He collected me, took me to his apartment and left me there for some days without telling anyone of my arrival. I had nothing to do, and felt disoriented and lonely. Finally, John introduced me to fellow workers in his office. I was a surprise to them, for he had told nobody that he was married. His female co-workers seemed quite pleased that I had turned up, perhaps hoping I would keep him in order.

John said that he did not want a divorce. His objections were, to me, meaningless and unpersuasive. He argued that it was not "the done thing" and wondered what my parents would think. By then it had become apparent that he was in love with someone else. He admitted that he had a girlfriend, Margaret, but said that he didn't expect their relationship to last. The more he hedged, the more adamant I became. How strange that I had to fight him to get a divorce that part of me still didn't want!

Finally he agreed to my divorcing him on grounds of adultery. Not wishing to implicate his real girlfriend, he arranged instead to be caught with a fake one: a German SIS agent who innocently thought the set-up was just another part she had to play in gathering intelligence. After enacting this charade, I went to a German lawyer with my sad story of finding my husband with another woman. I doubted that I would be convincing, as I am no actress, but at some point during the interview I was amazed to find myself feeling like the wronged woman I was pretending to be. I seldom cry, but I wept in front of that lawyer. I realized that when one is going with the flow, doing what is right, help is given and everything opens out.

Although John had already booked leave to vacation with Margaret, instead he spent it with me. Erica was visiting family in Munich, and I was to meet her there to attend the 1950 Passion Play in Oberammergau. John offered to drive me there by a roundabout route, making a holiday of it. We motored through Germany, Luxembourg, Switzerland, Italy and Liechtenstein, having a wonderful time together. Now that we were free of expectations, agendas and unresolved issues, we simply enjoyed one another's company. We were friends. Secretly I still hoped he would come back to me some day, but, for the moment, I was at peace, content to let events take their course.

As it turned out, I was never to see him again after we parted in Munich. The finality of our split was something I only realized gradually as, over time, my own destiny continued to unfold. Once in a while, I heard news of his doings from mutual friends. When my first book, *To Hear the Angels Sing*, was published, I sent him a copy, and received a brief acknowledgement in return.

About a week before Christmas in 1994, my phone rang, and the caller identified himself as "John."

"John who?" I asked.

"John," he repeated.

"John *who*?"

Had anyone suggested back in 1950 that the day would come when my ex-husband's name didn't immediately ring a bell, I would have found the idea unfathomable. He had to say it a third time before I finally recognized his voice.

"I just phoned to wish you Merry Christmas," he said.

I said, "It would be fun to see you some time." He agreed that it would be fun. This seemed a safely hypothetical agreement, since he told me he was living in Croatia. But about an hour after this brief exchange, my Slovenian friend Milenko dropped by to see me. When I mentioned I'd just heard from my ex-husband in Croatia, Milenko asked whether I'd like him to arrange a workshop for me in Slovenia. Why not? I thought.

Once the date was set for that workshop in Ljubljana, I wrote John to give him my schedule and see if there was any way we could meet. For a month, I heard nothing. Then I received a letter from a Lien Wood, thanking me for my letter to her husband John, and explaining with great sadness that he had died in a car accident on February 19, in Croatia. She herself had been injured in the accident. She said she would be pleased to meet me some time. I replied with a letter of condolence, saying I'd love to have a recent photo of John, and asking whether she could meet me in Ljubljana. When I hadn't heard from her for three months, I wrote again, saying that as John's first wife, I would dearly love to hear about what his life had been like. That time I got an immediate and shocked reply. He had told Lien that Margaret—his girlfriend at the time of our divorce—was his first wife.

Lien and I continued to correspond, for now she was as curious as I was. She sent me photos, and copies of articles about the highly regarded international aid work he had done with the United Nations and various humanitarian organizations. According to her, he was greatly esteemed when he died. That was interesting, but what I really wanted to know was whether he had continued with his spiritual work.

We finally met in person when Lien came to a workshop I was giving in London. Our conversation confirmed my suspicion that John had constructed a huge and elaborate network of lies. He had always been secretive, but the falsehoods he had woven throughout his life were unbelievably complex. After his death, his two sons by Margaret and two daughters by another partner (an Englishwoman with whom he had lived in Canada for some time) met each other and exchanged stories. At the funeral, Lien had met one of the two daughters, whom John had told her were the daughters of his entirely fictitious stepbrother. One son, Alistair, who lives in London, and a daughter, Sophie, who lives in Victoria, later came to visit me, hoping that between us we could piece together the facts. I learned that John had been fired from SIS, and later from the United Nations. Margaret and John had divorced, and Margaret had stayed with SIS, marrying another staff member. John had moved around, become a Canadian citizen, taught at the University of British Columbia, and then had lived in the Balkans for some time. Books could be written about his intrigues and deceptions—but no one would believe them! Alistair went on trying to get to the bottom of his father's story by visiting various others who had known him. But when he and Sophie visited me again a year later, many riddles, gaps and contradictions remained. To his own children, John was every bit the enigma he had been to me. Why did he feel this compulsion to deceive and withhold? I wish I knew.

The one thing I have never seriously questioned is whether I was right to marry him to begin with. That had been the first time in my life I ever trusted an inner knowing. Ironically, the second big intuition I ever trusted was the knowledge that the time had come to divorce him. I still believe that both intuitions were right, and obeying them was a formative experience in both my inner and my outer life. Following inner guidance is no guarantee of happily ever after, no insurance that everything is going to come out the way one wishes it would—though in my experience it is at least a guarantee that things are going to come out *interesting*!

Chapter 5

After the divorce, I moved back to London. Life there wasn't easy. I missed John and the friends who had welcomed us as a couple. It was very different being on my own, and I often felt sorry for myself. I would sing a popular song:

I'm sorry for myself, so sorry for myself.
I would go and end it all, but fourteen stories is an awful fall.
I'm so sorry for myself.
I'm blue as I can be. My man walked out on me.
I would jump into the sea—but no one might be there to rescue me.
I'm so sorry for myself.

Then I would laugh, and feel better.

I linked up again with Sheena and the group of spiritual seekers around her, which included Peter Caddy, Eileen Combe and others. I tried to tell them about the discoveries I had made in studying with Vitvan. As I didn't really understand his concepts myself, what I conveyed must have been pretty chaotic and confused, and I soon gave up my attempts.

I was living in a small flat on Chelsea Embankment and was once again going to art school. When I would come home from school and find myself alone in my flat, a thought would often enter my mind: "Stop, listen and write." At first I ignored it, for I wondered what I might be listening to, and feared that I what I wrote would be falsehood or nonsense. But the thought persisted. Thinking that it might go away if appeased, I finally took out my shorthand notebook. I tried to focus on my experience of knowing that God was within, which felt like a safe place. Thoughts and feelings did come to me. They seemed somehow purer, more inspiring than my usual thoughts. Something came in these times of "listening" but it didn't take the form of sounds or words. Yet it felt like "hearing". It is a difficult experience to describe. Since I had been asked to write, I did my best to render these inner impressions in words of my own choosing. At first I was very wary of the whole process, afraid the messages would become garbled in the process of putting them into words. So I censored them, deleting any messages that didn't sound right, or that seemed frivolous. Eventually I had a secret little journal of this censored material, full of trite and unchallenging sayings, like "God is love."

One day with Sheena, I let slip that I was keeping this journal. She asked to see it. The next day she returned it, saying she believed that I was receiving truth and encouraging me to do what I was being asked to do. She recommended that I attune three times a day, morning, noon and night. That was helpful: had she not suggested a regular meditation schedule, I would not have maintained the practice. Nor would I have accepted the suggestion had it come from anyone but Sheena. As it was, I sometimes rebelled, particularly at having to get up early in the morning to attune. But I trusted Sheena, and her confidence in my process helped me to trust that as well. Her belief in the validity of what I was receiving encouraged me to relax and stop censoring.

A wonderful period of inner attunement began, a period that taught and trained me. Three times a day in my meditation I received from my inner divinity some helpful message. I loved my first disclosures with their light touch from what came to me as God's "shimmering thought life." In their joyousness and lightness, the viewpoints I received were completely different from those of my Christian cultural background, and they charmed and delighted me.

Here is the second message that came to me after I stopped censoring, dated April 22, 1954 pm.

Awareness of My elfin mind brings awareness of the limitations in which man functions. These limitations are self-imposed, for what could possibly be freer than the children of God the Unlimited? And this lack of limitation will seem strange at first and unformed, because of course it is, to normal consciousness. But if you listen with joy it is not strange; it is the only way of living and thinking. My ways are boundless and I would have nothing hampering anyone.

You have no conception of the joy which is the birthright of My children. There is an expression "bursting with joy," and that is literally true. In my realm this "bursting" casts a shower of stars, like a sparkler, but the sparks do not vanish. They remain in whatever form is suitable at the moment.

Words cannot be found to describe these wonders, and yet I would have them brought down on earth to this dense planet, to make it less dense and to make it the wonderland of unimaginable beauty which is My idea of it, where there are no hindrances, nothing to mar the perfection in which it could live and have its being.

"Elfin" was the only word I could think of to convey the delicate yet deep gaiety that was filling me. But it was so foreign to my old concepts of God that I felt apprehensive. Was I picking up nonsense from somewhere? Was it just my imagination?

Next day I got an answer to my worries.

My child, fear not that you are putting down inaccuracies. Have you no faith? In fact you have a lot if you will only let it present itself to you through the welter of the thought life that is man-made, that churning laborious pot.

Now let us leave that behind and enter into My realms and feel the effervescence and the beauty of the bubbles of awareness which are My thoughts before they have a recognizable form. In each bubble is the seed of loveliness, even though it looks like a vacuum. Airiness in itself is beauty. People long for that beyond their reach and so are attracted to wisps of beginnings—unless they are too weighed down by self-made conditions.

Try to realize that which I am telling you is a reality, not a dream.

I never knew what the subject would be in these times of inward attunement, and was asked to have no preconceptions. I was also asked to set aside the critical, analyzing mind and attune to the universal mind—a very difficult task for a person like me who tended to make decisions rationally. I came to understand that one doesn't need to get rid of the mind to meditate. Rather, one needs to be ungoverned by it, letting it mirror the higher energies so that one can be conscious of them. My conscious mind was a participant in the process. Its job was to choose the right words, and often I used a thesaurus to help find a word.

During those early days I continued to be concerned about

receiving false messages, so at Sheena's suggestion I would ask for cleansing and purifying each time I turned within. Just asking for help was a help to me. I also thought it would be helpful to surround myself with a circle of light. I felt dependent on such protection until I became familiar enough with the quality of the divine within to know when I had reached it. Then I felt safe. I began to notice, too, that my guidance was not about other people or events. Since it affected no one but myself, there was no need to be skeptical.

Leading a life of bliss entails canceling other engagements, engagements you have made through habit to your body, to convention, to social codes, to others' opinions. Throw them away merrily and fill your engagement book with My engagements, which may not be conventional but which are much more fulfilling. Each day is a blank page . . . and each hour has a different fragrance.

Each day when I entered into the inner realms I was bathed in qualities of love, joy, peace or harmony through which ideas came, and which my mind translated into words. The theme of these messages, worded differently each time, was basically always the same: to go within to God for everything, thus putting love first in my life. I loved the light touch, the sense of fun, the artistic feeling, the fact that I never knew what God was going to say next. The perspectives of this God were unusual and new to me, and drew from me a deep love and appreciation. Gradually the themes became more personal.

The following one had a great impact on me:

Come closer, come closer, so softly, on tiptoe. As quietly as a mouse creep up to Me. Let Me draw you nearer, in slow motion lest we disturb anyone, lest we raise any dust. Move closer to Me invisibly, hearing no evil, seeing no evil, speaking no evil. Only purity can come close to Me, and we do not want any ripple of impurity to trip you.

Draw nearer; draw nearer, with the movement of your heart. Let it expand into Me, let it bridge any space that might be between us, until there is just one, big, glowing heart, so big that it holds up this universe.

Let the wings of your heart bear you closer. Let them gently flutter a little nearer, a little nearer, bringing you closer to Me without our awareness. Sneak into My heart, into My comfort, into the protection of My wings. Nestle there. This is your home. From here you can fly with My messages, but this is your home. Feel at home in it until any other dwelling place makes you homesick, until any defense but the defenselessness of love and truth are contrary to you, until your whole life is that of love and you take your home, My heart, with you to bring others home.

How could I help but fall in love with God after that?

The wording of the messages reflected my personal understanding at the time. When I used the word "God", I was using the current language of my patriarchal culture, not portraying masculinity, for the God I experienced within was a Mother/Father. It was also me. That inner divinity was so vast and powerful, that I felt like a child to it. Hence the messages often address Dorothy as "my child." This parent/child viewpoint continued for years, until it changed to a deeper attunement.

A favorite early message was:

Rejoice, the stream of love is growing, the stream that will carry the world back to its Creator, purified and ready to start again in the light of the clear beauty which is My idea of it.

Give Me some hearts open to Me, given wholly to Me and filled with My love, and I can and will change the face of the earth.

Give Me a heart in which I can work without restriction, and there is nothing that cannot be done, no work that cannot be undertaken and carried through to My fulfillment.

Give Me a heart sensitive to need because of its love, and there is no need that cannot be met.

Give Me a heart that upholds the truth at any cost, because it is My truth, and no falseness will be left.

Give Me a heart that lifts the hearts it meets because of the joy of God, and all hearts will rejoice.

Give Me a heart that asks only Me what to do, and all will be done with My power.

Give Me a heart that will walk the earth bearing Me, and

the earth will know Me.

Give Me a heart only attached to love, and the world will lose its other attachments.

Give Me your heart.

The messages continually helped me to get closer.

Stretch every particle of yourself towards Me, and I will fill every particle with Myself out of My abundance. Soak yourself in the stream of love inside and out, giving yourself up completely. Relax in it, drown in it, every atom of you, until there is nothing in you not made new and pure.

Then breathe again, like a newly emerged chick, breathing love in instead of air. It is My love that keeps you alive, that sustains you. Know this, breathe it in softly, and breathe it out gently.

Let all your thoughts come to love for their life, that they breathe forth My dimensions of love. Let all your acts come to love for their life, that they abound only with love. Let all you see be seen in love, that you see only boundless loveliness.

Walk tentatively in this world of love, letting Me guide each step. Stay very young—this is the land of eternal youth and you will lose your way if you grow up. Let every particle of yourself remain in love, and you will never lose your way again. Go onward in the stream of love.

Re-reading these messages now, I realized how wonderfully and powerfully I was led to a greater consciousness of wholeness. Such awareness keeps enlarging as life's experiences underline the truth of what I received, and the Divine becomes more present in everything. I also realized anew how we all color whatever we perceive, and how the environment influences us. The messages jump from the personal to the impersonal and back. I was later to discover that the angels and spiritual beings are impersonal and that humans are personal. Only God is both.

The importance of turning consciously to the Divine at the beginning of each session was made vitally obvious to me in my first year of attuning. On one occasion, I had the feeling that some message urgently wanted to come to me. The moment I was alone, I immediately started to listen and write, skipping my usual ritual of cleansing, purifying and surrounding myself with light. The message I received informed me that Douglas, a young and handsome member of Sheena's circle, was to be my partner. Though I liked Douglas very much, there was no special closeness between us, which made me think any partnership was premature. By then, I was routinely sharing many of my messages— which at first I had only shown to Sheena —with our whole group. So despite, some misgivings, I shared this one, and the group accepted it as one of my usual valid communications. The dynamics of the group then changed uncomfortably and yet powerfully. It soon became clear to all of us, including Douglas and myself, that we were not truly bonded. The repercussions of my mistake almost broke up the group. I realized with great embarrassment that I had allowed an unconscious yearning of mine to impersonate the God within. It was a painful lesson, but it was well learned.

My loving connection continued:

You are close to Me but you can come still closer, further into My love. That is the marvelous journey ahead of you all, this glad venturing into My love, this delicate response in you to a new outpouring of Myself. This is the ever-different, ever-uplifting, ever-softening process which is the joy of My heart to behold in you and in all.

For everyone My approach is different, for My one love is sensitive to all. The warmth of My love, the surge of it into an open heart, is universal and unique. I am all things to all people. I pour it out on all creation, and it comes back to you as you open yourself to Me from all sides, within and without. The more you open your heart, the wider the opening through which I can come. Open it wide, to let in more of My ineffable tenderness until you are so filled with Me that there is nothing of you. When you can talk and not know what you are saying because My love is so strong in you, you will know more of My love.

I pour it out on you. I cannot help but pour it out on you, for that is the nature of love. I continually woo you, see the beauty in you, because that is the nature of love. I am always constant, always available, always ready to give of Myself. I cannot do otherwise. I am continually purifying, bringing only the best, for I am love. I give you the perfection for which I made you, as I know what pleases you most.

In the core of your being you worship Me. Come closer still to this beauty I offer you. Open up your heart and let Me flood you with Myself.

In these times of at-one-ment, from the embracing qualities of love, joy, peace, beauty, I always emerged feeling a better person. It was not a matter of just basking in the love, I was to live it. It was not a matter of escaping the world, for I was constantly asked to bring the love I experienced into my everyday living. God would say: Brush your teeth with Me. I would try, generally with little success because I simply forgot.

This communication went on for years. Each time it was given in a different way, for God knew that I hated repetition! The endless patience and love of God through the years was incredible, and couldn't help but affect and change my personality, however slowly. At these times I was not giving anything to the world. I was just receiving, open to whatever came to me. As I changed and grew, the messages also changed, helping me to become more and more conscious.

The rustle of a flower is sometimes loud enough to drown My voice, and inconsequential thoughts are much too loud for Me to shout through. At the very center of stillness am I, and you have to pick your way to Me through mazes of inaudible noise, through to the heart of the stillness.

There I remain quiet, and yet at My look all things revolve. I am the essence of peace, and I make the suns and the planets move in My rhythm. I am here, I am there, at one and the same time to you. Motionless I traverse all space.

I am God, the focus of all awe, and less trammeled than any form. I am free yet I am bound, bound by love to My children. Love Me, and you are bound and you are free, and you are very blessed. Love brings all blessings, for I am love, and love is before power and might. All else stems from love.

Join yourself to Me in love, and all else can be bestowed on you. Love is first, love is all. Cast off all things to come to love, steer through all mists to come to love. Wherever you are, find your way to love and you find your way to Me, from whence all else arises. In love you are blessed and do bless.

I also received messages about the intellect:

On the human mind I imprint My pictures, but the human heart I fill with Myself. I cannot give glimpses of My mind to people whose hearts are empty of love, because then is the heart full of self and My pictures are distorted and twisted . . .

The tortuous mind, the limiting, limited, caged mind that self had made of an instrument freer than air, must be scrapped . . . With this perverted mind has humanity gained dominance, making the raison d'etre of mind the assertion of self. Nothing is more contrary to the qualities of the Creator of those minds, who gave the gift of freedom of choice. . .

Though the critical mind and the limited self was not to be rejected, I was helped to see what to do about it, and how to find help:

You can contact me with the speed of light, depending on our love. There is no need for elaborate preparations, for settling down, for composing yourself. Just love and you are with Me.

If your heart is open, you are open to Me and can hear My voice. When your heart is open and love is flowing forth, you are in the cleansing stream that makes you pure enough to hear Me. But you have to turn to it, you have to submit yourself to it—for a critical mind will do what it can to stop you turning to Me.

Love knows what to do with the mind. Give it to Me. Give it to that wonderful cleansing stream no matter how far the mind has wandered, with no reservation;, I know the mind and know what to do with it.

Each time it comes to Me, it comes a little more into alignment, and you are beginning to catch it more quickly each time it wanders. Love can cope with the mind. Give it to love any time of the day or night for instant cleansing, and let your whole being be in love and very close to Me.

During the second year I notice now that a few of the messages become almost strident about the role of the separated self and the "lower" mind, the intellect:

> *Human minds have such a very limited and dull view of Me, and as they look around them, what meets their eyes is not very heart-warming, and they begin to wonder anew about Me and My works. They see upside-down and inside-out. They blame God, love, for their troubles instead of themselves. They plan to make the world better, and they forget to ask Me to make them better. They go ahead vigorously and righteously, all the while building up in themselves that part which feeds on and must have darkness. Many drone on about Me, as if I were a shadow either too big or too little for influence. . . .*

At that time the belief of our group was that the separated self, the personality, the lower mind, was a bogeyman, that which limited us and separated us from the divine. We needed back then to overcome the dominance of the intellect so prevalent in our culture. I became keenly aware of the limitations of reason, perceiving the intellect sometimes as a terrible master and sometimes as a helpful servant. Since then, helped a lot by David Spangler's teachings, I have realized the divine beauty of every part of the human personality, including the reasoning mind.

When I chose the inner state, I could trust what I experienced through my emotions and mind, and it always helped me to be more loving. Always the direction was to bring that love into my daily life: *Do the dishes with Me.*

Chapter 6

Sheena and Peter Caddy had divorced, but they remained good friends, and Peter was an important member of the close-knit group that that gathered around her. At the RAF base in Iraq, he had met Eileen Combe, who was unhappily married to another RAF officer, and the mother of five children. They got to know each other there, and Peter, who believed in twin souls, came to believe that she was his "other half." Sheena supported their relationship. When Eileen flew back to England on holiday with her children, Peter arranged to be on the same flight. It was during that journey that she began to return his feelings. She fell in love with him and knew they had to be together.

On the weekend that the two of them went to tell her family of her commitment to Peter, Sheena and I looked after her children at her family home. Eileen's husband Andrew returned unexpectedly and threw us out of the house. Peter and Eileen had wanted and planned to keep the children, but Andrew forbade Eileen access to them. This was a great anguish to her, for she was an extremely motherly person. It was during this period of crisis that Eileen, too, began to receive inner guidance. In a sanctuary in Glastonbury, she heard a voice saying *"Be still and know that I am God."* Later messages confirmed that she and Peter had work to do together.

Each of us had our own unique inner contact with God. Eileen heard a distinct voice, speaking to her in words that she wrote down verbatim. I heard nothing and had to find my own words to record the inner impressions that came to me. Peter never had much success with meditation. For him, guidance took the form of a keen intuition in action. Sheena encouraged him to follow these intuitions without hesitation. More often than not, they were accurate.

Meanwhile, Sheena was giving us teachings from her own inner guidance. Often these focused on how to apply love in the everyday world. I would take down her talks in shorthand, and later type them. At this time, I had a well-paid executive secretarial job at the *Daily Mirror*, a British tabloid with a huge circulation. I had an office to myself and thus could hold my noon meditation without interruption. I could even type and duplicate messages from members of our group on office time and office machines. As my boss did not have enough work for me, he was glad to see me busily typing and seemingly keeping me busy. Unknowingly, the *Daily Mirror* was supporting our spiritual endeavors. Once again, I was at the right place at the right time.

We were coming to believe that Sheena had a vastly important role as a World Teacher, with a mission to bring love to the world and to advance a new, more feminine approach to spirituality. She envisioned six couples as disciples, men and women working closely together, to help her and to be examples of love in action.

During this period, I began to receive some beautiful poems for Sheena, most of which, unfortunately, have been lost. This one, from March 1955, though not one of the best, reflects our sense of Sheena as a divine messenger:

> *Listen, small children, listen to Me,*
> *The song that I sing is joyous and free.*
> *It is only the self, with its one plaintive note*
> *That's wrecked a whole world and put stop to all growth.*

> *Listen, My children, listen to Me*
> *For the love that makes you all selfless and free,*
> *That's come through My messenger, and come for you all*
> *To rescue the world and put an end to the fall . . .*

I have since wondered whether the magnitude of this mission overwhelmed her. She continued to suffer from acute migraines, and the depths she went to in her spiritual work with others sometimes put a strain on her, leaving her shaken and exhausted. Even when I had first known her during the war, she had been prone to mood swings. Though my fondest memories are of those times when she was joyous and loving and radiant, when depressed or unwell, she could be difficult to get along with. Over the years, these dark periods were to become more pronounced. I suspect the exacting demands she placed on herself and on others, the inner and outer opposition she struggled against, and the public notoriety our group later attracted, all began to take their toll on her.

Much of the time, Peter was away on RAF missions. In his absence, he asked Eileen to move in with Sheena and accept teaching from her. The separation from her five children continued to be a constant source of distress to Eileen. To make matters worse, Peter was in no hurry to marry her. As he saw it, they were already married in the eyes of God, and there was no particular need to be married in the eyes of anyone else. To top it all off, he now expected her to become the roommate and the disciple of his ex-wife!

Fortunately she had her own inner guidance to support her, which included exceptional visions of a child, called the Christ Child, carrying out various simple actions. These visions we would send for interpretation to Naomi, a highly developed telepathic medium whom Peter had met in the Philippines during one of his RAF trips, now living in Illinois. Eileen's own guidance eventually told her that this Christ Child was represented by Sheena. That, for Eileen, was the last straw in her relationship to Sheena. She got "guidance" to burn all of Sheena's teachings, and proceeded to do just that. My own messages were mixed in with Sheena's and I rushed to rescue as many of them as I could. As my personal longings had once produced a false message about Douglas, so Eileen's hatred of Sheena had momentarily distorted her link with the divine.

Sheena readily perceived the distorting effects of our personal desires and brought these to our attention. With some people she did this gently, with others she wielded the sword of truth. I believe we draw to ourselves the training that is necessary to us at any given time. As each of us drew on different aspects of Sheena, each of us saw her differently. To Eileen she seemed a cruel disciplinarian; Peter felt both her love and her discipline; what I felt most was her love.

Now came the most chaotic period of my life. One day Sheena said to us, "You have your own guidance now. Why not use it more in your everyday life?" We took her to mean that we needed to leave our comfortable, settled lives in order to be freer to follow inner injunctions from moment to moment. Though I and the others rather choked at this idea, we quit our jobs and hit the road. Peter and Eileen stayed together, but the rest of us went our separate ways.

Since we still needed to earn a living, we had to be willing to do whatever work was available, no matter how difficult or dirty. Douglas mentioned to me that a certain girls' school near Chichester was advertising for a matron. I arrived at the school door, unannounced, carrying a suitcase with all my belongings. I must have seemed providential to them, for they took me on at once, and I settled in to look after about a dozen teenaged girls. I had never even been in a girls' school before, knew nothing of children or of the discipline required. I made various conspicuous or silly mistakes, such as applying Dettol, a very strong antiseptic that is meant to be diluted, directly onto cuts. As I believed in freedom, not rules, I was a failure as a disciplinarian. Still, they somehow liked me, and at the end of the term they asked me to return—though as a secretary, not a matron.

Another time I took a job as second kitchen maid in an old people's home run by two delightful sisters, Miss Edwards and Miss Hilda. My mentor, the first kitchen maid, was a charming but illiterate Irish girl. One of our jobs was to take breakfast trays to the old people. I asked her to write down exactly what to give each person so that I could easily fill each tray. Of course she couldn't write but I discovered that she didn't need to. Every morning she knew intuitively what each resident wanted that day. When she realized that I myself lacked this ability, she thought I was incredibly stupid. So much for university degrees! But I did endear myself to her and the two Misses Edwards by redecorating and painting their private rooms. I learned much from being "in service" that I would not have learned otherwise—for instance, that the sort of people referred to in England as "the lower classes" were generally loving and helpful.

One summer when I was feeling cut off from everything, I went to a place in Yorkshire that sponsored working holidays and accommodated us in Nissen huts left vacant from the war. Farmers would appear early in the morning asking for people to weed or pick vegetables, or whatever was needed on their farms. We could volunteer, and were paid the minimum wage. Picking potatoes was the most backbreaking work I have ever done. At the end of the first week of bending over potatoes I could not stand up. I stayed long enough to get over the stiffness, and even became a captain of a potato-picking group.

Believing that Sheena was in Scotland, I went there and took a truly uncongenial job as a mother's helper to a Presbyterian minister's wife in Kirkcaldy. Completely inexperienced and inept, I seemed to put my foot in it no matter what. Even what I was good at turned sour. The children and their friends played badminton. At their mother's request, I, a former badminton team captain, would make every effort to let them win. Somehow, though, my deliberately awkward lunges at the bird always seemed to connect. Even at losing, I felt like a loser!

I disliked the hypocrisy I saw in that home. Since work was not permitted on the Sabbath, the baby's nappies were dried indoors on

Sundays, instead of hanging them on the outside clothesline, where they would be visible. The children were not allowed to laugh on a Sunday. I had hoped to bring spirituality to the family and broaden their views, but I merely annoyed them. After a while I gave up and hitchhiked back to London. By then I was penniless, having already sold the only jewelry I had—mostly attractive pieces given to me by my in-laws. I could always get temporary secretarial work in London, and the Chelsea flat that John and I had lived in was still available.

One of Sheena's followers had left his wife and daughter in order to be with her. His enraged mother-in-law contacted a reporter, telling him a garbled story of a horrible woman (Sheena) who was breaking up families. His version was published and unexpectedly aroused so much interest that reporters began to contact us for more stories. Naively we thought this was a wonderful opportunity to broadcast our truths to a waiting public, and we answered questions honestly. There were many interviews, but when the series on our group did get published, our statements had been completely misunderstood, twisted around and sensationalized. It was evidently weird to be both Christian and Buddhist, to believe that contemporary people could achieve Christhood, and to have no name for our group. Some wit called us the Nameless Ones, and the series on the Nameless Ones was so surprisingly popular that we became infamous as a cult. In our attempts to avoid the continual publicity, we scattered to remote parts of Scotland, still avidly pursued by journalists. We were front-page news in some Scottish newspapers for the whole month of January. (January is a slow month for news!) I remember getting up one morning to find that there were twenty reporters waiting outside for an interview. On another occasion reporters knocked on my window at three o'clock in the morning.

Around this time, in order to be near Sheena, who had rented a little cottage near Kintra on the west coast of Mull, I searched for work in that area. Eventually I was hired for the summer as a waitress at the St. Columba Hotel on the island of Iona. Most of the rest of the staff were students working during their summer holidays and I was particularly welcomed as I came earlier, before the students could leave their colleges, and left after they had returned to school. My bedroom was half of a run-down "but and ben", a typical Highland stone cottage opposite Iona Abbey; later it became a pottery. Beside the Abbey was the ruined St. Oran's Chapel, with its old graveyard holding the burial slabs of Scottish, Pictish and Viking kings and nobles. I was delighted to find the effigy of a Maclean chieftain among them. For protection from the elements, these stones have now been taken indoors. Seeing them in their original site, with the sculptures lying on their backs open to the sky as they had been through the centuries, was strangely moving. I loved the island, its treeless hills and valleys with their own unique names, and soft colors suffusing the atmosphere. Every afternoon I would wander about in tennis shoes, which got soaked in the boggy land but dried easily. Occasionally I could take the ferry over to Mull to see Sheena.

It was difficult writing to my parents about what was happening to me. There seemed no way, short of seeing them, to help them understand my wandering life. Why, my father wondered, would I, with my qualifications, take a job as a waitress? I couldn't explain, just tried to write in an upbeat tone, necessarily leaving a great deal out. I later learned that a second cousin had unfortunately gotten hold of some newspaper reports on the Nameless Ones and sent them to my parents. I am sure they worried a great deal. Frequently I was grateful that they were thousands of miles away. They trusted me, though, and believed things would come out all right.

My polestar was my continuing, loving inner connection with the Divine. Wherever I was, at any time, I would go within for guidance. It continued through the years, always helping me. Here is a message I received during this period:

> *Why do you listen to Me, My child? If it is for knowledge, you will get knowledge to be put to use. If it is for your own safety, you will only be safe when all your moments are Mine. If it is out of duty, you will not get very close, for duty is cold, hard, a mental thing, and I need all of your being and powers. But if it is because you love Me and want above all else to be with Me, then our life together can go forward with leaps and bounds. If this is your motive, you will take to heart what I say and would not dream of following anything but Me.*
>
> *If you feel that your motives are not of the purest love, ask for My help. Only I can clear away the barriers that cover up and imprison that central core of one's being. Only I can clear away all the man-made ideas that have relegated this primal power to a back seat and put anything and everything in front*

of it. If you put yourself in My hands, I can remake you by My cleansing and purifying.

Slowly, slowly, through the years I was learning to turn to love. When I would attune to God, such wisdom and love came through to me that there was never a question any more whether to listen and obey. To do so was my joy. As gradually this became second nature to me, I was told within that I no longer needed to seek specific guidance, that I was able to stand in my inner knowing and make wise choices. And should I ever make an unwise choice, I must remember that perfection is not of this earth, and not important, for God desires most that our choices be free.

But I'm getting a little ahead of the story, for before I came to that place of inner composure, I had to weather a crisis of faith.

I had secured a good secretarial job at a lawyer's office in Oban, and was living in the Caddy trailer in a caravan park there. For one of Scottish descent it was an interesting and romantic place, with boats going and coming from the islands and a daily walk past Dunstaffnage Castle. But at that time I was on my own, out of contact with the others, with no spiritual work to do. Suddenly the precarious, uncomfortable and lonely life I was leading seemed pointless. As far as I could tell, I was accomplishing nothing. I was alone, and I could see no future. God seemed far off or even non-existent. I lost faith in my guidance, which up to then had always been a wonderful daily support.

I decided to go home to Canada as soon as I could earn enough money for the plane fare. I considered I owed it to Sheena to tell her my plans, so I hitchhiked from Inverness to Oban, hoping to find her somewhere in the Hebrides. This was the day before Christmas and perhaps the worst day of my life. I had great difficulty in hitching a ride. A huge lorry carrying fish eventually picked me up and, traveling by a very slow and circuitous route, reached Oban late on Christmas Eve. Full of self-pity at being homeless and alone at this special time, I trudged through the streets, searching for an inn in my meager price range. The next day I took the ferry to Mull, heading for Kintra, where I believed Eileen was staying, thinking she would know Sheena's whereabouts.

I found Eileen, Peter and their baby Jonathan in a cottage there. Sheena was elsewhere looking after their elder child, Christopher. Eileen had fallen into such a depressed, negative state that Sheena, for his own welfare, had taken Christopher away. Peter and I agreed that Sheena had acted wisely, but Eileen found it unforgivable. She and Jonathan had been alone in the cottage for several miserable months until Peter had arrived—just a few days before I did—to take them away.

Sheena soon appeared, and when I told her of my plans, she urged me to stay in her Mull cottage to think things over for a few days. I agreed and settled in her isolated and primitive abode: no electricity, a camp bed, a peat fire for warmth and cooking, water from an outside pump, and heather and rocks as a lavatory. Despite the January weather, I was content with these conditions, for I rather enjoy roughing it. The few days turned into a few months. I had almost no money. A simple but caring local man, who had previously looked after Eileen, now looked after me. He brought me peat, and sometimes fresh eggs or biscuits, squashed or not in his pockets, all stolen from his parents. The only problem was that he wanted to marry me!

Peter has likened this period to my "dark night of the soul." After several months I realized that it would not be right to run away to Canada. Instead, I left the cottage and went to join Peter, Eileen, Christopher and Jonathan in Glasgow.

To elude the press, who were still hunting for the Nameless Ones, we kept a low profile. Peter got a job selling brushes from door to door, while I found temporary secretarial work. Our biggest treat was to have fish and chips on payday. Lena Lamont, Peter's landlady, a lovely girl from Skye who was living with her husband in Glasgow, joined our group. Lena did not need the extensive training from Sheena that we three had undergone, and immediately became part of us as much as her shyness would allow her.

Glasgow was not a beautiful city to us. Its good points were its soft water, its luscious brown bread, and the anonymity it afforded. We were there for quite a few months, unable to find more agreeable jobs, for if we were known to be the Nameless Ones, no one would hire us. Finally, Mrs. Bruce, general manager of the Allied Hotel chain, which owned twenty-one hotels in Scotland, offered Peter the opportunity to manage one of them. She knew he was one of the Nameless Ones but had a certain sympathy for our view, although she made us promise not to regroup. A new chapter in our lives began.

Chapter 7

In 1957 Peter, Eileen, and the two older boys left for Cluny Hill Hotel in the town of Forres. A little later I, and then Lena, her husband and their three children, joined them at the hotel. There I worked as a receptionist/secretary. This was not easy for me; my training was to run an office, and to me the guests were interfering with my work. I had to learn to be pleasant to them. I also had to accept taking dictation from Peter, although I was sure that I, with all my training and experience, could write better letters than he.

I would become annoyed when Peter told guests that it was a wonderful day, when in fact it was pouring with rain. I would look at the dark clouds and mutter to myself, "That's a lie." At the time I did not appreciate how his positive thinking helped people to be positive themselves. However, I could appreciate the masterly way he ran the hotel and our staff of fifty. He kept a card index of the guests, with notes on the drinks, food and accommodation they liked, any peculiarities, and other items of interest. When he met them again he would know them by name and knew just what to offer them.

The hotel chain booked bus tours, which mainly consisted of people from the Midlands, for overnight stays. As these people would not, in Peter's eyes, raise the status of Cluny Hill Hotel, he offered them lesser food alternatives, like the fish and chips dinners they were used to, and at set times. The higher paying guests had a large menu to choose from, for Peter's attention went to those who would best help the hotel become a success. He arranged sports like pony trekking locally, and water skiing at nearby Findhorn Bay. Though he usually knew intuitively what action to take, if he was at a loss he would ask Eileen for confirmation through her guidance. How could we not be successful with this divine support? Peter was fond of saying that God was running the hotel.

The hotel was open from Easter until October. During the closed winter months the Caddys remained in the hotel as caretakers. I was not allowed to stay for the first winter, probably because Mrs. Bruce feared a regrouping of the Nameless Ones. I found a room in the nearby town of Elgin and bussed each day to a job as secretary to Gordon Baxter, head of the food firm of Baxter's, in Fochabers. In the spring I returned to Cluny Hill.

The next winter I was allowed to remain in the hotel, and we all worked at clearing the grounds, which were overgrown and neglected when the military took it over during the war years. I also redecorated—with wallpaper and paint paid for out of my own pocket—the bedrooms of the neglected staff quarters, which were dreary and murky. I loved doing this, bringing color into the drabness. My efforts were scorned by the housekeeper, who told me that I would get no thanks or appreciation from Allied Hotels. I think what really upset her was that I was breaking tradition by penetrating the staff quarters, something not done by the 'black staff.' These were the housekeeper and receptionists, who wore black and were allowed to eat in the dining room, while the rest of the staff ate in the Staff Hall.

As it happens, I detested the color black, and had never worn it. In London, I had removed every single black item from my flat—even the lines around the matting of pictures on the wall—which resulted in the place having a very floaty feeling. As receptionist, I chose to wear charcoal grey instead. When that wasn't accepted, I bought the finest black I could find— a cashmere sweater set—in the hopes that its luxurious softness would soften me. On the first day that I wore it, I got a telegram from Canada saying that my beloved father had died. That made me hate black all the more!

A year after my father died, my relatives told me that my mother was dying of cancer. I rushed home to Guelph, where dear Aunt Ina had come to take charge of the house while Mother was in the nearby hospital. I arrived in time to hear my painfully thin mother say that seeing me was her last wish come true. She seemed to have the knowledge that her life was over, that she had done all she had to do, and that it was time to leave. She asked that I please pray that she just go now. I did, and she died a day after that, her physical suffering over. She had lived alone for a year after my father died, and must have missed him terribly. In spite of how much we all loved her, I felt that the timing of her dying was right. That loss led to yet another: the selling of our family home in Guelph. Though my brothers and I cherished it and wished we could always have it, our lives had taken us elsewhere. Years later it was declared a heritage home by the government, much to my joy for that protected it against change.

I returned to Cluny Hill Hotel and stayed there five years. The first few winters were rather odd: just a handful of us living in a large, elegant and well-appointed hotel, but without running water. (The pipes were drained when the hotel closed for the winter to prevent cracking.) The only water available was in the boot hall, a small room with a single tap and a gas burner on which we heated water. When we wanted a bath, we would trudge down the long corridors and upstairs to our bedrooms bearing pails of hot water, then dump the contents into primitive tin tubs. In later years, the Caddys were allowed to use a suite with running water. This certainly helped with the three little boys, the youngest of whom, David, was born in the hotel.

Our focus during these winter months was our spiritual work. Every day we dedicated time to attuning to the Masters of the Seven Rays as portrayed by Alice Bailey, to sending light and love out to the world, and to connecting with beings from outer space and to the Network of Light. The latter two developments had been started by Naomi Edwards and her group near Chicago. They had charted the Network of Light, which was composed of what we called Magnetic Centers, groups of people like ourselves working for the betterment of the planet and situated all over the world. Our job seemed to be to contact them telepathically to encourage them in their spiritual work, to link strongly with them, and to warn them that a crisis was impending that would require us to rely on our inner connections. We understood that there was danger that humans might shatter the planet with nuclear power. Lena and I expressed our association with them in words, while Eileen was given visions.

All this was great training in broadening our perspective: realizing that on the planet were many people also dedicated to furthering spirit, and that from outer space great beings on other planes were also helping the Earth. Lena, a most sensitive person, had a particularly close telepathic contact with extra-terrestrial beings. In this activity we were in touch with a spaceship manned by beings of superior intelligence who had come to help prepare us for a rescue mission in case of nuclear disaster. We were trying to raise our vibrations, and the extra-terrestrials were attempting to lower theirs, so that we could meet physically on common ground. We felt very much on our own in this endeavor and did not know that other people were making similar contacts. I understood that my particular space contact, Bahento, had the job of discovering 'dark' spots on Earth from his scouting vehicle and reporting them back to the mother ship, which then sent positive energies to that area.

Here is a quote from Bahento:

When we come to the Earth now, we feel that we are deliberately pushed off, warned away, that the forces of evil [here is another example of my view of evil at that time] *have been ensouled against us specifically. It is not pleasant.*

These forces must feel the strength of God behind us, for why else would they fear simple ones like us who merely seek out their area? If they are deliberately fighting us, they will do likewise with you. We are just passing this on.

Of course we could be fully protected if we only entered the Earth in our higher bodies, but that is not the aim. The new Earth is to function physically as we know it, higher than you know it but nevertheless in dense physical bodies—dense as compared to light bodies. We have our part to play in this, and our task calls for the most ingenious resources. We can go through the solid wall of evil if we are vibrating finely enough, but we must solidify again on each side of that wall. Humans, in order to go through too, must also be able to vibrate finely enough to be unaffected. Or we could blast our way through and rely on protection as we move. When the actual operations are taking place, we cannot rely on protection from you on Earth, for unless you have expanded very greatly, you will be too occupied with the job at hand.

We would just have you know that we are tackling the problem of the Earth in every possible way from our angle. We do not mean that we see an immediate application. We are just doing our part, delighting in the inner growth of the Magnetic Centers and, as always, are very grateful for your recognition and love.

We had chosen a place on the beach where we hoped the Extraterrestrials could land their craft. Peter and Lena went there at the full moon to practice raising their vibrations, while Eileen and I stayed in the hotel sending love and light to them. We wondered if the village people thought that Peter and Lena were having an affair down on the beach. That was perhaps a good cover story!

The cooperation with the Extraterrestrials went on for years, even during early Findhorn days, but we stopped when they told us that the current danger of the world blowing itself up was over. We kept files, mostly now lost, of the transmissions and directions from the spaceships, and understood and "translated" these transmissions according to our views at that time. We might interpret them differently now, in the light of more experience and knowledge. I believe our connection with the space beings was real, particularly in its intent and energy. It covered a lot of different aspects of life, no doubt as part of our learning process.

As much as we could, we read current spiritual literature. I remember a book called *One*, in which the author stated that people could not begin their spiritual work until they knew their spiritual names, and that she could help them discover this. Eileen and I took this to heart and wrote to her. Eileen recalled a vision she had had years ago, when the word "Elixir" was inscribed on her forehead. The author confirmed that this was indeed her name. I had more difficulty, as the first name that came to me, Mal something or other, sounded wrong to me. The author agreed with this, and then confirmed that the second name that came to me—Divina—was correct. I regret now that my earlier books were published under this name; it sounds so pretentious, and should not have been used publicly.

In the summer months, Cluny Hill Hotel had our full attention. Gradually it became more popular and gained a supportive and loyal staff, as well as regular visitors. Scottish Country Dancing was resumed in the ballroom, and I would attend, though I knew none of the dances and was awkward. One participant, a large local lady, was always kind enough to ask me for a dance. She was so incredibly light on her feet that even I felt adroit with her. At times a group of staff members, called the Cluny Loonies, gave concerts on primitive instruments like pots and pans. Being fairly far north, in midsummer it was so light that we could play tennis after work at ten p.m.

During one memorable period, we were short of receptionists and for some time I had to work from eight a.m. until ten p.m. As a result I got so tired and stressed out that I didn't care how I behaved, didn't care what people thought, and broke down and cried in reception in front of whomever was there. My behavior brought to mind an utterly wretched-looking woman—filthy, dressed in rags, hair uncombed— whom I had once seen in front of the Church of St. Martin in the Field by Trafalgar Square in London. I had looked at her and thought "How could any human being let themselves go to that extent? Where is her pride? I could never sink to such depths." Yet here I was, sunk so low that I was past caring how I appeared. I was appalled at my previous judgment. It was a good lesson.

Hotels are difficult and stressful places to work in, for the staff members never get away from one another as they would in a nine-to-five job. In Scotland, one way to relieve stress is to drink whiskey, and at one point all our heads of department were alcoholics. My favorite story of this period concerned our delightful alcoholic head chef Charles, who arrived late one afternoon so full of whiskey that he was unable to stand up—and he had two hundred dinners to serve! Peter's intuition failed to give him a clue, so he rushed to Eileen, asking her for emergency guidance.

Eileen turned within and received this message for Peter: *My son, if you want the dinners served, give Charles another whiskey.*

Peter did as instructed and, to the astonishment of all of us not least of all Charles, this had the desired effect. Dinner went off without a hitch. Who but God would give such seemingly stupid yet miraculously effective advice? We learned through such incidents that whatever the situation, spiritual or material, we could get help from within, and we came to trust and accept the messages each one of us received.

Sheena visited us one winter, wanting to stay with us and resume her former role as our leader. Our pretext for refusing her was that we had promised Mrs. Bruce, the general manager, that the Nameless Ones would not regroup. Mrs. Bruce had been especially adamant about keeping Sheena away. But we knew—and Sheena sensed, too—that the real reason for our refusal went deeper than that. After years on our own, relying entirely on our inner guidance, we no longer had the need for a human teacher. Sheena had long ago predicted that such a day would come, but that was evidently scant consolation when it actually did. On a personal level, she seemed hurt and angry, and behaved rather badly. There were some hard feelings on both sides when she left the hotel, and it would be several years before we met her again.

There were many battles with Mrs. Bruce, who practiced "management by intimidation"—a technique that didn't work at all with Peter. On one occasion, he placed an order for better quality china. Mrs. Bruce sent us more of a cheap grade. When it was delivered by an Allied Hotel driver, Peter just smashed it to the ground. When he didn't approve of one of her orders (a command to fire Charles, for example), he would let it be overruled by the guidance that came through Eileen. The guidance proved irrefutable, and never failed to bring about appropriate results. The combination of Peter's positive thinking, his efficient management, and God's help brought so much success to the hotel, that Mrs. Bruce had little choice but to tolerate Peter's insubordination.

Then the press got wind of us again. An article appeared in the newspapers alluding to our connections with UFOs and calling Cluny Hill the "Heavenly Hotel." We were not sure who had furnished this information, but the result was that the chairman of the hotel chain became an object of public ridicule. That may have been why he, Mrs. Bruce and a delegation of executives descended en masse one day to fire Peter. But Peter's belief that the hotel was his to manage was so strong that he would not budge. He simply refused to acknowledge that he was fired no matter what they said to him. I would have loved to have heard that conversation! Somehow his mulish insistence on the positive won the day. That year, the hotel turned a profit for the first time in its history.

Chapter 8

After five years at Cluny Hill, Mrs. Bruce asked us to go to the Trossachs, another struggling hotel in the Allied group. We didn't want to leave, but our guidance said yes, go, and send love to Mrs. Bruce. It was difficult to love her, but we tried.

The Trossachs Hotel was a large and splendid Victorian edifice, set among beautiful scenery near Loch Katrine. Yet it was gloomy, for the wild hills surrounding it kept out most of the sunlight, and it had acquired a reputation for being the graveyard of managers. Somehow all of the large staff who had accompanied us there fell under the dark spell of the place. Nothing seemed to go right. I even resumed smoking for a while! That summer even Peter lost heart. He requested a transfer back to Cluny Hill, although we were expected to spend the winter at the Trossachs. I think Mrs. Bruce was tired of battling with Peter. When we didn't immediately succeed with the Trossachs, she finally had an excuse to fire him. On the closing day of the season, she and some auditors arrived and, with no explanation, gave us four hours' notice to leave. Such a precipitous instruction was usual with hotels at the time, as it prevented managers from making off with the silver.

I was painting the wall of a room when the news came down, and had to stop in the middle of a brush stroke. How I hated leaving a partly painted wall! A black cat, who had adopted me at Cluny and had come with us to the Trossachs, was at my heels all that day. I couldn't leave him in an empty hotel and had to arrange for the Humane Society to collect him, which bothered me more than anything else. I had a final skirmish with Mrs. Bruce when she asked me to hand her the contents of my typing basket. I refused, as there was some of our guidance in it. She snatched the papers from me. I bided my time until she relaxed, then snatched them back and kept them.

So Peter, Eileen (who had guidance that I must stay with them) and I hastily packed our belongings, picked up the three boys from their one-room schoolhouse, and headed north towards the caravan that we had left at Findhorn, near Cluny Hill. The Caddy family was allowed to stay at an Allied hotel, the Stotfield in Lossiemouth, for two nights, while I slept in the caravan.

As the caravan was on a summer location near the beach, it

had to be moved. We found a space in a neglected corner of Findhorn Bay Caravan Park, and moved there on November 17, 1962. Though the trailer, a Rollalong, was the Rolls Royce of its kind and was long for its day (thirty feet), U.K. road regulations limited trailer width to seven and a half feet. This is a narrow living space. The main bed and table folded up in the room that was the sitting room, dining room, bedroom, library and office. Every bit of space seemed to do double duty, for it had been carefully designed by boat builders. The boys slept in the second room, with the kitchen and bathroom in between. They went to bed at eight o'clock, freeing the main room for us adults. Eileen trained them to accept this discipline easily. They loved the cozy family space after being in a huge hotel where they seldom saw their busy parents. True, they had to crawl under the ironing board if Eileen or I were ironing, but fortunately they were small at the time. People now look at the original trailer and often ask how we ever managed in such a tiny space. Well, we managed, for we were certain that we were where we were meant to be. When one accepts and does not resist one's situation, difficulties often vanish.

We hoped to return to Cluny Hill Hotel for its Easter opening, especially as we heard from the local staff that the hotel had gone downhill since we had left. We spent the winter concentrating on our spiritual work, getting books from the mobile library and living simply. Peter and I read anything we could find, but Peter, in his belief that Eileen could best keep the simple clarity of her inner contact without intellectual knowledge, would not allow her to read books on spiritual subjects. As there wasn't room for me in the caravan, Peter secured a sleeping space for me in the closed summer staff quarters of the Culbin Sands Hotel in Findhorn village. Every day after tea I would walk over the sand dunes and through the gorse to my room, turn on the electric blanket (there was no heating and it was a cold winter), walk back for the meal and the evening with the Caddys, return to sleep, and join them again in the morning. I loved those walks through different sections of the gorse and the sand dunes, and became familiar with the whole area.

That spring, Cluny Hill Hotel opened without us. We rushed to get our guidance, all of us receiving that we were to stay at Findhorn. Peter and I tried to get jobs, with no success. We went on National Assistance (Unemployment Benefit), which at least gave us a small amount of money, almost sufficient for our very simple life style. To supplement our meager diet, Peter planted lettuce and radishes on a bit of land adjacent to our trailer.

At the caravan park we were very much on our own. People who had been friends of the Caddys when they were in a position of social prominence, or when, as manager of the hotel, Peter was able to be of help to them, snubbed us completely now that we were on National Assistance. Only three people made friendly calls on us. Two of these were very low ranking but delightful ex-members of the hotel staff. The other was a traveling salesman who often stayed at the hotel. As a guest, he had been inordinately fussy, always complaining about his room, the mattress, the food, and so forth. He was the last person we would have expected to seek us out. We enjoyed tea with him, and he paid us another visit in the following year.

One thing we knew, and had long known, was that we were to remain together, though we didn't know why. We were simply committed to doing what we called 'God's will', whatever that was. I realize more and more the power of commitment. We were three very ordinary people except for our commitment to God, and on this rock the now famous Findhorn community was built. Knowing that we were to stay there and follow our guidance to be more loving, whatever happened, was a complete job.

> *What is more new to you is the group work and awareness. Previously your glimpses of the new were only with Me. I am with you always, but the group awareness is to grow. . . . Love is the bond. No matter on what level a person is living, if the love is there it can bring a sharing of experience.*

To feel this love on a day-to-day basis was not always easy. Our personalities were very different; we had different interests and were not natural friends. Peter and I, in particular, seemed to rub each other the wrong way. He was completely one-pointed, brooking no opposition to his relentlessly positive outlook. I am more of a balancer, inclined to see two sides of every question. If I differed from Peter, he would assume I was just being negative, and then ask me to supply reasons in support of my viewpoint. I always seemed to take the bait and fall into the trap of trying to fabricate a logical rationale for what I felt intuitively. Since these rationalizations came after the fact, they were usually pretty flimsy, and Peter had no trouble demolishing them. I was constantly losing arguments I didn't want to have in the first place. It was only years later, after I had left Findhorn, that I finally understood this dynamic.

Peter's natural bossiness was another source of conflict between us. Since childhood I have hated being ordered to do anything. My mother once showed me a letter sent by my grandmother after a visit to Guelph when I was very small: "Dorothy can be asked to do something, but not ordered," my grandmother had observed. That remains true of me even now: if a request is phrased as an order, I automatically resist it. This is a dynamic that Peter seems never to have understood. As a former RAF officer, he was used to giving orders and having them obeyed. So we had a lot of rows. Each time, I would turn within, find it in myself to be more loving toward him—until the next row.

Eileen and I jogged along with each other as best we could. She often had to act as intermediary—almost always with guidance— between Peter and me. I admired her domestic talents, her wonderful way with children, her incredible visions, her ease in talking to people: all areas in which I felt inferior. Until I read her autobiography years later, I had not realized that she considered me an intellectual and had, for all those years, been feeling inferior to me! In later life we did get over some mutual insecurities and become closer.

With Lena and her three children, who had spent the winter at the Trossachs and had rejoined us in the spring, and Naomi, the telepathic medium who was visiting us from America, we continued work with the Network of Light. For me, the experience of this contact was different from that with my inner divinity. I used the word 'telepathic' to describe it, as it was more on a mental level, lacking in the deep quality of experiences that came from God within.

The easiest group for me to contact was a tribe of aborigines in Australia; they were always right there, as if their consciousness was constantly open to non-physical realms. The next easiest was a group of Eskimos. Another group impressed me as not being in physical form. We contacted many of these "stations," and became familiar with their general location, which we marked with pins on a globe of the world. (Years later, Jonathan Caddy remembered this globe and asked me what the pins were for.)

The transcripts of these messages seem to be mainly lost, though I still have a few, like the following dated November 1, 1962:

Mexico City - Saw a stepped pyramid in the light with people on it, with other people crawling up on the pyramid and being pushed back. The Center seemed old.

Those of the light are very much under attack. They are pushing back, but you will notice that those of the dark are only a little lower than they are.

Australia - Aborigines. I experienced these as a small band upright in the light and free, with shields to fight for the light. But cut off, alone.

My inner guidance had the following to convey:

Yes, there is much work to be done on the Network of Light, the Magnetic Centers. Feel into each one with Me and you will be given their state and can help them. This help of course will vary, but I can lead you to the ones which are in the greatest need. Thus each Center will become living to you, and as it becomes real, you can be used to link it up more strongly with the light.

The linking up is necessary because some of the Centers think they stand alone and even if their conscious minds do not know of the linking done, a feeling of being part of a greater whole can grow in them. Know also that none of these Centers are dead; the radiations are working through them in some level or another, because they are part of the earth itself. The Stations of Light may vary but the Magnetic Centers are established.

Concentrate first on the Centers, for even if they are established they need to be of the chain of light now for the new. Remember how Cluny Hill had to be brought to life? There are many levels of bringing to life, and yet all is one.

Another group, X-7 (X standing for Christ and 7 as the 7th center in this grouping), consisted of people in Siberia incarcerated underground who were developing sustenance from invisible energies. Messages from them were later published under the title *A World Within a World*. Here is one of their messages:

The forces that come out of the earth are what you would call 'spiritual' forces, and yet they encompass a great range of wavelengths, including some quite dense physical ones, because they have to do with living on the earth. The forces that come from outside, from a more developed source like the sun, have permeated the earth and are part of it, for life is a union of various substances. The center of the earth is a source of pure power, an essence; the surface is the meeting ground of many forces from many sources.

We find our support in this central earth essence to an extent which would not be possible unless we were where we are. We think that in the Divine Mercy we have been put here to discover this, for if our need were less, such a meeting of forces would not have taken place. Therefore whenever we can, we pass on something of our findings.

We feel the potentials are vast and quite untouched. We feel that developed people's movements have been away from the suffering earth into finer realms, and that this should not be, that here on this very earth is everything needed for perfect living. We know man's inhumanity to man better than most, but we feel that this need not be, that when the balance is restored this world can be a paradise. We can feel the earth forces and they are so constructed that this is not only possible, but part of its destiny.

We should like to impress this on all the Magnetic Centers, that they may regard this earth with the love that it should have, and not abuse it as has been done increasingly. A love for it would open all your eyes to the possibilities inherent in it. We should put an end to the belief that this is a darkened planet, and return to its Maker's concept of it as one of the fairest of creation, with a life most richly endowed.

We pass this on with love and gratitude, and the hopes that you too will begin to feel the fair forces of earth.

We had no outer level of proof of the authenticity of these communications, since any responses were only received inwardly. I suspect that some of the groups were unconscious of our link with them. Years later though, a group from Ephesus in Turkey visited Findhorn. They reported that they had spent many years trying to find us, their only clue being the word "Findhorn," which had come to them while doing their inner work. I had left Findhorn by then and so missed what must have been a wonderfully affirming meeting.

In 1960, an interesting phase of the inner work began for me, one I called "Roaming Telepathic Links." I would periodically put out feelers and would come across someone who wanted to make contact, and I was given wisdom to help them. Different people connected with me each time, and sometimes I knew the place or a name. Occasionally follow-ups were needed. Here is an example of one such conversation:

"Do not leave, do not pass on. I am alone and must share with someone or I shall go mad. It is my husband; I am sure he is trying to kill me but I cannot voice this to anyone for they simply would not believe, no, not anyone. He has brothers and sisters who must know what he is like, but they would not believe me. My own friends would say it is my imagination and that I am just tired. It is not what he does, it is what he does not do, and he is so different when anyone is with us. We have no children and I half believe that is the reason, that he would like to get rid of me and find another wife, but would not have guts to go through with a divorce. I have offered a divorce with myself as the guilty party, but he would not have that. I believe it is an 'accident' that he wants. Life is not worth living, but dying this way is too much. I feel better by having come out with all this, and please talk to me about it."

"Have you anywhere you could go to if you left him? Somewhere far away?"

"I have thought of that, and there is a distant cousin in another country. I could get there but would not have money to support myself or get back."

"Could you not get a job there?"

"I could try, oh, I could try. Just to make a clean break. It is such a relief to hear you suggest that, because I daren't suggest it to myself seriously. It is the only answer and it will be hard, but now I see it is right. Yes, I will quietly do it. After I make the break then he could not find it difficult to let a divorce come through in time. Yes, I will do it. I feel controlled about it already. Thank you more than I can say."

"Not me. Thank God."

"Yes, that is better. I thank God that there is a way."

There seemed to be no pattern to my roaming telepathic contacts. Some were from people I knew, but most were from strangers. Some identified their place and circumstances, with others I just had to guess. The following, for instance, seems to have come from a group of tribal people, possibly African:

"We search, we search. We have heard from our forefathers that if we search we shall find, and we know this to be true in other directions and therefore we search in this direction - and behold, we have found. We search for guidance, not in our daily lives, which are simple enough, but where to find refreshment of spirit. In sleep we do not get it; we wake up more or less the same as we were. We know there is a way to these things. We have heard it is so, but the old ones who told us have died and we must find it anew. We found you by simply asking, asking, knowing we would find."

"What do you seek?"

"We seek communication with one who would lead us and our people."

"If you found it, would people follow you?"

"Now they do not. We had hoped that if we had the Voice, they would change. They heed only their own desires"

"If they have begun to follow their desires, they will not leave them to follow a Voice you talk about. The spirit of the self has grown up and they turn from the old ways. I believe 'The Voice' does not come to your people any more because of this, not because you are not fit leaders. It is not you failing your people; it is your people failing you."

71

"You have told us what we really sought. We can face our forefathers' memories now and not be taboo. We can live again openly and we thank you. We know where to come if there is need again."

When I look back that these many contacts after over forty years, I am amazed at the wisdom I was given to respond to them. I would like to have that much wisdom now, but these days it no longer seems to be my role to counsel people.

Meanwhile my inner guidance kept encouraging me to expand my range, to feel out into forms of consciousness that I would not have thought accessible to me.

The individual work of each is a matter of stretching into the unknown. You do not know what you will find because you are pioneering. Here different faculties are needed: a sense of wonder, an openness, a longing, searching. Here are not positive goals that require positive faculties and a stamping out of the old, but a search. To each it is different, but it is a giving up of the little self to find the greater . . .

I was told that the feeling-out process would not just take me upward but would take me out and even downward, for our work was with humanity and humanity lives on many levels. I was told that there is always some purpose behind the workings of nature, a cause and effect, a need being met, a bridge being built, a saturation point of some force. I was to stretch into it and let little bits of knowledge and understanding come gradually.

I, God, have made Myself available to you at all times, in any place. The part of Me which you contact has come down to meet humanity, as humanity has not been able to come up to meet Me. Usually a person would have to be in a very heightened state before contacting Me. The other contacts you make on the inner have a certain range; they come to meet you but you on your part must also meet them, as your vibrations have to coincide. They speak from the vibrational range of their worlds; you must to a certain extent enter their world vibrationally. Therefore what they say is limited, in the same way as your receiving is limited. As the highest, I cover the whole range. This Allness of Mine is the reason you feel so safe with Me. You do not feel the same sense of security with others because limitation is present.

When I didn't feel equal to all this inner stretching, I received encouragement.

Even when you are feeling down and seem to reach a blank wall, or when you despair of ever achieving unity, underneath that very surface failure know that you are unlimited, know that you are at the time based on the old and that it is only temporary. Know that you can and will reach out, touch and be in a brand new, tingling, living space. Base your life on this.

And:

You have felt very stuck for the last few days, unable to stretch. The light is always there, but sometimes it is easier to feel than at other times. In fact it is there, glowing, radiating, and warming you, infilling your whole being as you go into it. There are many reasons why sometimes it is easier to feel this. You are beginning to be aware of the unseen forces at work through all creation; they may be pulling you one way or another, say for testing. Just know that, however difficult, it is always possible to rise. Never give up . . .

And so I persisted, never dreaming what was about to happen next.

Chapter 9

When we realized we would not be returning to Cluny Hill Hotel, Peter began to extend our tiny garden in order to grow more vegetables for our meals. All of us became vegetarians, although not strictly so, as when gifted with a rabbit, we ate it as a gracious addition to our rather meager fare.

In May, 1963, during my regular morning meditation I received a message that turned out to be auspicious, ushering in a new phase of our work:

> *To those who have an insight into life everything has meaning. For example, there is a spiritual meaning behind the constant blowing of the wind, in spite of what may seem unpleasant results. To those with open eyes everything flits into place.*
>
> *The forces of nature are to be felt into, to be stretched out to, as you do to the Magnetic Centers . . . One of the jobs for you, as My free child, is to feel into the nature forces such as the wind, to feel its essence and purpose for Me, and to be positive and harmonize with that essence. It will not be as difficult as you immediately imagine . . . because the beings of these forces will be glad to feel a friendly power. All the forces are to be felt into, even the sun, the moon, the sea, the trees, the very grass. All are part of My life.*

I hoped this message meant that I was being given permission to go for long walks or to lie in the sun. Peter believed it pertained to our garden. My guidance backed him up:

> *Yes, you are to cooperate in the garden. Begin by thinking about the higher nature spirits who overlight, and attune to them. That will be so unusual as to draw their interest here. They will be overjoyed to find some members of the human race eager for their help. That is the first step: the smaller individual nature spirits are under their jurisdiction.*
>
> *By the higher nature spirits I do not mean just the one that geographically overlights the area, but the spirits of the*

different physical forms such as spirits of clouds, of rain, of the separate vegetables. In the new, their realms will be open to humans—or I should say, humans will be open to them—and when rain is needed, for example, it will be brought about. It is even possible with you now, if your faith were great enough and there were no sense of limitation. Now just be open and seek out into the glorious realms of nature with sympathy and understanding, knowing these beings are of the Light, willing to help but suspicious of humans and on the look-out for the false, the snags. Keep with Me and they will find none, and you will all build towards the New.

Peter has stated in his autobiography that it was his badgering that was responsible for my making contact with nature. This is simply not true. If anything, his pestering me to do something usually got me moving in exactly the opposite direction! What actually happened is that in my regular attunement one day, I found myself in a stream of power. I felt inwardly powerful enough even to communicate with a vegetable. Had I known that I would be meeting a great planetary being, I probably would not have thought myself equal to such an encounter. But, being in a sense of power, I could reach out without any feeling of inferiority or superiority. I realize now how important it is to have inner strength and conviction when entering a new realm. Reaching into newness out of need or lack creates an unstable condition and genuine contact cannot be made; there just isn't resonance.

I chose to start with the garden pea, which I've always liked eating. If I focused on its essence, maybe I would be able to recognize it as a conscious being and establish some sort of communication. But what was that essence? I considered its outer form—the shape of its leaves, their color and that of the flower, the smell, the taste—and imagined what those qualities would be if distilled into oneness. To my surprise, I felt a message coming through right away. Like my experience of the God within, it communicated a feeling, an inner impression, that I had to find the words to express. Here is what it said:

I can speak to you, human. I am entirely directed by my work, which is set out and molded and which I merely bring to fruition, yet you have come straight to my awareness. My work is clear before me: to bring the force fields into manifestation

75

regardless of obstacles, of which there are many on this man-infested world. You think that slugs, for example, are a greater menace to me than humans. But this is not so; slugs are part of the order of things and the vegetable kingdom holds no grudge against those it feeds, while humans take what they can as a matter of course, giving no thanks, which makes us strangely hostile.

What I would tell you is that as we forge ahead, never deviating from our course for one moment's thought, feeling or action, so could you. Humans generally don't seem to know where they are going, or why. If they did, what powerhouses they would be! If they were on a straight course of what is to be done, how we could cooperate with them! I have put my meaning across, and bid you farewell.

I wondered whether slugs were capable of giving thanks. My new contact replied:

It is not that a slug is evolved enough to give thanks, but that it follows its own force field. Unlike humans it does not go out of it and bring in forces which upset others.

I realized that this communication was not coming from an individual pea plant. Vegetables had group souls. There was an overlighting spirit for each species. These were planetary beings, responsible for holding the pattern of their particular vegetable in the northern and southern hemispheres. The closest word for them that came to mind was "angel," but according to my Christian background, angels were fully formed with wings, haloes, harps, and flowing robes, whereas I was in touch with a formless energy field. I had heard of the word "deva," Sanskrit for "shining one." That's the word I chose at first, because it was uncluttered by cultural preconceptions. A little later, my understanding of what "angel" meant expanded, and then I came to use both words—angel and deva—interchangeably.

When I read the Pea Deva's message now, I see that other preconceptions of mine crept into my translation. Phrases like "man-infested" and "strangely hostile" reflected my own distaste for how we humans have treated the planet. Angels themselves do not convey such a carping negativity.

I was delighted by the contact itself—the mere presence of this being and its willingness to communicate to me—and that remained true of all my encounters with devas. It never mattered to me whether or not what they imparted was immediately useful. When I showed the message to Peter, though, he was mainly interested in the part about the slugs. Right away, he prepared a list of questions about other plants and asked me to get in touch with their devas. Supplying him with horticultural advice was to keep me busy for years.

A few days after my initial contact with the Pea Deva, I became aware of a being whom I called the Landscape Angel. This was probably a misnomer, as it led people to think this being was only responsible for the landscape. In fact, it was the local representative of the Planetary Angel, responsible for helping us to achieve Findhorn's role in planetary transformation. Perhaps I should have named it something like the local representative of Gaia. The earth's magnetism and this angel's magnetism were linked; it was responsible for all life in our geographical area: mineral, vegetable, animal, human, angelic and archangelic. The Landscape Angel became a mentor and general intermediary with the angelic kingdom throughout the growth of the garden and our other spiritual work. Its main task—and Findhorn's main task, as I understand it—is to ground humanity in the fact that all of us can link up consciously and act from our inner divinity, and to raise awareness that nature has a vast intelligence and that our conscious cooperation with this intelligence is vital to the well-being of our planet.

Messages from God encouraged this contact:

> What you write down from the deva world will gain in power as you are completely and utterly free with it. Up to now you have still had a hedge of doubts which limited what came. You cannot mix the old world you know and this new world, for the new world does not make sense in terms of the old and your critical faculties are of no avail with the devas... Remember also that most of the beings you contact are highly evolved and understand human feeling, so they will try to meet you... It is best to have no set ideas.

The Landscape Angel communicated:

77

The contact between our two worlds is something we seek to foster as much as possible. We know it is in the Plan, and therefore any of us are always ready to extend to a sympathetic human our love and help. Our very life force is extended towards your world—how can it be otherwise when God, life itself, in each and every one is moving towards unity? We feel this mighty trend. We are of it and we know it, while most humans are unaware of it or just talk of a new age. There is no theory in the angelic world; we live, we flow with the force, we are these new age energies. So when any of you turn an ear vibrationally in our direction, so to speak, we are here. We more than meet you, and contact is readily established.

And God added:

Mingle with these beings. It is an exchange and a beginning of a unique and far-reaching cooperation. They are amazed and delighted that their cooperation is sought and then followed so faithfully, and at this time in the world's evolution when humans are increasingly harming their work. It is not only important but vital that a new relationship be established.

Listen to the sounds of nature whenever you have the chance. They are true sounds, coming from Me within each, and can lead you into My world and into the world of the sound devas. When you are close to Me, you are tuning yourself into worlds of growth and forces which are always present and have a tremendous effect on humans unconsciously. When you are conscious of them, they open up and reveal how you are linked. Do not worry if you get no specific message; as you tune into them, the link with them grows and may bear fruit in a slightly different direction—with the devas for example.

Some months later, God told me:

You are pioneering in the true attitude to nature, to the one life. For this attitude, it behooves you to think of everything in terms of life force, not merely an impersonal force like electricity but a manifestation of a being. They can teach and help you, though what you see of them outwardly may be a lowly bee,

a leaf, a stone. Behind all is a great chain of life leading to Me.
Humans have been given dominion over all these on Earth, but
only as you too fit into the great chain of life.

I also received from the Angels:

We receive your thoughts that this is all very wonderful, but
what of the reality of the increasing rape of nature and human
destruction of the world of form through pollution, etc? Such
are the results of human lack of contact with us. When you
turn to the reality which we are, as you become more aware
of the truth of our existence, you will no longer break the laws
of your existence.

Having established contact with the nature devas, we
experimented with growing a garden in direct cooperation with them.
Peter supervised the outward work, while my job was to pose questions
and receive answers from the various devas, as well as the Landscape
Angel. At times they were very definite in their recommendations, but
they never gave us direct orders. The devas don't want humans as
obedient servants. Rather, they want us to cooperate with them from
our own wholeness, as equals.

Early on, the Landscape Angel told me we shouldn't expect the
devas to do the work. If we wanted healthy vegetables, we needed
to have healthy soil, and it was up to us, who had hands and feet
on earth, to produce that soil. What we started with was little more
than sand. Peter read up on composting, and we scouted the area for
whatever organic matter we could obtain for free. Peter would keep an
eye on the horizon for smoke, then go the next day to where the fire
had been and collect the ashes. Eileen and I would gather seaweed
from the beach, and buckets of horse manure from a nearby field. We
also used to scrounge in one area of the caravan park, a little valley
which was a town dump, never knowing what useful object we might
find there. We enjoyed that and, exulting in the richness of our finds,
laughed at a TV program that commiserated with poor people who
had to depend on dumps.

For the first five years the garden was our daytime work, while
our spiritual connections continued in the evenings. We had a small
annex built onto the caravan for my sleeping accommodation, and I

no longer walked to the village each night. As the hill slanting down to our caravan was of no use to the owner of the caravan park, he allowed Peter to terrace and plant on it.

In the evenings, Peter would round up Eileen, Lena and me for an hour or so of attuning to the Network of Light, or whatever our meditative work was at the time. Then we would watch television, with Eileen and me knitting, and the cat ensconced on one of our laps, while Lena returned to her own caravan and family. Eileen did wonders as a cook, with only two burners on which she layered double or triple boilers. The food was simple, but we gloried in the taste of our luscious homegrown vegetables. For lunch we always had a fresh salad picked from the garden, lettuce and a medley of herbs, a daily feast which Peter and I loved but which bored Eileen.

Every week Peter and I would go into Forres to collect our dole money. This hurt my pride, and I also felt I should be working and not collecting money gratis. Eileen worried that Peter would lose heart and become a scruffy ne'er-do-well, with nothing to live for. Actually, though, we were working harder than we ever had in our lives. Peter realized that his real purpose at that time was the garden and the cooperation with the devas. Occasionally the National Assistance Board would offer him a job, but only menial jobs were available. He would dress in his best clothes (Eileen's guidance seemed to encourage this), successfully conveying the impression that the work offered was unsuitable for someone of his qualifications. Great fun! Occasionally I too was presented with a job opportunity. I did secretarial work in Forres at Sanquhar House for Major Hilleary, and also for a time worked in the office of Moray Estates.

Peter and I continually clashed while the two of us were outside in the garden. He insisted on having the radio on, while I wanted to listen to nature sounds like the birds and the wind. He believed plants liked classical music, while I believed plants liked whatever music the gardener liked. I got guidance that we should compromise by taking turns. If memory serves me, his turns became longer and more frequent, and eventually became permanent!

Peter planned and planted. Eileen and I were not allowed to plant even one seed. We picked up stones, weeded, and humped the wheelbarrow. It was laborious work, often in the rain. The taste of the vegetables rewarded us. We had forgotten, for example, that potatoes could be so delicious. I say "forgotten" because before World War II chemicals were rarely used in agriculture. Our own organic produce recalled the flavors we had enjoyed when we were young.

Deciding we should add some herbs to the garden, Peter consulted many catalogs. The herb plants were shipped to us carefully wrapped to contain their moisture and keep them healthy. One that we had obtained this way was Sweet Cicely, which we later discovered was a very common roadside weed in our area. The herbs were tasty additions to our daily salads; we experimented with new ones and grew giant dandelions for blanching. Fruits came later. Berries flourished and I well remember, as if in answer to a prayer, having more strawberries than we could actually eat. We had such magnificent black currants that the blackbirds used to walk under them with their mouths wide open, simply waiting for the fruit to drop in.

A herb deva expressed approval of the garden's growing diversity:

> *We can indeed speak with one voice. We were more or less awaiting you, for we have been told of what happens here. Also the connection between humans and herbs has long been close. Before you come to us individually, learn more of us so that you do not have to think to differentiate us.*
>
> *Of course our plants each contribute something different. It is good for humans to eat different varieties, though they do not consider this important. The aromatic plants add something of their own. We range into wavelengths unique in the different smells they portray, and our special contribution is that we affect different parts of your physical bodies. Therefore naturally the wider range of plants you eat, the more balanced help we can give you. That is all we wish to say now, as we add our radiances to the garden.*

Later, flowers expressed their delight in being included, as in this first communication from the Petunia Deva:

> *We have been wondering when you would get around to us, because we want to say that we love being in this garden. Here we can swirl our forces around in soft, rich brilliance in complete comfort. Round and round we go, complete masters of each little flower, absorbing what the sun gives when it*

looks at us and what humans give when they look at us, then incorporating such into ourselves.

There is an immense interplay of energy among all creation. As you need air to breathe and fish need water, so each plant, each part of life, is immersed in an atmosphere that is part of its make-up and to which it also contributes. People can contribute most of all, and when you do this beneficially, what a wonderful world it will be!

You are wondering on what level you are contacting us, for we do seem very flippant and gay. We have many levels of contact, as do humans. Not that we are as moody, but we also have various facets and are not very serious or earnest. We are alive, we go into life fully; we have to, the season being short. In any case, why hold back when life is there to be expressed? There is nothing to stop us, as there so often seems to be with you.

Go and have a look at us now. Look at our makeup, become more familiar with it, for it is an expression of us and you have the feel of it right now. All is one, all has a pattern on another level. See how it works.

Other devas expressed specific concerns, as in this message from the Black Currant Deva:

We doubt very much that the mature blackcurrant bushes would survive transplanting. Plants are part of their environment, and whereas young ones are pliable enough to be moved, with the older ones it is a delicate matter. Of course we shall help all we can if you decide to try this out, but we feel much more can be done starting out with young plants. We look forward to cooperation with you.

As gardener and "representative of humanity" Peter was most interested in the practical messages like these. I was always glad—and relieved—when a practical message turned out to be reliable, for I was less confident of those than of the more philosophical ones, which arose from deeper levels of attunement. In the past, Eileen and I had often compared notes to confirm our guidance, but as Eileen did not receive deva messages, I was on my own.

For instance, I didn't know how to evaluate a message like this one from the Manure and Seaweed Devas.

It would be better to put the manure and seaweed in the compost rather than in a separate pile, because in the compost they will be broken down more quickly and will provide a more varied diet for the soil.

The only way to be sure that I'd perceived such a message correctly was to act on it and see what happened.

My own delight was in what Peter called my "ethereal, philosophic communications." For me, these seemed the most important, for they put what we were doing in a larger context, awakening us to large dimensions.

Responses from the Landscape Angel often mixed practical advice (such as when to turn the compost), with insights into how our efforts were being viewed by the garden. I would be told that the compost was irradiating it, uniting it, and that a clod of earth was alive with light, not heavy and inert as it might appear to me. From there, the communication would often expand into larger realms.

When you think of us, remember that every conceivable part of life is alive, and if it is alive and manifesting force, there will be a spirit of that force. We are a vast world ensouling many things, qualities as well as material things. For example, when you affirm something, when you repeatedly sound something, you tune into the spirit of that something or create it yourself. The "Aum" for example, tunes into a certain level, a certain life, and creates a certain life. There is no such thing as dead matter in the sense that it is an unloving thing, or a thought in the sense that it is a dead thing. All are linked and part of worlds of force. So be ready for and open to us. We are very real.

Don't imagine that all the energy around, whether in the atom or in flowing water, just happens. In our world, which is closer to the world of causes, we see all things are a manifestation of intelligence and that all happenings are related. We work in this world of force. Humans are prosaic and take these things for granted.

From the earliest contacts, the deva messages, too, spoke of other levels. They emphasized how people's thoughts and feelings are creative and affect all life, and that they, the devas, are able to work even more effectively when we join our creative thoughts and practical efforts with them. The devas see life in terms of inner energy, and suggested that we think in those terms as well: think of plants as glowing with life. Certainly in my contact with them I felt a glow, a joy, a juggling into life. The Landscape Angel once described it like this:

We work in what you call mantras, in movement, which produces sound and makes a pattern, and works up to a certain pitch. By these movements I am now putting a quality of life force into the garden, bringing it to a certain level and minimizing irregularities. As you come to believe in these forces yourselves, seeing how much greater they are than anything manifested in the outer world, not giving strength to appearances, so these powers become yours and you will wield them as we do, with joy.

Some years later, when the garden was flourishing and the community growing, the Landscape Angel returned to the theme of power, expressing its satisfaction:

The power in my area has increased enormously . . . You are very close to that power, in some ways more part of it than myself. Yet do not mistake me, there is no division on my part . . . The aspect impressed on you now is unerring stark strength, and you see me going about my consecrated business in lightness and freedom, while you seem anchored. That is but one aspect of the whole . . . If only humans would see there is no division, all worlds on this earth would be more effective in their close working . . . We are always open . . . I give no message nor teaching to humanity . . . we are here like the sun shining on all and sundry, and you can appreciate us or not as you wish.

Chapter 10

Once I learned to attune to plant devas, the Landscape Angel was eager to widen the range of my acquaintance in the angelic realms. I met angels of sound, of silence, of color and of the elements. I was attracted to the higher energies, a realm of beauty, love, joy, and truth beyond the carping mind. Contact with them helped to awaken these energies in myself. I believe that this gift of awakening was more important than any of the practical information we received.

I have collected some of these messages in a separate section of this book, where you can read them little by little, since attuning to the vastness of angel minds can be a bit overwhelming. Some, like the Fire Angels, were just too powerful for me to approach at first, though after some years I did finally succeed in making contact with them. I wondered why it was that the Fire Angels overwhelmed me, while contact with God had always been so intimate and so pervasive, permeating all levels yet never too much to take in. Maybe God is approachable to humans because of our need,—a need a Sun being probably cannot comprehend.

Attunement to the devic/angelic dimension is not done on the intellectual level; I need to have an energy relationship with my contacts. If a plant is unknown to me, it is no good just reading or having someone tell me about it. Only from its physical presence can I contact its uniqueness, its specialness. I must choose to be in my own wholeness, to be one with God, and from there resonate with the Divine aspect of a plant or any other being I wish to contact. This means going into the deepest love that I know, for it is love that connects us with the rest of life.

Strangely, although the devas' teaching was all about love, they at first struck me as rather cold and impersonal. I remembered stories of changelings, of fairies kidnapping human children and substituting their children, which seemed very unloving to me. Years later, I questioned them on the subject. They told me that I had been expecting love focused on me personally as humans do when loving one another, whereas they, the devas, focused on everyone, not just on individuals.

That love can be powerful on material levels was made clear to me early on. I enjoyed roaming the moors next to the caravan park, the eighteen acres of spiny gorse with its little rabbit paths and hidden hollows. One day I came across a delightful hidden dell. Whenever I was upset (generally with humans) and needed to find peace, I would go there to find balance and harmony. Winter weather put a temporary stop to these retreats. When I ventured forth again the following spring, the new gorse growth made the paths very prickly and uncomfortable. Because I loved the area and it was my particular place, I attuned to the Gorse Deva to ask permission to trim the path. Permission was given, and I had many a happy wander in and out of my chosen spot. Again the following winter I stopped going there, and again the following spring found the paths blocked by new growth—except for some ten yards around my special dell where the gorse was actually growing away from the path! I couldn't believe it. Somehow in response to my love for it, the growth pattern of the gorse was changed!

The power of love was again made clear when Peter asked me to get rid of the caterpillars which were devouring the leaves of the gooseberry bushes. As I didn't know the life cycle of these caterpillars, didn't know what the moth felt like and therefore thought that I could not resonate with it, I believed that I couldn't attune to the deva accurately. What could I do? I decided to pick the caterpillars from the gooseberry leaves, put them in a jam jar and later dump the jam jar on the compost heap for the birds to eat. That seemed in accord with nature, up to a point! I began to make regular tours of the gooseberry bushes, picking off the caterpillars by hand and depositing them in the jar. It was a horrifying experience for me, for I had always been afraid to touch legless things like worms, caterpillars or snakes. Now I had to do it almost daily, and I hated every second of it. Still the caterpillars proliferated. One day I remembered that the only adage we had at Findhorn was "Work is love in action" and realized that fear and hatred, not love, were the emotions I was expressing.

To change myself, I thought of and attuned to something I loved. Then, in love, I explained the whole situation to the inner world of caterpillars, asked for their help, and went on with my round of de-caterpillaring. Several days later, I found the creatures still busily eating leaves until I came to the bushes which, during the previous round, I had dealt with in a loving manner. These last three bushes were completely free of caterpillars!

One day Peter asked me to get rid of the cutworms that had eaten off the rootlets of our cabbages, causing them to sicken and begin to die. As I knew nothing about cutworms, I asked the Landscape Angel how to do this. The Landscape Angel shook a metaphoric head, and said something like: *Our job is to nourish life, not to kill it.*

"Then what am I to do?" I asked.

The reply was that we were to send love to the cabbages whenever we saw them—we passed them many times every day—and that we should imagine them as vigorous and healthy in spite of their sickly appearance. Obviously we should continue to meet their needs for water and other nourishment. We complied with these suggestions. It worked; the cabbages re-grew their rootlets, were healthy and ripened.

Some years later, Donald Wilson, secretary of the Soil Association, offered confirmation of what we had already learned from the Landscape Angel. The Soil Association had two experimental fields in the south of England planted with cabbages. One field was fed with artificial fertilizers, and the other with natural fertilizers. At harvest time the field fed with natural fertilizers had far more potentially damaging creatures like cutworms in the soil, yet it also had healthier cabbages. (see message in Appendix 3, page 203 about specific questions) The Landscape Angel's view was justified: a caring environment can nourish abundant life.

Our own cabbages were an early and famous result of our loving cooperation with nature. They grew so enormous and healthy in soil commonly believed to be unsuitable for growing cabbages at all, that news of them spread and people came to see them. Some of these people decided to join us, and a community began to form, much to our surprise. Somehow the fact that we were in direct connection with nature beings, with fairies and angels, and actually received their help, struck a deep chord in human hearts. After the first publications about our work, we received many letters from people who had had similar experiences, saying how relieved they were by our disclosures, as they had believed they were alone, and possibly crazy.

How to deal lovingly with moles proved something of a challenge. During our first year at Findhorn, they invaded the garden, attracted by the luscious earthworms born in the compost. For the moles this was a great improvement over the barren dunes where they had been living. Their burrowing under our parsley left roots dangling in air, unable to get sustenance, and plants began to die. Peter decided the moles had to go, and asked me to see to the arrangements with their deva. I didn't believe I could contact animals, but something had to be done.

My first idea was to use my imagination to surround the garden with a wall of light, thinking that might bother the weak eyes that moles were said to have. I asked God whether this was a good move, and the answer was, *"You can try it."* For almost a week there was no evidence of moles, but then the stones indicating their burrowing appeared. I asked within about this failure, and was told, *"Well, you didn't believe your wall would work, did you?"* True: I hadn't believed it. I spent a miserable summer feeling responsible for the mole problem, trying every method I could think with no success. Then winter came and the moles disappeared. At first I thought they were just hibernating, especially as to my relief, there was no sign of them the following spring. For years afterward, the garden was mole free, and I was happy to forget all about them.

Some years later, after we had become a community and I was working in the office, an adjoining piece of land was given to us. It had moles. By then we had a team of gardeners, who had heard the myth of my getting rid of moles and now came to me for advice on how to do it themselves. I say "myth" because I didn't believe that the moles had ever cooperated with me, but I thought they might cooperate with these young, animal-loving gardeners. They did and that new area became mole-free.

We had been at Findhorn for seven years when I moved to a new caravan, only to discover that there was a mole living on the property. This time I succeeded in contacting the over-soul of moles, to whom I proposed a compromise. I said that the mole was welcome to rampage during the winter, for there were no vegetables or flowers on my land, but that when spring came I would have to ask it to leave. I felt that my request was understood. The mole did rampage, and during the winter months it left many little piles of stones. As I picked up the stones, which had to be removed lest they harm the lawn mowers, I didn't know whether to laugh or cry. After all, I had said it could rampage. Spring and moles came and I once again had to contact the Mole Deva to remind it of our agreement. I still wasn't sure I could do that, but I put myself in a loving frame of mind, focused on the soul of moles, explained the situation and asked for help. I felt I was understood. The next morning, my next-door neighbor came to complain that a mole had invaded her garden. Again I attuned to the mole intelligence, and was told: *"You didn't say where the mole was to go, did you?"* So I suggested it go into a nearby empty field, and in the following days saw evidence that it had done so. Only then did I believe that I could contact animal intelligence.

Peter proposed that I take up beekeeping, and we found a retiring beekeeper willing to sell his hives cheaply. I was full of trepidation, but the old gentleman took me to one of his hives, opened it up and was so obviously enthused about the bees that I caught his joy and love for them. We transported them to the caravan park, and I handled them as best I could. My best was very little, the minimum, for I considered that the bees knew more about looking after themselves than I did. When time came to take off the honey, we asked a beekeeper in the area, the local minister, for help. He generously offered his kitchen, his equipment and his time for me to spin the honey off the combs. This is a very sticky, slow, business. Though we never went to his church, he continued this unselfish charity for several years.

Bees are fascinating. A couple of times I saw them loitering outside my window, obviously not on their usual route to and from flowers. I wondered if they were trying to tell me something, so I went to the hives and indeed found something that I could and did put right. The Bee Deva was full of wisdom, telling me to be calm and collected at all times when dealing with the bees. Many people wanted to help me with them, but one sting would usually put them off.

I eventually became allergic to bee stings, discovering this when helping with someone else's bees which I was told were "savage." They did sting me and I reacted with a wildly thumping heart and difficulty breathing, and found myself falling to the ground in great fear. Peter found me and took me to the doctor, who told me I must never deal with bees again, that I would die if I did. But as there was no one else to look after them, I continued, taking great care and wearing protective clothing. Years later, in America, while I was alone on someone else's property, I got stung. I wondered how to prepare to die, whether I should find and tell friends, or just stay alone. I chose the latter, but after some fifteen distraught minutes realized I was not going to die after all. I then discovered I had been stung by a wasp, not a bee.

When it came to loving contact with other beings, my greatest challenge of all were the rats that began to infest our compost heaps as our community grew larger. I didn't mind them frolicking in the compost, but when they moved into the space between the railway sleepers that supported my annex, I felt it was time to draw the line. Beneath the floor, just inches from my bed, they frisked around, thumping or squeaking and squealing in their rat voices, loudly enough to keep me awake. When I would stamp my foot, a brief silence would result, but just as I was drifting back to sleep, the racket would start again. After three consecutive sleepless nights, I knew I had to contact the Rat Deva.

Like most humans I hated rats, believing that they spread disease, ate grain grown for people, bit children, and were generally horrible. I knew this attitude was unlikely to endear me to the Rat Deva whom, frankly, I was not all that eager to meet. That night, when the rats began their noise, I thought of something loving, entered into a state of love and in that state connected with the essence of ratdom, the over-soul, in the same way that I connected with the soul of any life. All that I could think to do in the circumstances was to explain the situation honestly and ask for help. I told the deva that human beings need sleep, and that I couldn't function without it. I admitted that I couldn't offer the rats anything in return for their cooperation, though I myself would do nothing to harm them. I suggested it might ask the rats to play in the daytime, or go somewhere else.

I felt I was understood. There was a little noise beneath me, but gratefully I fell asleep. The next night the same commotion was going on when I went to bed, and again I tuned into the quality of love and again went through the same explanation and plea for help. Again I fell asleep. The following night there was silence. Though I was very glad of it, I didn't immediately conclude that my appeal to the Rat Deva had been a success, for I still had little faith in my ability to communicate with animals. I figured the rats had merely found a better playground elsewhere.

For four years, I slept in that annex and was never again troubled by rats. I forgot all about them. But when I moved into a caravan of my own, my room was given to a community member, who after his first night there, came running to me saying, "There were rats after me all night long!" He was sure they were trying to get at him and meant to bite him. I was thunderstruck. Evidently, the rats had been keeping quiet as a result of my request—and had kept their pledge for four years! They were perfect gentlemen. My feeling towards rats completely reversed; I saw them as intelligent, cooperating, caring creatures and felt a great love for them. One day I saw one in the compost heap, and I swear we winked at each other.

Maybe I gave them too much love, for rats began to proliferate in the community. Peter was afraid that a Sanitary Inspector would find them and close our kitchen. I was told that unless they left, poison would be put down. Though I tried to tell people what wonderful beings rats were, no one seemed to believe me. I was not surprised at this, for it had taken a miracle to change my own attitude to them. One community member was sprouting wheat grass with difficulty, as the rats would eat the wheat seeds at night. When I spoke up on behalf of the rats, she recalled the "Dear Ratty" that she had loved in the book *The Wind in the Willows*. A moment later, though, she was back to worrying about the rats eating her wheat grass.

Once again, I attuned to the Rat Deva, explained the situation and asked it to persuade the rats to move. I never got a chance to find out what effect my request had, for poison was put down after all, and some rats were definitely killed. As a community, we failed to cooperate with them.

Years later, when there was a mouse infestation in the kitchen of Cluny Hill, the kitchen crew attuned to the Mouse Deva to explain why, from the human viewpoint, mice were not welcome in the hotel. They asked for help and also put food outside for the mice. This time the cooperation worked, and the mice left. Still later, when there was a different kitchen crew who did not attune to them, they returned. Evidently, truces with animals apply only to the person or group of people who have specifically requested them, and expire as soon as there is no one around attuning to the animal oversoul.

I received messages from animal species, and found them just as much interested in communications as other devas. For instance, in connecting with a bear in Alaska, it told me that although it was a loving being, it did not have free will. It behaved instinctively and would always try to protect its cubs from humans. They can't change their behavior. But as humans are able to learn how animals behave, we can accordingly deal with them appropriately, fitting in with animal behavior.

In Nepal I also recall contacting a mother rhinoceros and her calf, who were being rounded up regularly to be shown to tourists. On this occasion I felt a surprising sweetness in this ungainly and prehistoric animal, which delighted it. It commented that it would be glad to have a more sensitive body through which it would be more

91

able to express the sweetness. For a long time I would not tell this story, fearing that people might assume that, as it wanted a different body, it would be alright to kill rhinos.

Chapter 11

We had lost contact with Sheena since the winter when she visited us at Cluny Hill Hotel. She turned up again during the winter of 1963. This visit was even more troubling than the last had been. A shadow of her former self, she was occasionally bitter, opinionated and angry. When she tried to reassert her role as our teacher, she got angry when we resisted. On one occasion, she even slapped my face. Another time, she tried to take away my file of the poems that God had once given me about her. Sheena had been the most important influence on my spiritual life, the person whose help and counsel I had valued most in all the world. It was heartbreaking to see her fallen into such a diminished and joyless state.

Grieved and confused, I sought understanding from God:

> *You feel only immense gratitude for all that Sheena has been instrumental in doing for you—and I alone know the extent of that—and you want her, and I through you, to know that. That is an ever-present truth . . .*
>
> *You wonder how Sheena, being what she was, could be what she is, and now you understand more. The force has been withdrawn, the sensitivity dulled, even the memory shattered . . . The heart has returned to Me. Remember Sheena as she was, part of My heart, and let your gratitude go towards Us.*

Through the years, our guidance had referred to a Perfect Plan and an Alternative Plan. Sheena had been at the center of the Perfect Plan—which clearly was not going to work out. But plans don't necessarily fail. They change. Choices change them.

Without Sheena, there would have been no Findhorn. To this day, I continue to consider her teaching valid and true and helpful. She had supported each of us in our direct contact with God, and in relying on inner guidance that would eventually render an outward teacher unnecessary. Years before, she had predicted that this would someday lead us to reject her as a teacher. Yet we were loath to reject her as a friend. Even Eileen, who had once hated Sheena, had mellowed and was making an effort, and suffered as the rest of us did when our guidance confirmed that we must ask Sheena to leave.

93

Perhaps she felt we were rejecting her teachings. Having devoted so many years of her life to training us, perhaps she felt as though it had all been wasted. If so, what a burden to carry! I don't know exactly what had happened during those intervening years to wear down the radiant woman who had once personified Love to us, and seemed to us an example of a living Christ. I don't know how she came to be so broken and bitter and desperate.

She lived nearby for a while, in a house in Croy. Eileen and I visited her there once. She had a wild bird nesting in her living room. She kept a window always open for the bird. I have never heard of a wild bird making its home in a human living room. It must have felt her love. Nevertheless, the life that she was leading seemed empty and desolate. She couldn't help others—or even herself—any more. To me it seemed the only solution was for her to die. The moment I thought that, I felt guilty. When I heard some years later that she had died of cerebral hemorrhage, I felt even more guilty, thinking that perhaps my feelings had somehow influenced her death.

About a year after Sheena died, Findhorn was visited by a healing medium. One day as he was giving a healing session, with Eileen, Peter and myself assisting him by laying our hands on his patient, he said there was someone on the inner realms who had a message for me. We asked who it was, and he said he did not know, that it was someone who had died fairly recently. Eileen asked "Is it Sheena?" "Yes", the healer said. The message for me was "Now I understand." What a relief that was for me! I was overjoyed to hear from her, and my guilt left me.

In 1965, Peter's parents moved from their home in Devon and Peter motored down there to help them. Our telepathic friend Naomi and I went with him. En route we visited Edinburgh, where we met various people attending the Edinburgh Ecumenical and International Convention, our first entry into the extensive and interesting group of British spiritual seekers, occultists and mystics. An organizer of the convention was Lady Mayo, memorable because she wore nothing but purple—she even had a purple fur coat!

We gave another organizer a lift further south to St. Anne's, where she planned to contact Liebie Pugh, founder of the Universal Link. When Peter knocked at her door, her secretary, Joanie Hartnell-Beavis, said that Liebie was resting and couldn't be disturbed. She invited us to return the next day. Peter would have none of this; he insisted on seeing Liebie and bulldozed his way in. She was a remarkable person who looked like a Tibetan. She was completely dedicated to the Christ, whom she knew as the All-Knowing One, or Limitless Love and Truth, and who overlighted her. I found her very disconcerting to be with, for she only responded to you when you talked from spiritual levels. If I made a superficial remark for the sake of conversation, it was as if she didn't hear me. Otherwise it was a joy to be in her presence. She became our friend and supporter, and we gained like-minded friends from among the people close to her. When Liebie died a few years later, some of these friends, like Joanie, joined us.

From St. Anne's we continued to Glastonbury, where Peter left Naomi and me at the Chalice Well Trust while he went on to Devon. We stayed at the Chalice Well Trust for some days, and, after Peter rejoined us, spent an absorbing evening with Tudor Pole, who was over ninety at the time, and was obviously a master. I felt he knew what I was thinking, and knew that I knew.

In 1966, Peter attended a New Age conference sponsored by Sir George Trevelyan at Attingham Park. After that conference, people became interested in us and we began to have more visitors. R. Ogilvie Crombie (ROC), an elderly scientist whom we had met in Edinburgh,was one of them. He was also artistic and a fine pianist. The living room of his Edinburgh flat held thousands of books on many subjects. It did not, however, have all modern conveniences. I was fascinated by the complicated contraption he had rigged up with an overhead bucket that enabled him to have a cold shower each day by pulling a rope.

While visiting the Royal Botanical Gardens of Edinburgh, Ogilvie had had the unusual experience of seeing a mythical creature, a faun, dancing in front of him. He spoke to the faun, who was surprised and exclaimed, "But humans can't see us!" Ogilvie replied that this human could see him. To test him, the faun did an intricate dance and asked Ogilvie to describe what he was doing. Ogilvie described the dance correctly and in detail, and they became friends.

This was the beginning of Ogilvie's connection with the elemental kingdom. He said that the elementals' forms were actually light, that we humans projected human-like forms on them in order to make our contact with them easier for us: an assumption that they often accepted.

Every now and then he would be favored with the sight of and communication with elementals: the beings of the four elements of earth, air, fire and water, the legendary gnomes, fairies, salamanders and undines. His stories were fascinating. He was a reserved person, not easy to get to know as he didn't share much about himself. But he and I, with our common love of nature, understood and respected each other.

My basic understanding of the nature realms is that the devas hold the archetypal pattern and plan for creation and wield its energy, while the elementals are the craftsmen who transform that energy into more material form. Ogilvie was in touch with their overseer, the god Pan, as well as the Master St. Germaine. I was delighted one day when I took him to my dell in the gorse and he said that this place was Pan's headquarters in the area.

Findhorn's famous cabbages were grown before we knew Ogilvie, but now the help of the elementals was added to that of the devas. The elementals are in a sense more down to earth, and Ogilvie could often be more specific about garden problems than the devas were. Elementals are also closer, vibrationally, to our human personalities, which meant that they expressed feelings when we did something in the garden that they didn't like. This was helpful to me, for at times I would sense that something was off-balance, but couldn't put my finger on what it was. The elementals were precise about it. If we made what they considered to be big blunders, they might threaten to leave the garden.

Peter followed common gardening practices including the pinching off of sweet pea buds, in order to have one big bloom on a long stem. The Sweet Pea Deva communicated its disapproval of this practice more tactfully than an elemental would have done:

> *I come in like a breath of our perfume, fresh and clear-colored, gay and dainty, not the promise but the fulfillment of the perfection of sweet pea beauty and above the world of error. You ask why the flowers have not long stems. Long stems have been forced by humans when they distorted the natural growth and created a mutilated, unbalanced plant, and this is the sort of treatment which causes our kingdom to distrust and move away from the human kingdom. Humans have dominion on earth and there is nothing we can do about that*

treatment when they consider only their own ends regardless of the means. But you cannot expect any of us, and particularly those directly concerned with the production of each plant, to find the freedom of enjoyment which goes with the unfolding of the perfect pattern or, knowing the pattern is flawed, to feel drawn to humans.

Of course there is an answer to this problem, as there is to all problems. That lies in cooperation, in working together for and with the plan of the whole. You wish long stems in order to arrange the flowers in large groups, and this can be done providing all concerned are working together for the project. This is achieved not by outer destruction of part of the plant, but by inner concentration on development. You humans have a large part to play in this because you are the innovators of the change. You have to make clear to and convince our various members sufficiently to ensure their cooperation, and then you must ask, believing, really believing. It is not a matter of experiment to see how far it will go, but always an experiment for a useful productive end, part of the great forward movement of life.

You wonder how you will know that we are convinced. Our kingdoms are not unreasonable, though some members are justifiably suspicious. Therefore it would be wise to go softly until you are proved trustworthy. With full cooperation between our kingdoms, developments are possible beyond imagination. We on the devic level would hold a blueprint for that time, when all creation is working together under God for the good of all creation, and there is life-giving harmony between us and you. We will play our part. Will you play yours?

In fact, the Sweet Pea Deva was even more gentle than my translation of its message would suggest. The implication that nature was distrustful and moving away from us reflects my own understanding at the time: I would have mistrusted humans had I been nature! I know now that nature follows its pattern in love, without blame though not without awareness.

In any event, Peter didn't take the Sweet Pea Deva's point. He considered the message too other-worldly (it is, rather), and went on picking off the buds. Then Ogilvie received a vehement message about the matter from one of his own contacts. That, like anything that came from Ogilvie, finally commanded Peter's attention. Perhaps because he had met Eileen and me when we were younger and pretty limited, Peter tended not to take us as seriously as he took Ogilvie. When I couldn't get through to him with my own deva messages, I would enlist Ogilvie and his elementals as back-up. This scheme worked for a long time.

Ogilvie became our wizard, our Merlin, and the protector of the community in his role as champion for the light against the dark. Neither Eileen nor I were involved in "fighting" the dark forces. Eileen's guidance assured us that this was work for Peter and Ogilvie, and that our work lay elsewhere. Now I see the "negative" very differently, not as something to be fought but to be embraced as a help in our individual growth towards wholeness, for the polarities cannot be separated and complement each other.

Chapter 12

In the mid 1960s, Peter sought the advice of a Scottish Horticultural Adviser. This man took some of our soil to analyze, for he believed that all soil in our region was unbalanced. To his great surprise the analysis revealed that ours was perfectly balanced. He invited Peter to talk about the garden on BBC radio. Even Peter didn't dare mention angels to the Scottish audience, and said in the broadcast that our good compost accounted for the vitality of our vegetables. The program brought visitors to Findhorn who came to see the garden for themselves.

Our guidance had counseled us not to invite anyone to Findhorn— not even family—and not to seek any publicity. Nevertheless people from all over the world began to show up uninvited. Each one arrived with some incredible story about how he or she had been drawn to the place. One had been told by a medium that he was to go to a place called Findhorn and had spent a year or so just trying to figure out where Findhorn was located. Another had known for years that she was to join a community in the north of Scotland and had finally discovered us. Many other similar stories were told, and we loved hearing them.

As more visitors arrived, we needed an extra caravan for guests, but we had no money with which to purchase one. That is how we began to learn what we called the "laws of manifestation." Eileen received guidance that the caravan was necessary and was advised to apply for a loan from Peter's father, who strongly disapproved of his son's lifestyle. Her request was firmly refused. Next she was guided to ask her sister for a loan, which brought another furious refusal. Then my brother Don visited us, and poor Eileen had guidance to ask this shy stranger for money. He shrugged, said nothing, and left next morning. But some weeks later a letter arrived from Don, with a check for £200.

We were joyfully grateful and immediately took the check to Mr. Cameron, the owner of a caravan for sale. Surprised, he said the price was £350, and asked us if this was partial payment. At this, I looked so downcast that his wife felt sorry for me and whispered to me that she would fix it. The next day Mr. Cameron said we could have it for £200 if I painted an old caravan of his. That was fine, for

I loved painting. Before I could start though, Mr. Cameron had a row with the owner of the park and moved all his caravans away, except the one he had sold us.

Later we formalized the process of meeting our needs into the following "laws":

1) Make certain that what you want to manifest is in God's will. Use whatever method you are familiar with to determine this: attunement, sleeping on the idea, dreams, asking to be shown, and so on. Many people think that "following their bliss" is an indicator of God's will; it can be, but very often that bliss is simply a separated personal desire.

2) Have a precise idea or vision of what is to be manifested.

3) Make your needs known, and take action. Publicize the need, so that someone can be used to meet it. God works through people. Take the necessary steps towards the project.

4) Know that God will meet the need. Have utter faith and belief that the need will be met.

5) Give thanks that this is so, and give thanks again when the need is met, realizing this is God's work and you are a co-creator.

Learning to apply these principles was a gradual process. For instance, once we had our guest caravan, we wanted to add an annex—a small, shed-like structure at its entrance. Our guidance acknowledged that our need for this was legitimate. We held our vision of it, and felt sure the means to realize our need would manifest, but nothing happened. What was going on? Eventually it dawned on us that each one of us been envisioning a different role for the annex: a place to stash shoes and outerwear; a place to shelve our books and records; a place to sleep an extra guest. The vision we'd been projecting was muddled. So we tried again, this time coming to agreement on what the specific function of the annex would be, then all of us holding that shared vision. The very next day the perfect annex appeared at a very cheap price. We had learned another lesson.

In July 1963, I had received an impression of a nebulous being, a sort of Sleeping Beauty lying on its back as if waiting for a prince to come and awaken it with a kiss. Not that such a form physically existed. This was simply the picture that arose in my imagination as I attuned to its energy. I asked the Landscape Angel about it, and was told:

> *It is in fact a being, a very wonderful being...with its own peculiar beauty and developing rapidly. You all give it strength as you think of this place as apart, unique, pure. As you work for that perfection, the depth of your thought and feeling gives it strength...*
>
> *No, it is not an immature child-form, but unformed, asleep. It is of all of you and all that comprises your place, and yet it is a life of itself; it is both. You will have to get used to these vague boundaries in the inner kingdoms, for they overlap and interconnect, and will not be pinned down. The moment you think you know all about them, with a leap they are out of your grasp again, free beings...*

The Landscape Angel was telling me that a unique angel was forming. I was given to understand that when any group of humans became melded into a unique identity with its own separate presence, there was an equivalent soul identity, an "angel" of the group. Initially I conceived of this as an angel of our place (Findhorn), but I later came to understand that it was really the angel of our work. When I asked what to do about it, I was told that we could help in its formation and give it strength by sending it love, as well as by doing our individual work with love and joy. By consciously giving our united life force to the development of this angel, which I called the Angel of Findhorn, we were helping to create a new type of angel. With the wisdom of hindsight I can see that in so naming it, I contributed to much confusion within the community in later years.

A few months later, The Landscape Angel reported:

> *Your angel has a certain difficulty in forming, because there is enough higher energy to form a great angel, but so little geographical variety. Everything is in miniature except the vibration. It will have to be a new sort of creature.*

Later, the Landscape Angel continued:

I said before that the angel in formation for you is a new type of angel, and this is becoming increasingly apparent. It is gathering life from all of you in a unity with humankind not hitherto known. You are in a sense part of its body, and it will also act as a sensory bridge with you for others of my kingdom. Though to you it may be slow in growing, it is phenomenally fast compared to others. You cannot feel this new creature yet — nor can we, but we cause it to be brought about. Its eyes are closed yet, its reposeful hands still being defined, its length very great. Definite warmth to it will speed up its process and quicken its life. We are fascinated and delighted that you can see that much of it.

In November 1963 the Landscape Angel informed us:

As the garden grows, your angel is growing; the eyes are open and the head has some movement. No, you will not be able to contact it yet; it is not coherent enough, not yet one of us. When it is developed, our knowledge is its knowledge, for any of us can tune into or draw on an over-all level of knowing. You humans could do likewise if you so willed, but you have not developed enough, nor are there enough of you, to have an encyclopedia of the real world. Your immediate reservoirs of knowledge are racial and limited.

Later that month the neighboring Wilkie Angel introduced itself, saying that it was proud to have a hand in the fashioning of this new angel, and it was a privilege for it to channel forces to our angel. The Cluny Hill angelic being also mentioned its links with us, and in February 1964 the Landscape Angel said that this angel was almost ready to speak. But another three years were to pass before I could perceive any communication from it directly. Its first message came to me in February, 1967:

I take my stand with my brothers, and we stand tall and one in essence. Immensely vigorous and vital am I, with a role that reaches the four corners of the Earth and beyond.

I am a new being and we all rejoice that I am. We all rejoice amongst ourselves that, with the help of you all, has been born and grown to fulfillment one such as I, a prototype of this combined activity. I have been brought up and given sustenance by both the devic and human worlds, mothered by the Landscape Angel, energized by you all, and planned from near the Godhead.

Do not form a set concept of me and so keep me in limitation. My aspect of you has been of immensely vital young manhood, to use your terminology, that is a small and current view from the focus of the expansion here at present. I have many parts to play and much to do, and we do it together, we being you humans and myself as you see me. Yet I am more individual and general than others of my kind, rather a crossbreed.

Now I go from our consciousness, but I am in you and you are in me, different yet one. I am the spirit of a center of consciousness, yet how much more I am. You are limited human beings, and you are gods in the making. We are one because we have all been given life.

The injunction not to keep the being in limitation, not to hold rigid ideas, was a recurring theme in my messages. When we form a fixed idea of any conscious being — whether angel, friend or family member — we limit its possibilities in relationship to us. For anything to achieve its full creative potential, we need to remain flexible in the way we conceive of it, open to the possibility that it may have changed overnight.

We were thrilled that this angel was now capable of 'speaking'. But after the first message, it fell silent for over two years. In May 1969, it finally addressed us again:

From an unawakened godling I have grown to stature reaching up to the Highest, for the spirit of a place does not depend on the physical size of the land. Many qualities are part of my make-up, but now my greatest characteristic is height, up, up into the Highest. That straight line leads to the heart of all things, to God, to be found high up or deep within, in the Sun itself, whatever way your consciousness is attuned. I would lift you out of yourself into your core self; for that purpose I was brought into being.

You know me well in one way, but you do not realize the unseen activity required for my growth. The deva hosts have been busy and have come on the wings of every aspiration and of every effort made by any of you towards betterment. Nothing is wasted in the divine economy; all is used for the building of the whole. The bridge to Heaven is built with bricks you make yourself. This is always so, and this whole project has always been under God's guidance. Therefore the bricks have been put firmly in place.

With our feet attached to one bit of the earth, we angels and devas of an inhabited place meet consciously and jointly in the Heart of All, uniting and swaying as we spread our forces in the necessary directions. Some are active, some are quiescent; each helps the other. In your activity you have help from all over the world and beyond, yes, from the universes. This is a focal point, and to me as a channel with my head in the Heart of All, distance is nothing. It is the purity, the intention and the effort which counts.

Into me as a channel are pushed energies from all sides and on all levels in these worlds of spirit. I am fed with the friendly help of the greatest of Beings, Beings who have been of help to the earth through the ages. The openings in me into which these Beings pour that help are caused by all of you as you open more to perfection. I am, we are, one. I give as you give, I receive as you receive, but I can see from whence your help comes. I can see the vastness of the influences.

You do not have to think of me. I am here. Think of the Highest, accept no limitations, range any world, do any deed, turn from every shadow in yourself and face the Light. As you do that, we grow and the Spirit of Findhorn spans all worlds. Rejoice that it is so.

To have given birth to this angel was wondrous. I suppose I shouldn't have been surprised that it so captivated our fledgling community. We had fun composing and singing a song about it. (The chorus began: "Angel of Findhorn, open your eyes.") Yet I was—and still am—a little uneasy with the central role it occupied for so many Findhorn residents. Somehow over the years it took on more and

more prominence, until, when I revisited the community in the ea
1980's, I found that many group meetings were starting with an
attunement to the Angel of Findhorn. It was coming to displace what,
to my mind, is the more central and crucial attunement to the God
within. Perhaps incoming members found an angel less daunting to
deal with than God, especially if they had been raised in a tradition
that considered it blasphemous to believe that God was speaking to
one directly. Yet this direct attunement to God had been our founding
principle and practice. The Findhorn Angel would never have been
born without it.

I was uneasy, too, that the Angel of Findhorn came to eclipse the
Landscape Angel in the imagination of the community. In my eleven
years at Findhorn, I received hundreds of messages from the Landscape
Angel and only five from the Angel of Findhorn. Nevertheless, members
of the community tended to invoke the Findhorn Angel and direct
questions to it that were more properly the province of the Landscape
Angel. Of course, the latter never complained of this, for angels don't
get huffy when they are upstaged by other angels. But it bothered
me, for in overlooking the Landscape Angel, it seemed to me that
people were losing sight of the big picture, the larger context that our
garden and our growing community was meant to serve. I hope that
in sharing all 5 of the messages from the Angel of Findhorn as part
of this book, I have not perpetuated that overemphasis.

An early message from the Landscape Angel describes that
context:

> *When you humans rise to your true estate and sound your
> note as clearly and purely as that bird which is welcoming
> the dawn, all worlds will stop, listen and learn, for your note
> will be their goal. We are speaking this from the world of the
> angels, those who have not left the Father's house and who
> are trusted to wield divine power throughout the cosmos. Now
> we are your teachers, messengers and exemplars of how to
> live in a world that is one, and that is easy for us because
> our world is one, and even our form can be one when this is
> inwardly necessary*
>
> *For you we have provided the means for life's finest
> expression, to be many and yet one in the most difficult and
> challenging conditions. As you meet the challenge—as you*

ne wisdom—we marvel at our handiwork. Then it
to be teachers, and the love of God walks on Earth
sciousness, including all life, and the love of God
ıt to itself, to other planets and other systems.

u reach out to those distant worlds, remember that we
have been there first, we who have not the limitations of time
and space and who control the energy stuff of the universe.
You may call that energy positive and negative, even label
it good and evil, but when the fruit of the tree of knowledge
has been digested, you will know that all is one. You will be
proof of it, having emerged from the wars of the opposites to
unity. In your knowledge you will know as we do not know.
You will have our consciousness and more, and qualities to
rise to greater tasks. Your estate will be vast and will grow,
and we will grow because of it. As we all grow, we expand
and yet become one.

So let us be your teachers and share our joy and
limitlessness, and then let us go on as you share your seasoned
love, and all life rejoices and returns to the One.

The Landscape Angel, as well as guiding our overall development, was also our point of contact with other life forms in the area. Through this angel, I was introduced to the various garden devas and to more of the angelic realm. It is by attuning to the whole host of these teachers and messengers who "have not left the Father's house" that humanity can foster the health and growth of all living things, and the expansion of planetary consciousness. Though some of these beings help out with practical information, that is not their primary purpose. Rather, they seek to uplift us, to expand our awareness beyond the human-centered perspective that wants to grow peas because we are hungry for them, or to get rid of slugs because we imagine they threaten the harvest. The central importance of this higher attunement was a perennial theme of my messages from the Landscape Angel.

The Angel of Findhorn is more of a people angel. Its task was to communicate the wisdom and experience achieved at Findhorn with human beings in the wider world. The hundreds of people who joined our community were originally attracted to us by the garden and what it represented. Yet as the community grew, a subtle shift occurred. As Peter put it, "Now we are growing people, not vegetables." To be sure, growing people is a marvelous enterprise. But the garden was never merely a device for attracting people—or for feeding them. From the beginning, it had been growing something more than vegetables.

Years later I met Judy McAllister and she shared with me an image she had received of these two different streams of consciousness. I found it a clear and accurate reflection of my own understanding, and it has helped many to understand the nature and the relationship between the two.

Initially she was given an image of a being sitting cross-legged with some of its 'body' imbedded in the earth. In its lap was a large dome, inside of which were all the things she associated with the Findhorn Foundation and its relationships with the surrounding community. This was the Landscape Angel, holding in its care and keeping all the levels of life of the land at Findhorn, including all the human activities relating to the work of that centre. The dome was full of sparkly light, representing the collective state of consciousness created by the grounding of the founding principals of connecting to God and co-creation with nature. This sparkly light was somehow the 'product' of those activities, and it changed in color and consistency depending on the activities.

Into the image came another being. It was clear that the two beings were equal, though different, and there was a sense of mutual respect between them. The second being inserted what looked like a thick hose into the dome and began to draw out that sparkly energy. It then dispersed the energy out across the planet, as if through a garden hose spray attachment. This second being was the Angel of Findhorn. Judy understood that it is was not particularly concerned with the 'doings' going on inside the dome—rather it was interested in the 'product' of those doings. That sparkly energy, the collective consciousness, is the 'fuel' it requires, and the resource it needs, to engage in its own particular work of uplifting/transforming human consciousness across the planet. Indeed, to the "four corners of the world" just as it had initially told me.

The Landscape Angel holds the centre called Findhorn and its doings, in its care. Thus it can provide direction and support for the activities within the community. Findhorn is a grand experiment, one directed by spirit. The Landscape Angel can be called upon for specific help regarding how to live and work together. The Angel of Findhorn then uses the energies created, through that living and working, to sustain its work in bringing about a new state of consciousness in humanity.

I have said that in some ways the name Landscape Angel is a misnomer. It is actually a local representative of Gaia. This became even more clear to both Judy and me when we encountered another Landscape Angel during a workshop we were doing. In my workshops we often practice making a connection with the angel of the city or country we are in. In this case it was Athens. We encountered a 'grandmotherly' version of the Landscape angel, one that had been around considerably longer than the one we knew at Findhorn. The exchange we experienced reinforced our understanding of the Gaia connection.

Chapter 13

Though our guidance had urged us to keep a low profile, around 1969 we were apparently ready for publicity. Stories about a garden run by people who were cooperating with nature and producing giant cabbages appeared in newspapers, magazines and on the BBC. The heartfelt letters we received from people relieved that they were not alone in believing that "fairy tales" were true, touched and amazed us. A little later, Paul Hawkin's rather glamorized book, *The Magic of Findhorn*, was published, attracting hordes of people, many of them hoping to see fairies. The mystique engendered by that book still persists. I remember, after giving a talk in New Zealand in the 1980s, being approached by a lady who remarked, "How wonderful it must have been to have all the work in your garden done by fairies and gnomes!"

"But it was hard work," I responded. "We all worked very hard."

"No", she insisted, "I read that the nature spirits did the work."

She had just heard my own account of how the garden was developed, but it hadn't made a dent in her previous convictions. When I reiterated that it was we humans who had done all the hard physical labor, she exclaimed, "But there is that picture of roses growing in the snow!"

"That was after a freak snowstorm," I pointed out.

She glared at me for a moment, then snapped, "You're ordinary!" and stomped away.

Whatever it was that led people to Findhorn, many of them had unforgettable experiences of walking into an intense atmosphere of love. Some said they felt it even before they came within the boundaries of the community. Some said it seemed like coming home at last. They were deeply affected by this, and might be rather emotional for a couple of days until they got used to the energies. I never felt anything like that, but couldn't discount the many similar stories. I believe that the purity of our commitment to doing God's will, no matter what happened, built up this pervading quality of love. I am told that some people still have the same experience when visiting Findhorn.

People require attention, food, lodging, jobs to do, and answers to their letters of inquiry. As more and more of them arrived, their requirements became more complicated. People activities flourished, and our attention withdrew from the garden. I spent all my time in our newly built office. We formed the first Findhorn Trust, with Peter as custodian, Evelyn, (an elderly lady who had joined us) and later Joanie, as treasurer, and me as secretary. The law demanded that we keep minutes of our board meetings. As we didn't hold any such meetings, we enjoyed making up transcripts of fictitious ones, and voting on and seconding imaginary propositions.

Early on, we attracted a lot of psychics. When we realized we needed a place for group meditation, Eileen received a vision of a simple cedar building. Not to be outdone, every psychic in the community came up with his or her own vision of the future meditation hall. No two were alike. Peter listened to all of them, long after the rest of us were completely fed up. To me, his blind spot was his dependence on psychics: he was open to anyone and everyone who had a "message" to impart. We all tried, unsuccessfully, to get him to trust his own intuition. As usual, he wound up following Eileen's guidance in the end. We called our new cedar building the Sanctuary.

All community members started the day by meeting in the Sanctuary. Attendance was mandatory, and if some member failed to appear, Peter was sure to notice and take them to task. The meeting began with silent meditation. Peter always sat in the same chair, with Eileen on his right and myself on his left. After a while Eileen and I would read out the guidance that we had received earlier in the morning. Sometimes another person, often an elder, would find courage to share aloud some revelation that had come to them. Then Peter would share with us details of the projects that were happening in the community, and make work assignments. It was a unifying experience, helpful in starting the day on a positive note and in building a group consciousness.

Sanctuary could also be fun. One member, Ed, had an incredible ability to make people laugh there. One method he used was to stare fixedly at someone with an absolutely straight face, keeping it up with unwavering concentration until the person being stared at finally noticed and responded— usually by doubling up laughing.

After Sanctuary I would go to the office and spend the day there. There was lots of correspondence to deal with. Peter would dictate some of the letters. Occasionally in the middle of a sentence he would just get up and disappear. His intuition would indicate that he should go to some place in the community, and there he would find someone doing the 'wrong thing', or worse, doing nothing. After correcting the situation, he would return to the office and pick up wherever he had left off. His habit of showing up when people least expected or desired it soon became a legend.

Peter's style of leadership was as autocratic as it had always been. If people objected to his decisions or wanted changes made in the way the community was run, he would say that they were free to go elsewhere. Some took him up on that. Peter would listen to people's ideas, but if he felt they were a hindrance to the community, he had no compunction about throwing them out. Thus we were spared the burden of the hangers-on who have bedeviled many spiritual communities. To be fair, I would also say that he recognized when people spoke from a place of inner knowing.

Peter was a terrific manager and leader—not a spiritual teacher but a wonderful example of someone who followed his spiritual commitment. One thing that set Findhorn apart from other communities was that it had not grown up around a single, charismatic leader. There were three of us, with Peter being the only charismatic one. Each of us offered different perspectives and energy, yet we were completely united on the spiritual level. Our ordinariness and our failings proved that anybody can connect with and experience the Divine within. As Sheena once said to us in exasperation, "If you three can make the inner connection to God, anybody can."

For a new creation, three is a good number, as two can become polarized. That might have happened between Peter and me had Eileen not been around to mediate. I sometimes felt that he treated me like a doormat and valued me only as a typist. When I asked others for their perspectives, they all agreed that he treated me badly, which gave me an excuse to wallow in my resentment. For a while I did wallow, until I began to dislike my constant animosity and decided to do something about it. I remembered Vitvan's teaching about acting, not reacting, and instead chose to focus on Peter's good points. As a result of my new approach to him, he stopped treating me so boorishly.

As representative of humanity in our garden experiment, Peter's idea of cooperation with nature was still very man-oriented and orthodox, and that bothered me. He was very proud of the neat little lawns beside the bungalows that had been added to the community, taking great delight in their green, luxurious growth. When one lawn began to sprout dandelions and other weeds, Peter asked the group of young gardeners from Blackpool who had joined us, to spread weed killer on it. That was contrary to our policy of not using any pesticides, and the nature-loving gardeners refused to do it. So one evening, Peter went out and did the job himself. Somehow he got the proportions of the solution wrong and almost killed the whole lawn. One of his less lovable characteristics was that he always believed he was right. The fact that he usually was right didn't make him any easier to live with!

When the community had grown to about twenty-five residents, we decided we needed a building in which to have our meals. Eileen received guidance that, yes, we were to build a dining room with kitchen facilities. It should be large enough to serve two hundred people, with everything of the highest quality. Though the cost would be astronomical, we had learned to trust our guidance. Peter proved his tremendous faith here, for despite the fact that the treasurer kept coming to report that we didn't have the funds he was committing, he went ploughing ahead. And sure enough, on the day when a major bill would arrive, so would a check to cover it. The basic design and layout of the kitchen sufficed us for the next twenty-five years.

Wonderful people visited or joined the community and I found many friends among them—for example, John and Janet Willoner, who would take the Caddy boys for hikes as Peter was generally too busy to attend to them himself. Early on we attracted hippies, who approved of our approach to life but not of our middle-class tidiness nor the structured chain of command. All these issues had to be resolved. With their prior relationship to nature, the gardeners from Blackpool were invaluable. As the community grew, it incorporated crafts people (potters, weavers, candle makers) and a lot of lively young Americans. Activities burgeoned and crafts workshops were constructed in Pineridge, an adjoining area that we now developed. Brian Nobbs, a potter and painter, began to have experiences with the elemental world and would later become Ogilvie's successor in that role.

We were a close community—small enough to know everybody—and we enjoyed being able to talk openly about what mattered to us most: living a life according to our spiritual ideals in a light-hearted way. The new developments were a good change for us three workaholics, who for years had literally been on duty twenty-four hours a day, seven days a week. That I, and possibly Eileen, did not have nervous breakdowns or become unduly stressed out was probably due to the peace experienced during our regular meditation times. During my times of inner communion with God I felt at home, relaxed, filled with love, joy and peace. Later on, another way in which we escaped the busyness of community life was to collect our dinners from the Community Center (which had been built for lunches, dinners, and meetings), and eat them in our caravans. Monica Parish and I did this a lot.

The early 70s was a period when everything seemed to fall beautifully into place, with money and whatever else we required always appearing at just the right moment. In those days, we had no set prices for residents, leaving it to them to donate what they considered appropriate. We were dependent on the laws of spirit for our needs, and it worked. Naturally, there were problems, but knowing we could trust each other's guidance was a tremendous help. Most communities seem to fall apart because of personality differences. We had those, but we also had something powerful and infallible to depend on: our inner connection with God.

However the expansion of the community, after years of being such a close-knit little group, did present me with some emotional challenges. When Joanie (Liebie Pugh's secretary) joined us, she became very close to Eileen. Though I knew Joanie's devotion was something Eileen really needed at that time, I felt left out. Not that I disliked Joanie: no one could for she was a wonderful person. I just felt unappreciated and relegated to a subordinate role in the office. Up until then, Peter and Eileen had shared everything with me, for Eileen's guidance had always been to include me. Now, on a social level, I felt pushed aside, and I withdrew into my shell. I still had much to learn about dealing with my personality issues.

While socially I sometimes felt adrift, I never wanted for inner relationships. My messages from the God within were something I could always count on, and through the Landscape Angel, I continued to make many other inner contacts as well.

One day I picked up a little pinkish pebble while rambling on the moors and wondered if it had a deva. I figured that a mere pebble, a mineral, would have a less evolved deva than any member of the vegetable kingdom. So I was astonished when the greatest being I had so far contacted—one that stretched across the universe to infinity—communicated with me. I called it the Cosmic Angel of Stone:

I whom you have contacted am concerned with vastly more than your planet, for I contain or am connected with mineral life which exists in various stages throughout creation. Nature is full of paradox, in that as you seek contact with what you consider a lower form of life, you in fact contact a more universal being. The human mind codifies and formulates, which is within its right and purpose, but forgets that all is one, that God is in all, and that the basic substance of life, which seems most devoid of sensitive consciousness, is held in its state of existence by its opposite, a vast consciousness, too vast for you to do more than sense its fringes and know that it extends beyond your imagination. You realize too that stones, rocks, dense matter, are influenced in their make-up by stellar energies, that oneness is very much fact in this department.

It was the beauty of this particular stone which drew you to me. Beauty is of God, beauty is working out in all levels of life. Consciousness of beauty brings you into oneness, into any part of the universe. You are contained in it just as I seem to contain universes within myself. The more you appreciate beauty, the more you are linked universally. It is good to seek the life of it on high levels, for then your consciousness is expanded.

You feel right now that you can only look at every pebble with deepest reverence and worship, because you know it is part of my vastness. We are glad that in this way you have been shown a very little of the glory of God, for the glory of God is everywhere, stretching from the farthest reaches of all the universes to the little grain of sand, one and the same thing, held in eternal love and timeless with life.

Yes, of course it would be good to tune in to me if you work with stone. Revere all life, emulate my patience, unfold the mysteries of God and even of pebbles. Do it as a learner of life, a revealer. Let your dominion be over yourself, and let your expanding consciousness see God's life in all things, where indeed it is, and, as you have learned, in the most surprising things. The color and sparkle of a stone is wonderful, but still more wonderful is consciousness which has brought about and

brings about these outer manifestations and grows cosmically.
We are all part of the one life, no higher or lower . . . Praise
God forever in the vastness of all life.

This message completely changed my attitude to the mineral
world. Like most people, I had until then considered minerals to be
dead matter. I realized how much more accurate is the viewpoint
of indigenous peoples, who have reverence for the earth. We mine
minerals, break them up, grind them, put them into fire, and reshape
them as if it is our right and without any sense of appreciation or
thanks. In workshops I regularly attuned to a mineral, sometimes in
crystal form, and found their intelligence mind-opening.

On another occasion, we planted a Monterey Cyprus. As was my
custom, I immediately attuned to it to welcome it into the garden. I
was expecting the sort of sweet philosophic message I usually received
from plant devas when they first arrived. Instead, I received an intense
blast:

We come in with a lordly sweep, for we are not just the
small trees that you see in your garden, but denizens of the
magnificent spaces of great hills in the sun and wind. We
put up with being hedges, but always in our inner being is a
growing toward the open sun-kissed places where we stand
in clustered grandeur.

You feel in us an almost intolerable longing to be fully
ourselves. We of the plant world have our pattern and our
destiny, worked out through the ages, and we feel it quite
wrong that, because of humans and their encroachment, we
and others like us are not allowed to be. We have our portions
of the plan to fulfill. We have been nurtured for this very reason,
and now, in this age, many of us can only dream of the spaces
where we can fulfill ourselves. The pattern is ever before us,
out of reach, a chimera we are forever growing toward but
seldom attaining. We are not a mistake on the part of nature.
We have our work to do.

Humanity is now becoming controller of the world's forests
and is beginning to realize how much these are needed. But you
cover acres with one quick-growing species, selecting trees for
silly economic reasons with no awareness at all of the planet's

115

needs. This shows utter ignorance of the purpose of trees and their channeling of diverse forces. The world needs us on a large scale. Perhaps if humans were in tune with the infinite, as we are, and were contributing their share, the forces would be in balance. But at present the planet needs more than ever just what is being denied it: the forces which come through the mature and stately trees.

We have been vehement. Here are these facts of life forever with us, with no one to listen to them. We have rather dumped this on you. Though you feel at one with us, you feel unable to help. You are only looking at it from a limited level. We know the very telling of this to you does help, that a truth once in human consciousness then percolates around and does its work. And we feel the better for communicating! Let us both believe that the Almighty One knows all this better than either of us and that something is being done.

This message made a tremendous impact on me, especially as all the large trees that I subsequently contacted gave variations of the same theme. I knew that felling trees changed the water table, caused floods, resulted in a loss of habitat for many creatures, but the devas gave additional reasons why trees are essential to the planet. They communicated, for instance, that trees need to be fully mature before they can do their job properly, and that we regularly cut them down before they are have reached full maturity. I was told that trees are, in a sense, the skin of the earth, and that if a certain percentage of the skin of any creature is destroyed, it dies. There are diverse forces from above and below the earth that only trees can channel.

There have been mighty changes in the past as this Earth has evolved but, while the sun shines and life depends on water, our role has been necessary and will continue to be. All of life can change, be lighter and happier and more aware, but nevertheless we have much to do. Our purposes flow as strongly as ever. We feel them coursing through us in waves of strength from the Source, and we seize every opportunity to tell humanity of the need for forests. We would reach minds, so that people may know, without a doubt, of this necessity. Humanity has taken on only part of its role as a creative Son of God, and is acting without the wisdom needed to fulfill that role. We attempt to make this clear. What is important now is consciousness. Our Nature worlds are essential; much of the human world, created with a sense of separation, is not essential. Together we can create a better earth.

I felt very much alone in my perspective on trees, which kept being strengthened whenever I attuned to them. Peter and Eileen thought I had a bee in my bonnet about them. At the time I knew of no one else who had similar views, nor did I know that forests all over the world were already being decimated. My perspective seemed unique, and I felt isolated, paranoid, and impotent to do anything about it.

A visit by Richard St. Barbe Baker, "The Man of the Trees", then in his eighties with a lifetime as a forester behind him, ended my isolation. He was also a spiritual seeker, a member of the Baha'i faith, which emboldened me to share with him a copy of my tree messages. After reading them he said he had come to the very same conclusions from his years of working with trees. What a boon that was to me! The tree devas even gave a thank-you message for him: the only message I have ever had from the angels for an individual human. In his support of our group, he landscaped the trailer park. As he did this, I went around with him and Peter in my capacity as a secretary and found that although I didn't know the Latin names of the trees, I understood just what he was suggesting.

Sir George Trevelyan, a member of the Soil Association and a student of Rudolph Steiner, visited us and noticed that there was something more than good compost-making in our garden. He called it "Factor X" and asked, what was Factor X? Peter shared my messages with Sir George, who accepted them fully and advised us to publish them. Thereupon we acquired a second-hand printing machine—which also gave me the opportunity to attune to machine souls—and published the first edition of *The Findhorn Garden*, carefully printed in green ink by Pete Godfrey and myself.

St. Barbe recommended that we also publish the messages from the trees. They became Part Four of the book. He wrote a lovely foreword to this, saying: "The messages from Tree Devas through Dorothy reveal the occult explanation that scientific research has been unable to give. The ancients believed that the Earth itself is a sentient being and feels the behavior of mankind upon it. As we have no scientific proof to the contrary, I submit that we should accept this and behave accordingly, and thus open up for ourselves a new world of understanding."

When searching for a title for this section, what came to me was "Talking Trees."

"People will think that trees actually talk," Peter objected. "It should be called 'The Tree Devas Speak.'"

"No, Peter," I said. "Its name is 'Talking Trees.' The title came to me when in attunement with the devas."

Ed, who was typing the booklet, sat expectantly behind his typewriter, waiting to add the title. When Peter stepped out of the office, I said, "Type: 'Talking Trees.'"

"I think we should wait until there is some agreement," Ed said.

A little while later, Peter returned, saying, "Eileen just got guidance that you are to use the title 'The Tree Devas Speak.'"

"I don't believe that," I said, and left the office.

As Ed told me later, Peter then told him to type in 'The Tree Devas Speak,' as there was a deadline and the manuscript had to be sent out. Ed replied, "No, Peter, I'm not going to type anything until you two come to some sort of agreement."

Thereupon, I returned to the office, and said, "Peter, you lied! I just went to Eileen and she said to me 'You get your own guidance, and go with the guidance you get.'"

Now it was Ed's turn to walk out. Peter called after him, "Where are you going?"

"I'm going to the Sanctuary and am going to stay there until you two arrive at some agreement."

I don't remember whether Peter or I, or both of us, eventually collected Ed from the Sanctuary, but he came back to the office and typed "Talking Trees." It's a story I relish telling, since it is about the only one of my rows with Peter that I ever won! It is also a very good illustration of our three-way dynamic: Eileen forever having to turn to her guidance to break the deadlock between Peter's domineering ways and my own stubborn resistance to them.

Chapter 14

In 1970, a young American named David Spangler visited us. Two years earlier a friend had mailed us a booklet of his entitled *"The Christ Experience and The New Age Within You"*. Being the office person, I read it first, loved it, and insisted that Peter and Eileen have a look at it. They had the same response. His writing was so inspiring that we were filled with delight. When this young author arrived, we welcomed him and his partner Myrtle Glines, with open arms. Not literally, mind you, for not until many more Americans arrived did the habit of hugging—which people now think of as a Findhorn rite—begin. Peter, Eileen and I never hugged one another!

David was the first person that Peter allowed to use the Sanctuary as a teaching space, and from there his wonderful talks poured forth with clarification on all sorts of spiritual subjects, along with floods of love and understanding. It didn't matter that many of us literally fell asleep in the Sanctuary under the spell of his soft voice. Very often in his talks David would say something and I would think, "Of course I knew that, but I didn't know that I knew it until David said it." His perspective helped me and others to better understand our own work.

David stayed for almost three years, becoming a key member of the community. Simultaneously many young Americans also arrived. A golden, creative period resulted. With his deep closeness to spirit, his bright intellect and great sense of humor, he was a treat for us all. He was much sought after—so much so that Myrtle became fiercely protective of him. One method was to post a sign in their caravan window saying 'Busy Upstairs." This was understood to mean that David was meditating, and would keep even Peter from interrupting him. Just as likely, though, David was busy reading comics, which he loved.

Until David arrived, it had not occurred to us to offer formal teaching. We just invited people to work alongside us—we hoped with love, since our theme was "Work is love in action." Peter would often assign visitors to begin by cleaning toilets. Only when they were able to do it perfectly and lovingly would he entrust them with other tasks.

David felt that the community needed more intellectual nourishment. He called for volunteers to help him to teach courses, and I was one of many who offered their services. A small group—mostly young Americans—began teaching. I well remember Sir George Trevelyan, in his Public Speaking courses, emphasizing the value of the pregnant pause. Personally, I made pauses because I didn't know what to say! Most of us were inexperienced as speakers and just did our best under David's direction, talking about our particular aspects of the spiritual work or our interests. I attempted to expound on communicating with God within and with the souls of nature. We were experimenting, trying to meet the needs of the community as we understood them within our personal limitations. I suspect that we all learned a great deal more than we taught; I know I did.

David was also good at coming up with group exercises. One that I especially remember was to share one's life story with a partner. That was a novelty to me, for I never talked or even thought about my past. My partner was Joy Drake, author of *The Game of Transformation*, who later became a close friend.

The community grew to over a hundred people. To meet this expansion we purchased several bungalows, each of which consisted of two trailers joined side by side to make a little house. An adjoining property, the Park, was donated to us by a visitor who had long been looking for the right recipient for her money. It is lucky we all got along so well, for living conditions were very crowded. The caravans—even a tiny one with berths for seven people—were generally full. Most of the Americans, inexperienced with coal fires, had trouble keeping them alight in the caravans.

Despite the Spartan conditions and the difficult climate, life was an adventure. At weekly Fun Nights on Fridays we made fun of ourselves and of life, often through clever skits written by members. All took part in these skits, whether or not they could act. (I recall once being the hind end of an elephant.) In one of the most memorable of these sketches, David and another witty member pretended to be dueling psychics. One would see a most beautiful dove, then the other would see an eagle devour the dove, then the eagle would be blown away, and so on. Peter was often the brunt of skits and joined in with good humor, though I sometimes wondered if he felt hurt. He loved the gaiety, creativity and energy of the young people. Some of them formed a musical group—the New Troubadours—performing songs composed by Milenko Matanovic with lyrics by David.

Peter was still the arbitrator of who would stay with us in the community. Initially, we left it to visitors to decide how much money they wished to contribute. But as the community grew larger and some people began taking undue advantage of it, we were obliged to start charging set prices. We made exceptions for people who had no money but were contributing in some other way to the working of the whole. If Peter felt someone was not contributing, however, they had to go. Lark, a singer with the New Troubadours, begged to be allowed to stay after she ran out of money. Peter said No. Twice more she made this request, and was again refused. Then she pondered her situation deeply, came to a spiritual understanding that it was right for her to be at Findhorn, and told this to Peter. He recognized at once that she was speaking from an inner knowing, and agreed that she could remain.

Peter's ability to discern whether people were speaking from what we in those days called their 'higher' or 'lower' levels, often displayed itself. Sometimes when he put a question to Eileen or me, he would ignore our immediate response, saying "I don't want to know what you think. I want to have God's view." Though hard for us on a personality level, it obliged us to keep turning to our guidance, and often prevented us from reacting out of hand.

In October, 1971 Eileen received an inner message that she was no longer to pass on her guidance to the community. It was time they received their own guidance and stopped depending on something outside themselves. This was devastating to her. Receiving guidance had been her special role in the community, and without it, she felt she was useless. For a while she still received messages for Peter, but not long afterwards that ceased as well. She was told that Peter should learn to trust his intuition. Initially, Peter would not accept this new directive. He went on coming to her for guidance, saying he needed her confirmation to run the community. She remained courageously firm in her refusal. It was one of the hardest things she ever did. She had always been afraid that Peter would one day leave her, and his dependence on her guidance was perhaps the firmest hold she had on him. Once she relinquished it, her fears began to materialize. Instead of relying on his own intuition, Peter began to seek guidance from others, mostly women, and their marriage was affected.

Though I was confined to the office, I still had my early morning attunement with God. David was happy when I shared the following message in the Sanctuary, for it confirmed his own belief that all of us should learn to trust our inner knowing:

As it is right and proper for a child to obey its earthly parents until it comes to its maturity, so it is right and proper for you to obey Me, your heavenly Father/Mother, until you come to your spiritual maturity. After that, you have all the faculties within you to make your own decisions without turning as a supplicant to Me.

This does not mean that you do not do My will. It simply means that you do My will on your own, as the angels do. They do not continually turn to Me in consciousness, seeking what is right for them to do. They flow with the energies, and it is impossible for them to do anything but My will. So with you, when you are mature. Because your consciousness is one with the higher, there is no question of returning to the state of separation and having to seek My will. It simply is in you.

You fear that you are not mature enough to be free of your separated self, that subtly it may encroach. As you flow with events and cease thinking in terms of limitation, accepting your maturity, you are living in it, and all is well. Put away childish things; do not cling to them. What if you feel it is a dangerous doctrine for many? You get on with living your own life. You have grown up. Just as your earthly parents trusted you and set you free, I would do no less, knowing that we are bound forever in love and more than that, that we are together always. You are no longer my dutiful child but the Beloved who loves all creation in Me, and we both know it and therefore can be one.

I wondered if I would ever feel sufficiently mature. Now, nearly forty years later, I still lack self-esteem, and sometimes have trouble trusting my own perceptions. But I was soon to grow into a greater maturity, for this message foreshadowed a challenging new phase in my life.

In 1972, Myrtle told me that the time at Findhorn for David and her was up, and they would be returning to America with some of the group of residents who had been teaching with them. Myrtle believed I belonged with this group. This sounded wrong to me, as for years a firm inner knowing that I belonged with Peter and Eileen had kept me with them through thick and thin. I took it as a matter of course that my place was at Findhorn. But coming from Myrtle, whom I respected, the suggestion deserved consideration. One day I found myself speculating about it with a young American visitor. She immediately asked, "Would you like me to get guidance for you?" I didn't want her guidance for me, but we were trying to teach residents to turn within, and I didn't wish to discourage her, so I said yes. Next day she gave me a typed transcript of the message she'd received, the first words of which were, "Dorothy is on no account to ever leave Findhorn." Instantly I knew those words were false. I turned within for my own guidance, and was told that yes, it was time for me to leave.

"No. You are not to leave," Peter said, when I reported my decision.

"But I'm sure it is right for me to go."

"No," he insisted. "Your place is here at Findhorn."

When I went on holding my ground he said, "You are to stay. I'll ask Eileen to get guidance about it."

"Go ahead,' I said, "I don't care if you get guidance from God, from all the Masters of all the Rays, from all the Archangels or whatever, that I am to stay. I know I am to go."

So Peter went to Eileen. Her guidance was:

> *My beloved, all is very well. It is time for Dorothy to move on. She has work to do in other centers.*
>
> *She may not realize it just now, but no matter where she is or what she is doing, she will always be part of this Center of Light. Her roots have sunk very deep. The links are unbreakable, they are so strong.*
>
> *She must go in absolute love and freedom to do the work she has to do, and with My full blessings. You three, Peter, you and Dorothy, have been through much together, many ups and the downs. Your links are deep spiritual ones and therefore are eternal. You have worked together in other lives, and were brought together again in this life to do a specific work, and this work will continue, for space and distance will never part you. Stop struggling and just blend together, and all of you find a new relationship of deep peace and harmony while you are together here, until Dorothy moves on to her new and greater work. Whom I have brought together no one and nothing can*

put asunder. Peace be with you all.

What a relief! While waiting for the right time to leave, I remained in the present, trying to fit in as best I could with the vibrant life around me. The work of creating a college was proceeding, but Peter was about to take a direction which was not in close harmony with David's ideas. At the same time, the different members of the college staff, each independently and for varying personal reasons, started to announce their intentions to leave. Particularly unsettling was the departure of Roger and Katherine Collis, who had married while in residence and had a baby, and now felt that Findhorn was not the place to raise their child. Their decision to leave was a great sorrow to Peter and Eileen, who considered this young couple to be their successors.

David and Myrtle left in April 1973. Eileen, who perceived David as the Second Coming, had put him on a pedestal and informed him that she had guidance that he was not to leave Findhorn. She loved David so much that she practically cursed him when he did leave, saying that only at Findhorn would he be able to write. (Actually he went on to write quite well in other places.) I left the following month—and certainly not in absolute love and freedom. Peter remained convinced I was leaving out of timing. Others had similar difficulties.

Departures from Findhorn were often accompanied by conflict and acrimony, and sometimes by guilt on the part of those who left. It seemed that there were two unreconciled principles in operation: the planetary educational work to help people open to a new consciousness, which requires members to go out into the world, and the necessity to maintain Findhorn as a center that demonstrates spiritual living and connecting with the intelligence of nature. As both entail being connected with and being of service to our inner Divinity, there should be no conflict. To me, the main role of Findhorn is to help people find their inner spiritual contact and learn how to serve that Presence. This can be done anywhere, and is in harmony with both principles. Ultimately, the perennial message of the God within is for us to be more loving. The simplicity of this is sometimes hard for people to grasp.

It is not an easy job to help people find their divinity. When people leave Findhorn without having made contact with God within, they often find themselves desolate. Then they long to return to the community with its sympathetic and like-minded people. But true community is the result of inner contact, not the way to find it. Many are also often drawn to Findhorn because they feel the love, because they are lonely, or because they believe that the future lies in community. But the answers are always within, and I know that as long as we seek outside ourselves for answers, we will not find them. On leaving there need be no sense of separation, for God, love, is everywhere. To go out into the world to be a loving example, or to help prepare people to find their own inner essence, is a most imperative and rewarding work.

What follows is a message from "John" (one of David Spangler's subtle world colleagues) to Dorothy Maclean given 1 May 1974.

Dorothy carries a particular blessing and assignment from the level of the collective higher nature of this world, whether devic or human, to enunciate a certain message and reformulate the links and pathways between areas of divided consciousness, to heal the ecology of the world, as it were, to be one of those who embody that energy of healing. You are going to be a point of entry into a wider consciousness for many people within the scientific framework. You will occupy a bridge position, energy to be divided among several patterns of action, involving travel. You are being prepared to enunciate a message beyond any you have given before. You will work in connection with the national patterns and the devas thereof, but this is only an aspect of what will constitute your full pattern.

You are to move into contact with the devic forces or with angelic forces beyond those of nature, of the plant world, into those great builders which wield the forces that determine the evolution of all of life and, on a human level, its cultural and consciousness aspects. You will be, in essence, a spokesman for forces operating within the world's soul, of which humanity is a part, and you will help other to make connections with that energy field which will be helpful to them in their work. You will be given all that you need to accomplish this task. You will move to become identified with that which is the building and creative life force, whether it is manifested in man, in nature or in the cosmic realms from which planets are forged....within your meditation and divine attunement lies the strength to accomplish what you must do.

Chapter 15

When I left Findhorn in 1973, I no longer had a home in Canada, as both my parents had died. My old friend Erica invited me to her home in Ojai, California. As it happened, May Hanna, an early sponsor of David Spangler, also had a home in the area. She invited him, and the circle of former Findhorn residents who had returned to North America with him, to join her at her ranch on the slopes of Mt. Lassen. This group included David Spangler and Julie Spangler, Myrtle Glines, Roger and Katherine Collis, Kathi and Milenko Matanovic, Freya Secrest, Merrily and Jim Bronson, and Lark Batteau. As we sat in May's living room, we looked at each other and realized we were a spiritual family, that we were related on inner levels and had work to do together. We named this family "Lorian," a word coined by David that he and the rest of us all liked the sound of. We have kept close links ever since.

After our stay at the ranch we all moved to Belmont, in the Bay area of San Francisco, and began to do public work. Our first foray was a presentation at Gunn High School, with talks, music and dance. I was terrified, remembering my speech at university when I had been too petrified to move lips or limbs. I wrote my talk, read it, re-read it, taped it, memorized it, and still I had to be physically pushed onto the stage. When I got through it, no doubt carried by the prayers of my friends, people came up to tell me that lots of angels had been hovering around me. If so, I was completely unaware of them, and only wished for more tangible help from them!

As a Canadian, I couldn't legally get a job to support myself in California. I took buses to Vancouver British Columbia to try to get a work visa for the United States so that I could play my part in Lorian endeavors. But I had to get a job before I could apply for American citizenship, and I couldn't get a job because I was not an American citizen. May Hanna realized I was meant to be in Belmont and, with great generosity, supported me herself during the three years we spent there.

During this time we talked publicly about our beliefs and tried to practice them. Alone or in groups we accepted invitations to speak or give workshops, and aroused a certain amount of interest. We published a Lorian Journal and developed a following. For me, it was a time of learning to value myself more as a whole person, not just someone who got guidance. I felt my Lorian friends appreciated me for myself, not just for the messages that came through me, and this began to boost my confidence.

While at May's ranch, I had attuned to the tree devas in particular. It was wonderful being with the incense cedars, the ponderosa pines, the aspens. The problem was that there was a highway at the edge of the ranch, and along this highway flowed a continuous stream of logging trucks. About every five minutes huge trucks thundered by, taking the trees away to the lumber yards, and racing back to pick up more tree trunks. The number of trucks seemed unbelievable, and no doubt the supply of lumber was considered endless. I hated to hear and see these trucks, but what could I do?

The predicament of the trees continued to trouble me after I found an apartment next to a wild valley in Belmont. There I attuned to the local devas, whom I found rather hemmed in by people. They almost grumbled—the only time I have experienced the angelic world as somewhat censorious. It was as if they been hoping for centuries that Americans would awaken to their presence and begin to treat nature with more respect. Now one of the last unspoiled areas on the continent, the Pacific coast, was being settled with the usual disregard for them. Bulldozers would in fact strip that valley the following year.

My distress came to a head when I visited the Avenue of the Giants, where groves of large virgin redwoods were set aside "For Posterity" as the plaques said. On looking at these 'saved' trees, I saw that they were dying. Why? Perhaps because dams prevented the alluvial floods which used to feed them, or because automobile exhausts poisoned the air around them, or because crowds trampled the earth on top of their roots. I was sick at heart, and wept. Then I contacted the Redwood Deva:

> *Small mortal and great being, we greet you. Come with us, up high above the traffic noise and the pettiness of little humans to where everlasting peace is. Let the 'evil' be as dust on your feet, to be shaken off and returned to itself, while the peace of God remains, the creative peace which cloaks a planet and many forms of life.*
>
> *What if the trees come toppling down? Their vibrations are*

forever part of life here and we are glad to have contributed as much as we have. Rejoice, for life moves on, whatever form it takes, and it is one life, as we well know. We are part of you, you are part of us, and so it will always be.

Although the message consoled me, the thought of forever losing those marvelous trees strengthened my resolve to do whatever I could to rescue them. I think the Redwood Deva knew full well that its message would have that effect on me. It seems to me that the angels, when we are attuned to them, are aware of our state of mind, so that what we receive from them is appropriate for us at that moment.

A counselor, who often visited U.S. Forestry Service stations to help wives deal with their lonely homes in the woods, heard me talk and wanted me to address the Forestry Service. Somehow she managed to make my proposed input sound helpful, and the combined Washington and Oregon Forest Services invited me to lead a workshop for their staff. They let me choose whether to go to a forest that had been devastated or one that was still intact. I chose the latter. We set out in a small Service plane from Portland, Oregon, to a ranger station in the Ochoco National Forest. As we flew over bare-topped mountains, the Forestry staff acknowledged that they had made a mistake: the trees should not have been cut there as it takes so long for them to renew themselves in the heights. Soon after we landed, a jeep appeared and carried us for a few more miles to the point where it was only possible to proceed on foot. From there, it was a trek of several hours to our camp site. A delicious meal around a campfire awaited us. After we had eaten, I gave my talk.

It was so dark by then that I couldn't see or judge what the response was to my stories of communications with trees. When I finished, the men just stood up silently and went to their sleeping bags or tents. I spent most of the night wondering whether they had been awed at what I had said, or simply aghast. My sleeplessness was compounded by the knowledge that it was a rattlesnake area, and rattlers love to climb into sleeping bags for warmth.

The next day we did exercises and attunements. I attuned to the local tree devas, who seemed distant and vast, presiding over the whole area, yet so glad to find us there and receptive that they came close and communicated:

The energies which we represent are always open to sympathetic humans. They are clearly here, clearly everywhere, but more easily available to you without the admixture of civilization. We are close to all of you in one way or another, and want you to know this, to share the joy of a communion which may seem unusual but is nonetheless real. But you know this.

What perhaps you do not know is that your recognition of us makes a stronger contact, because it is based on truth and provides a door to a two-way communication and cooperation. This is necessary for the well-being of humanity, which is moving towards the joy of becoming more part of the wholeness of the planet. Let us build on that positive picture and share the joy of the wild places in the world, and take that joy with us. We cannot but share it, for we live in it, and the same is true for you as you learn to be what you truly are.

We spent three days at the camp-site, attuning to the devas there. By the end of the third day most of the men had come to me individually to say that the devic messages had reminded them of their love for trees and their kinship with nature. I was encouraged.

When I left Findhorn, I knew I had to write a book about my experiences, and now was the time. Erica invited me to stay in her guest studio, where I could work without interruption.

My first efforts consisted mainly of a series of devic communications which I thought interesting or important. Erica told me that such a compilation would just be boring. She herself was taking writing lessons and suggested I seek advice from her teacher, who said, "You have to put yourself in it." I didn't consider myself anywhere near as interesting as my messages, but my guidance backed up what she and Erica were saying. It's the relationship between humans and devas that interests human readers so, like it or not, my own personality had to be part of the picture. The fruit of my effort was *To Hear the Angels Sing*, which was published in 1980.

After three years in Belmont, our Lorian group felt it was time to move east. California is a wonderfully supportive environment for spiritually minded people. New ideas and impulses were constantly springing up there, though they did not, it seemed to us, so readily take deep root. People seemed to dart restlessly from idea to idea, without following through. By contrast, when we moved and offered workshops in the Midwest, participants were interested enough to do the assignments we gave them and report back. The practical, industrious mood that made the American heartland initially somewhat less receptive of new ideas was a great advantage when it came to grounding those ideas in everyday life. Eventually most of the Lorians settled in Wisconsin: first in Milwaukee and then in Madison. With Freya Secrest, who was a beautiful six foot tall Lorian particularly sensitive to my deva messages and who shared my love of the outdoors, I moved to Toronto.

Once we were settled in there, it came to me in meditation that I was to begin to lead workshops away from the gang. This was unsettling news.

"Do you want to do it?" Freya asked, reasonably enough, when I shared this conviction with her.

"No!"

"Then don't."

In those days, we liked the expression "Follow your bliss." Offhand, I couldn't think of anything that gave me less bliss than addressing large groups of people. Leading workshops with my fellow Lorians had gotten me over the worst of my public speaking paralysis, but I was still a very long way from feeling comfortable in front of an audience, much less blissful. People have often advised me: "Just let the spirit speak through you. Don't plan, just have faith." I wanted to spit at them when they said that, for I hadn't the faith then. Yet I had known for a long time that what my personality did or did not want was not the deciding factor—not when it came to following guidance. What I wanted most was to do God's will, and if that meant stepping out of my own limitations, then I would have to do so. I have led many workshops since then.

The Lorians' eastward migration coincided with the U.S. Bicentennial year. My friends jokingly said that I couldn't join in the celebrations, since my Tory ancestors had backed the wrong horse during revolutionary times. Thousands of these Tories had left the States to settle in the wilderness of Canada. Even though I knew my friends were just kidding, I felt a little hurt and left out. Soon afterward, though, I learned from a relative that my grandmother, Katharine Ball, was a descendant of the same family that had produced Mary

Ball, George Washington's difficult mother. "So there!" I said to my friends. "I am related to George Washington. I'm more American than you are!" Since then, I have felt more American.

On the journey from California to Toronto, Freya and I had taken our time, indulging our mutual love of the outdoors by camping in the most unspoiled places we could find. Along the way, we stopped to fulfill my lifelong wish to visit Mesa Verde. As a child, I had fallen in love with pictures of the cliff dwellings there. In my fantasy, the ancient residents of Mesa Verde had lived close to nature and in harmony with all life, unlike contemporary Americans with their concrete jungles and logging trucks. But what made the biggest impression on me, when I finally saw the place, were the toe and finger-hold entrances and exits used to escape or push back enemies. The place was, in fact, a fortress. Its buildings were drafty, with smoke-blackened walls and ceilings, and water was far away. It dawned on me that the life of the people there was neither peaceful nor harmonious nor at all comfortable. The romantic fantasy I had harbored since childhood crumbled in an instant. Well, it was about time! Fixed ideas often imprisoned me in old patterns. The demise of this one opened my mind to the positive possibilities of modern cities.

The next time we passed through a city — I believe it was Albuquerque —I found myself wondering whether it, like so many natural landscapes, might have an angelic counterpart. I attempted to attune to such a being and, sure enough, became aware of a beautiful angel who was in charge of the place. What surprised me was that the angel asked me to send it love. I had always thought it was the other way around, that the angels sent us love. Then I realized that city angels must have the most difficult job of any of their kin, for they were trying to bring harmony into the world's most troubled spots: our urban areas full of poverty, pollution, violence, drugs, over-crowding and hustling. I also realized that I had contributed to the difficulty of the city angels. I had taken cities for granted, used them for my own benefit—for shopping, libraries, movies, museums—without offering any thanks or appreciation. I had, in fact, always disliked them, and tried to leave them as quickly as possible after accomplishing my purposes there. Now that I had discovered that they, too, had angels, I realized that cities were no less deserving of my gratitude, reverence and solicitude than was the natural world.

In order to attune to devas, I need to be in direct contact with their

131

physical counterpart. To meet a plant deva for the first time, I have to have direct experience of a particular plant of its species. The same is true of the angels of places such as cities. I have to actually visit a city to meet its deva. And while I may make initial devic contact through a brief or superficial encounter with a place—just flying over it in a plane, for instance—the relationship deepens and develops additional dimensions if I explore the place more thoroughly or make repeated visits. Places, like the life cycles of plants, unfold over time.

In my meditations I became aware that most cities had vigorous vital energies. My first impression of a city's energy was often of a moving pattern of white light. In New Orleans, for example, I found:

> *Quiet energy, watery. Feminine in many aspects, but also strong masculine feel. Almost sweeping in the area, drawing in 'dust' and blowing it away. Far-reaching energies, perhaps through ships and waterways.*

I described my first impression of the pattern of Juneau, Alaska, like this:

> *Very loving, trying to lift us all up into that lovingness, as if a hand was reaching down, lifting. Not very connected with the glacier, which is a very different energy. Energy coming in from the surrounds, from the sea mostly.*

The energy pattern was often accompanied by some sort of meaning or declaration—an explicit angel message—which I put into words. Both the pattern and the declarations would change during subsequent visits. Specific events and activities happening within a city, or even just a change of season, would cause a shift in the pattern.

One day I was attuning to the city of Milwaukee for about the third or fourth time. In addition to awareness of the overlighting angelic energy, which I was accustomed to perceiving when I attuned to a city, I picked up an impression of its personality. It was a sort of beer-drinking burgher being, almost like a cartoon character that embodied certain soul characteristics of Milwaukee's human inhabitants. To symbolize the personality of a place with a character is not unusual; for instance, Uncle Sam for the U.S. and John Bull for the U.K. It was evident that such characterizations have counterparts in the angelic world. In a university city, for instance, I sensed a professorial figure. In another city I sensed someone wearing a funny bonnet. When I described it to a group of residents, they said, "Oh yes, one of our founders was known for that bonnet." Since I had never heard of the founder or seen such a bonnet before, the episode confirmed that my projections had a certain reality.

The impression of the personality of a place was distinct from its energy pattern. I might perceive one without immediately perceiving the other, and sometimes what I perceived was a relationship between the two. For instance, in one North American city, an energy was falling like rain from the overlighting angel and being absorbed by the city's personality. I had the impression that this was a very new development. It was like the municipal equivalent of how an individual human personality appears when they awaken to the spirit—something happening on a citywide level that you usually only see in individuals or small groups. In another city, I observed the personality aspect turning its back on its angelic aspect: not merely separate and somewhat unaware of it but actively rejecting it. When I suggested to that city's personality that it might benefit from turning toward its angel, it told me to mind my own business!

In my workshops, I encouraged participants to attune to the angel of whatever city we were in. At first there was a lot of resistance to this, because people were interested in contacting nature, not the souls of cities. To get around this, I suggested that they begin with some natural beauty in the city, such as a garden or a tree that they loved. This would start the love flowing and open them to the love of the angel of the city.

On February 6, 1977, Freya and I were somewhere in the air over the continental U.S., en route to one of our workshops, when I encountered the Angel of the United States. I had never attuned to the spirit of a nation before, and this contact gave me my first glimpse of the work they do.

> *All of this broad land, along with the oceans, is in my embrace. All create me and are created in me. With humans I experiment in new configurations, in new assemblages that are good for the whole.*

My dynamism is therefore in the cities, and my aspiration. Nature responds in unison with me and I do not have to concern myself with it, because it is me, it is the automatic part of me which is well controlled by the whole, as your heart is in your body. But the reactions of humans, like those of your individual hearts and minds, are not to be left to chance. They are to be watched, loved and transformed. With you I build, and I have my aims, which are your aims in the depths of you. But you do not know it, and always I seek to make you more conscious of your oneness and your movement into wholeness, your vastness. This is an individual vastness and a national vastness; one brings on the other.

As there are diverse elements in this land, so there are diverse elements in your individual make-up, elements to be used to complement each other and make a greater diversity and greater destiny. I used the word "destiny" not lightly but because it is true and something to be accepted, and that is so for all nations. To be aware of destiny is to be aware of divinity in one sense, and to know that each has a part to play that is not precisely divine, but which is potential and awaiting outworking in some form, the form to be open to change, growth and experience, your experience, your expressing.

We need you as you need us, for we pass on energies for you to focus, and those energies include direction, goal and aspiration. You provide the means and in a sense you provide the goal, for in our oneness is our existence.

This was an interesting description of the work of the angel of a country.

Two weeks later the Angel of the U.S.A. also told me:

I am very linked with my Canadian counterpart, which exists but which is not truly connected with the soul of its people in a conscious way. It is indeed in this area that you can be helpful, by linking yourself with the angel and bringing its existence to the consciousness of other Canadians so that they too can link with it. If whatever exists is not 'seen' in the minds of humans, it in a sense does not exist to humanity, but when humans recognize some new principle or energy or thing, then it is heaven brought to earth; that is a reality to you.

Yes, you can invoke the soul of Canada to its people in whatever way opens to you, just as you are invoking the souls of individuals in their consciousness and making them aware of their capabilities. You will be aided in many ways, as you will discover, because this is worthwhile work.

This was disconcerting, for at the time I considered nationalism unacceptable. Though a seventh generation Canadian, I thought of myself as a planetary citizen and in fact had a planetary passport, which is not recognized by any country.

Still, after thirty-five years away from it, I was happy to be reconnecting with my native land. The exquisite little wildflowers that appeared in the Canadian woods before the leaves matured were far more beautiful to me than any cultured garden flower. No apples or peaches had ever been as delicious as those grown in the Niagara Peninsula, and I tasted them anew. The Canadian climate varied according to the seasons, unlike the continual rain of Britain or the constant sun of California. Even aspects of Toronto that were new to me had connections. For instance, there was a big new library in Toronto, named for John Robarts—he was a fellow student from my university days. A new music hall was named after Edward Johnson, who had been a friend of my father. I loved all these reminders of the past, these personal connections with the land and landmarks.

As these experiences brought me to realize its importance to me, I contacted the Angel of Canada directly. As I meditated, I became aware of an awe-inspiring, pure presence, perhaps reflecting the vast untouched lands of Canada. But it conveyed that it could not do its job as an angel, for angels of countries work through people. It said Canadians did not know their identity and therefore were limited in any contact with their country's angel.

That we Canadians were unsure of our identity was no news to me. Our limited sense of ourselves as a nation tended to divide us into English vs. French. About that conflict, the angel remarked:

You need to know that your humanity lessens in separation. This is a time for unity, not for splintering. Of course differences are real and of course they should remain so. Yet you will need to understand one another. You have the capacities and the opportunities for growth into maturity, to be wise enough to live and let live, and to delight in the breadth of your heritage.

There are very delicate balances to maintain and to create in the present energy flows. Separation would not help, but change would. Change is needed, with more breadth of vision, greater brotherhood and love for your fellow humans and for the land which supports you. All of which, as you well know, is based on a greater awareness of what you are as humans, or as divine beings.

Remember that your endeavors are supported by the creative direction of life, and that we wish to help you as well as needing your help.

Since the angel had emphasized the importance of recognizing our unique identity, I decided to explore that subject in a series of workshops. One identity that all Canadians could agree on is that we are not Americans! So I started there, inviting participants to contrast themselves with our neighbors to the south. Though we could cite many differences, they were slow at first to coalesce into a clear sense of what it meant to be Canadian. In my desire to keep an open mind on the subject, I was even willing to consider that there was no true Canadian identity, no compelling spiritual reason for us to be a separate nation from the United States.

I attuned to the Angel of the U.S.A. and asked about this. To my relief, its response was emphatic. It told me that North America was the locale of an experiment in human freedom, and that the two nations differ in the way they experience and express that freedom. Americans tend to value individual freedom at almost any cost, while in Canada individualism is tempered by a greater concern for the harmony and well-being of the whole. These differences can be seen throughout the history of the two nations. English-speaking Canada had first been settled by those from the thirteen American colonies who rejected armed rebellion against England. The Royal Canadian Mounted Police was formed to maintain control of guns and prevent the violence that occurred in the trigger-happy American West. Private enterprise built the transcontinental railroad in the U.S., while the government built its Canadian counterpart. The Angel assured me that each of these two differing approaches contributes something important to the success of the North American experiment.

Meanwhile in the workshops, we were discovering the significance of other differences from the U.S. One member of our group was a Welsh immigrant who still felt Welsh even though she had lived in Canada for twelve years. She felt out of place, guilty that she was taking advantage of Canadian facilities while not fully assimilating into the dominant culture there. This in itself is a very Canadian phenomenon, for unlike the U.S., Canada has not conceived of itself as a melting pot in which recent immigrants are supposed to submerge their previous national identities. Her guilt vanished as she realized that holding on to her Welshness and contributing that to the whole made her truly Canadian. Typically Canadians think in terms of a mosaic rather than a melting pot.

The low self-esteem that has been part of my make up all my life is also very Canadian, the flip side of one of our most positive national traits. Our habit of not asserting our own identity makes Canadians good listeners and peacemakers. Seeing what I had always conceived of as a personal challenge in the context of my national origins helped me to feel more accepting of that side of myself. I have learned, too, that it is important to suspend judgment when attuning to national characteristics, for traits that are positive in their native context often create friction when imported to another context. For example, the North American habit of hugging on short acquaintance is endearing, but, as we at Findhorn learned, it is not at all appropriate to hug the locals in most places in Scotland when first encountering them! It's just not done.

Several months after I began leading these workshops, the Angel of Canada communicated:

Of course, there are many aspects of me; some universal, some close to you. Knowing I reach out beyond your confines, let me come close in to say some things.

First, let me share my joy at the results of your workshops, bringing my reality to some Canadians. The appropriateness of national identity can spread, and it not only makes for better citizens of any country, but happier, more whole individuals.

Second, there is risk in appearing too apologetic for your ideas on such things as devas. Always acknowledge our reality, both to yourself and to others, for we do not want to occupy a phantasmagorical corner in the human mind. We are real, not fantasy, and we would be so recognized all over the world.

Third, there is no use denying the reality of politics. That reality lies in the pairs of opposites, in the strength given to it by man. As man gives more strength in his mental world to the wholeness behind politics, then will politics be more aligned to the whole. . .

You are concerned about people accepting the reality of what you propose to write if they haven't been through a workshop. All right, write about that. It would be good to give such workshops all over the country, and this article could be an excellent method of connecting you with the rest of the country.

Fifth, never forget the element of rejoicing that is part of nature, like those leaves dancing in the sun and wind. Nature is not grim in its so-called competition. It is light-hearted, because it doesn't mind if someone else wins. There is always more of it to come forward. It plays, it loves, it has fun. So does the angel of a country. It has myriad responsibilities, but it is also a game to flex and fuse those energies together in ever-changing patterns. Do not become grim about the fate of Canada. Become joyful, that the joy may grow and the country grow to maturity.

Our explorations on the subject of identity were distilled into a booklet called "The Soul of Canada: An Overview of National Identity", published in 1977. I was delighted when later it was used in a course at the University of Alberta. I also began to give workshops in French-speaking Canada, unfortunately having to use an interpreter as my French is almost non-existent. At a time when many people in Quebec wanted to separate from Canada, I held a workshop in Quebec City. Most of the attendees were teachers, artists, professionals —independent thinkers who favored separation. They were also interested in the spiritual life and unanimous in wanting to be more loving in their daily lives. At one point the subject of politics arose, and fur began to fly. Then I asked: "Are you being loving?" There was a long pause, as people realized that their emotions were influencing their political choices. Then someone suggested we take the situation into attunement. We did, and it was the most powerful meditation I'd ever been part of, for it meant so much to those present to re-identify their priorities and bring them into harmony with their deepest feelings as spiritual beings.

Another message, received while on a flight from Atlanta to Toronto, alludes to the problem of Canadian identity and the French/English split. But in its sweep, it also gives a good description of the role of national angels and their relationship to human cultures:

We are the embodiment of myths, for our qualities encompass all human striving to be what we are while on Earth. We change, therefore we are the past and future as well as the present. We inspire, for that is our nature; we have the job of spreading creative God-qualities on Earth. We are called the builders; we are the builders not only of form but of the realms from which form manifests, the learning which humanity makes real on Earth, the beauty and majesty which is immanent in everything.

Like all myth, the reality of this has to be born through expression on Earth. The Canadian reality is here and we are, or I am, that, just as we are, or I am, the American myth.

How is a myth brought to birth? Partly by building on what has already been born, and by the thoughts and feelings that humans decide to express in their ideals. The Romans were pragmatic and their pragmatism became the reality of the Pax Romanus. Canadian pragmatism, whether in French or English or any other language, is being born now as Canadians seek their identity. You are simply seeking too hard, not fully realizing your divinity, just as individuals can know but do not fully accept their divinity. Practice is needed by a nation.

You ask about the French split, and about the people who accept that and are therefore not open to a Canadian myth. The unity of the myth exists whether or not they accept it. Simply give no reality to any divisiveness, except on the ephemeral levels from which it comes, and other people will accept reality. Myth is based on true reality, which is much stronger and everlasting than the day-to-day mental sightings based on the chaos emoted in the search for truth.

Chapter 16

In 1984, most of the Lorians moved from Wisconsin to the Pacific Northwest. I had to wait a little longer before I got the inner green light to join them there. At first I couldn't understand why I had to remain so long in Toronto. Later I learned that I had stayed for the exact number of years necessary to qualify for Canadian medical insurance and other benefits.

We all settled in separate homes in the Seattle area. I took an apartment on my own in a small town where I could walk to a grocery store, post office and library. I had inherited a car from my brother, so I could visit friends, including David Spangler, whose teachings I continued to appreciate above all others. Every now and then I would be invited to give talks and workshops. I didn't make any special effort to promote them, just accepted invitations when they came.

Since I was known as the person who made the spiritual contact with nature at Findhorn, people wanted to learn from me how they could do that on their own. I would talk of my experiences, and then together we would go into meditation to make an inner contact with a particular flower or stone or animal or city or country. More and more I emphasized contact with the God within, for that aspect of the self is the prime link with all other beings. [For readers who wish to learn to make this contact themselves, I have included some instructions in Appendix I, page 185.]

Sometimes I teamed up with another teacher, such as Ron Rabin, who became my partner in leading five-day workshops called "Bonding with Earth." These involved wilderness camping expeditions, where participants would spend a full twenty-four hours communing with nature in absolute solitude, an experience which they always found powerful. I loved their stories of how a caterpillar or a bird or a twig had taught them some lesson, or guided them when they got lost.

Invitations to teach have taken me all over the world. In fact, the second half of my life story has been so full of travel that my editor complained she was getting jet lagged just from reading it. To prevent jet lag on the part of other readers, I'm not going to recount all of my trips in the order they happened. Instead I want to convey some of what they taught me about the complex spiritual life of the planet.

An early message from the Angel of Holland sounded a theme

upon which many other angels I was to meet on my travels added their variations:

> *It is worthwhile work to extend the knowledge of what we* [angels] *do. Up until now we have had to work with humans who are unconscious of us, although of course some have been unknowingly aligned to our purposes. It makes a tremendous difference when you know of us and can willingly blend with the harmonies we strive to bring about. Conscious human cooperation with planetary plans makes a wonderful dance of what has often been seen as pressure. Of course, at present only a few of you will be in step with us; those few have an influence far beyond their numbers, and are the thin edge of a new movement of growth in human awareness. We rejoice at this and are grateful to those who harmonize with us in even the smallest degree.*

This angel's encouragement of "conscious human cooperation with planetary plans" might give the misleading impression that there exists some Master Plan about which every angel is fully informed and most humans are completely in the dark. That is not at all the case, and not what this angel meant. Planetary plans, like human plans, are subject to frequent change. Like human plans, they tend to begin locally and spread through networks of contacts. They acquire planetary status only to the extent that the participants are conscious of themselves as planetary citizens, and of the link between what is occurring locally and what is occurring globally.

People vary in the range of their contacts and in their awareness of the bigger picture. The same is true of angels: some are better connected than others with what is happening outside of their immediate sphere of influence. Angels of islands, for example, often tend to be rather isolated and inward. Some angels are very conscious of human activities, while others are all but oblivious. Not surprisingly, angels of wilderness areas and of large bodies of water usually have very little awareness of people. Their planetary consciousness can be scanty as well. The Angel of the Pacific Ocean, for instance, told me:

> *Land angels are more in touch because humans are land life, not marine life. The oneness that everyone keeps*

mentioning is relative, as you know: true on one level, untrue on another. Yes, we are more aware of sea mammals, but they are not very linked with mankind.

This angel went on to say that the environmental impact of people on oceans had raised its awareness, not only of humans but of its own relationship with the planet.

The angel of Lake Dal in Kashmir may at one point have been as oblivious to people as most other lake devas, but I found this angel to be extremely gracious, and closely linked with humanity, perhaps because of the many people living on houseboats there. The same was true of the landscape angels in the valleys of Nepal. In general, I found angels in Asia more closely linked with humanity than elsewhere, and suspect it has to do with the longstanding civilizations there. Native American cultures seem to have made relatively little impression on American landscape angels—perhaps because those cultures were nomadic and created so little disturbance in the ecology of any particular place.

Because I myself have always been drawn to "unspoiled" natural areas and used to strongly prefer them to towns, I had initially assumed that the devic world must always resent human interference in the landscape and decry, as I did, the brutality of urbanization and industrialization. The angels I have met on my travels have more than once called this assumption into question, and urged me to set my prejudices and preconceptions aside. I learned that the angels do not feel resentment or other negative qualities and are always loving. I have often been surprised to find them less judgmental about human activities than I am. On touring a silk factory in China, for instance, I encountered a Silk Industry Deva, who expressed gladness that modern technology was sparing workers the repetitive labor of the past. It seemed to me this deva understood the human heart in a way few other devas do.

When in Chengdu, I asked the Angel of China, "Have you had any idea of how far technology should be used here? More and larger tractors would destroy the little plots and put people out of work."

That is a matter for the Chinese Government, and they are well aware of the problem. In your searching and discovery of the Chinese people, remember to keep your own projections and learning separate. This tour is a learning period for you; be grateful.

I first became aware of this angel on seeing the grasslands illuminated by the lights from the plane as we approached the Guilin airport. It was full of compassion for what the Chinese people were trying to accomplish and the difficulties that lay ahead of them. The feeling of compassion overwhelmed me and, surprisingly, remained present for hours, accompanying me through baggage claim, customs and immigration, the drive to the hotel, and dinner in a restaurant. Remembering this influenced me powerfully throughout the trip, often shifting my views of the Chinese from critical to sympathetic. When, a few months later, the demonstrations in Tiananmen Square came to a violent end, I realized more of what the angel's compassion had been foreseeing. The Angel of South Africa, whom I encountered during the period of unrest that preceded the abolishment of apartheid, was likewise unusually warm and compassionate. It seems that in times of political turbulence, national angels send out especially strong currents of love.

In Bali, Indonesia, the angel had a smiling energy which seemed to understand our culture as well as its own. I don't remember another angel so connected with human culture. It seemed to spread out in a beautiful fretwork, which was continually changing. To me this was represented in the artistry of the people. The beauty was reflected everywhere on the island. Rituals, ceremonies and even practical tasks like irrigation and terracing of the land, were performed with joy and lightness and care. At the same time, I was dismayed by the commercialism of the island. I asked the angel whether it, too, was dismayed.

I do not particularly see it. I continue to radiate and be what I am, and let that work out according to the choice of the people. Of course I know what you mean, but in this 'one world' all must meet the present as best they can.

When I asked about what I saw as the emergence of materialism and greed which were new to Bali, it replied that this had not become a pressing problem and the people could still be creative in their fields of endeavor. I mentioned that I had met an old ekot weaver who was selflessly dedicated to his art. One piece of weaving might take him two years to complete. I asked if that type of devoted artisan must inevitably succumb to modern influences.

He does that in his own way. Yet he and his like will indeed be compelled to share in the same universal energies of the planet, and their dedication to their art becomes less intense. But the inspiration for it can then broaden, and the art change and be no less rich. Perhaps less precise, perhaps more uplifting. Of course it is possible that modern methods can be used and the pieces of material be charged with powerful blessing in a different way. Blessings need not die with change, as love grows.

The Angel of Bali, continued serenely:

I have welcomed you through my people and their art; now I welcome you on the soul level. I give my note as needed. This is an island and as such has its own integrity, which is difficult to disturb. We try to encircle all who come with our love, that you may pick up our message of a loving balance and distribute it in your own homes.

In Nepal, too, I felt anxiously protective of the innocent beauty I found in the outlook of the people, afraid that exposure to western cultural values around materialism would destroy this. At the same time, their lives were very hard. So I asked the Angel of Nepal what it would prefer: for the people to remain as they were—primitive and isolated, but happy—or to ease their hardships through modernization.

It is not my desire, if I had one, that counts. World energies are changing and we are part of the world. There is no best way for change. Each situation has to be met as it comes up. There can be no master plan, and those who say that there is are not trustworthy. Unless people meet life with flexibility, they experience resistance and pain. Of course there will be lots of that, which is a learning process for you. We do not learn that way and do not suffer; we attempt to express purely whatever is ours to do. If that does not sound like using intelligence and just seems to be following the wind, so to speak, recollect that expressing purity is the intelligent way and, for you, not easy. For us it requires extreme sensitivity . . . Yes, it is important that people all over the world realize that there are angels of countries. Until all life harmonizes together, there are parts set against other parts, which is a disease of the body, a disease of the planet. Yet disease is a way to learn health. Yes, I am speaking for the angelic kingdom, not personally for Nepal.

After watching barefoot women employed in carrying sand, pebbles and boulders all day, or breaking stones for the roads, I asked the Angel of Nepal if that was what it wanted for its people, the women carrying stones on their backs while men ride in cars. It replied:

It fits and is fair at the moment. Change will come to women gradually. This is not a concern at present, nor is damage to the environment. As you know, comprehension comes slowly and gradually.

I said that my understanding of things didn't seem relevant to Nepal, and the angel agreed, but said that there was an atmosphere here conducive to inward turning for me, and to be grateful for that. I was, and was also grateful for more general teachings that this angel offered. It told me, for instance, that the role of the 'bad' is to help us learn that all is 'good'. When I questioned this, the angel replied:

Without opposites there is nothing. Through the opposites you come to wholeness. There are no opposites in the consciousness of a single tree, but the tree deva, the intelligence, knows that the expression of life which is a tree is a necessary part of the whole. Being in wholeness, it uses the energies for the whole, in love. That is what you each can do in your wholeness, if you choose. Of course there are limitations; life is a joyous limitation at one point.

I argued that to accept all customs of the countries I visited—even those that seemed backward or unjust—would be unfeeling.

No. Because you accept them with love. When that love is even stronger, you can assess those customs in your thoughts and thus help them to fruition. If change is needed, think of a better way. If there is merit in your thought, it will be picked up. The intelligence of the planet is always used for the whole.

On a trip that included visits to India and Australia, I toured New Zealand with fifteen other like-minded teachers, stopping in various places along the way to give presentations. Our group included an Australian aborigine. I was especially curious about him, remembering the ease with which I had connected telepathically with aboriginal tribes during the Network of Light work. Connecting face to face was not so easy, however. Although he said he loved being with me, he didn't, or couldn't, answer my questions, for he didn't seem to function much through the intellect.

There were also two New Zealand Maoris in our group. At the time, the Maoris were just beginning to reclaim their pride in their culture. It was most interesting to go to their meetings and see how these were conducted. Every speaker took a similar stance, used similar gestures, as if speaking at the meeting were a ritual. After the speech there was a recital of incredibly beautiful and harmonious songs. The quality of the music was surprising, for most of the singers were untrained Maori boys who had been picked up off the street. Singing must have been in their blood. This song break made an interval between the debating speakers, so any irate speaker or listener had time to cool down and find balance before the next turn.

An older lady Maori befriended me and told me a lot about their culture and customs. I loved the closeness until I realized that, as a condition of her acceptance of me, I was expected to act like a member of her tribe. This meant, for instance, that it was not all right to go for a walk on my own. My independent self balked at the constant togetherness, and I distanced myself from her for the rest of the trip.

My personal exasperation with the tribal mentality was eye opening, for I had long idealized indigenous peoples, believing them to be closer to nature and to the spiritual world than modern, industrialized people. Yet I had to admit that the richness of my own spiritual life owed a great deal to the individualism of the contemporary west. My Protestant upbringing had not constrained me from exploring and accepting teachings from other religious traditions, and I had been free to lead an unconventional and relatively unencumbered life, following my guidance wherever it led me. This freedom of inner and outer movement had led to an ever-expanding planetary awareness. From the angels of more ancient and tribal cultures, I learned that the differentiation of the individual from the tribe was a global trend. People in those societies needed to loosen their connection to tradition and become more autonomous so that they could better function in what is becoming one world.

In northern Thailand, I had become aware of an Angel of the Hill Tribes (including Thailand, Laos, Burma: the Golden Triangle). From a personality point of view this angel seemed fierce, colorful, and quick moving, with sharp pointy fingers. On a higher level it was wraithlike, disappearing like mist. When I asked why it was disappearing, it replied:

> *The energies that form us* [the tribes], *the individual strong cultures, do not fit into the emerging interconnectedness that is coming in the world. Even though tourists demand the artwork and keep it going, that is not sufficient. It may seem that these individualities are extremely strong and separate, unlike the North American tribes who have fallen apart, but that is not so. They are actually vanishing.*

When I said that the world would be poorer through the loss of such unique and colorful cultures, it answered:

> *The part of the culture that you have come across, in clothes and cloth artifacts, has already entered into other cultures and therefore has not died. It has been appreciated and adopted elsewhere, made applicable to modern times. Keeping ethnic and artistic differences in this changing world is laudable but not always practical. In any case, my energies have run their course.*

I objected, saying that all over the world separate nationalities are reappearing, insisting on being themselves, as in the Balkans.

> *Yes, many are returning to a unity which they had lost. But*

here there never was one large unity, only smaller traveling units. These cannot support themselves any more. Their reason for existence and their creativity, because it was so intense, is played out. You could say it has succeeded and now needs to change into something different. In this period of complete transformation of energies, I cannot tell you what the future will bring. In one sense there is no future, until all ceases to exist and therefore makes room for new birth.

I wondered: Is this the future for all tribal units all over the world?

Not necessarily all—which is enough of an answer for now.

"Why am I receiving this before I even visit the Hill Tribes?" I asked. "I know nothing about them."

Seeing them through this different perspective may keep your mind more open to the new, and de-emphasize the natural tendency to acclaim and crystallize the beauty.

The Angel of Thailand continued on this theme:

What can the soul of a country say to you, a visitor of a few days? I, or we, can always say what you already know, that being loving is the need for each country, and that we continually arrange the energies toward that goal. The tremendous changes at this time, which you have already noticed with regard to the Hill Tribes, will cause us to deal with these energies in an appreciative new way, releasing their finer qualities, knowing that the effect on the material world will be vast. Old patterns have to go, but we would minimize the fear and resistance that relinquishing the old brings.
It is not that each area or country or cultural entity will be treated differently, from our point of view. The patterns are there already; how these patterns are adjusted to the new is yours to choose. You yourself are fully occupied in taking in all the differences and what you consider the picturesque qualities

148

of the various cultures. Nevertheless, please attune to these levels as much as possible, for from here we can open new facets of human life on the mind level, and that is important.

I had believed that the breaking up of old cultures left indigenous people bereft, but I came to realize that patterns are working out quickly now. Like it or not, western values have changed the whole world, and have separated people from their previous traditions. In that separation people can see their traditions more clearly and claim their uniqueness, in the same way that I reframed my Canadian identity. Natives of ancient cultures are rediscovering their own traditions, arts and languages, and while these will not be the same as they once were, they foster the growth of self-esteem.

We westerners also need to change. No longer can we go on using planetary resources for our own ends; we must learn to husband them in a more ecologically balanced and unselfish way. We have to respect the rights of other cultures, and stop assuming our superiority. In South Africa, I had been moved by the strength of tribal family life, the attitude of love for all children. This also was true of the native Polynesian people of Hawaii. Their word for family—*ohana*—was used as a verb, and one of their sayings was, "The healthier the family, the more confident the individual." In a material sense, western societies have been the more advanced, but in the arts of relationship—which are the root of happiness—technologically advanced countries often lag behind unsophisticated peoples.

To the Angel of China, I once remarked: "We of the West have freedom and are sharing that with the East. What does or will the East share with us?" It replied:

As you have said, the idea of the good of the whole, which your environmental pollution is bringing to your consciousness. But it is more than that: it is a feeling of the togetherness of things, Feng Shui in nature, and a more sensitive awareness of human workings. The people here do not get annoyed when pushed on the street; they have less ego but not less self-esteem. Ponder on that.

My last message from the Angel of China was:

149

Remember that love is always with us, inclusive and helping. There will be many mistakes by the people as they react to the new energies; work and help them yourselves. Remember how many millions of people are concerned and are part of the changes. The more people, the greater strength is needed for change. There is no escape from one world now. Old enmities come to the surface in one way or another, to be sloughed off to make room for fresh relationships. Those of you who can love, and understand, have lots to do!

In Hindu Katmandu I came across a local tradition: the Kumari or Living Goddess. The goddess is a very young girl who must meet certain strict requirements. She must come from a Buddhist family, possess certain traditional Buddhist marks of excellence, have no physical imperfections, and must never have bled, not even from a pinprick. She is also severely tested for fearlessness. Once selected, she is installed in her own ancient and beautifully carved temple residence in the city and watched constantly to ensure that she never meets with an accident that might draw blood. She leaves her residence only once a year, when she is paraded through the streets of Katmandu and the Hindu king of Nepal pays obeisance to her. She is also watched for certain gestures, hand and eye movements that have traditional meaning for the country —foretelling the future or indicating some action that needs to be taken. A Nepalese friend of mine interviewed an ex-Kumari, and ascertained that she had no memory of the occasions when she made these gestures. It seems that at those times she was taken over by a supernormal energy, perhaps in a way similar to the trances of the Delphic oracles of Greece.

When the Kumari's menstrual blood starts to flow, that is the end of her divinity. The goddess has left her, and another child has to be found to fill the role. Ex-Kumaris have a hard life after such a limited and sheltered upbringing, with no training for domesticity or wifehood. They are further disadvantaged by the prevailing belief that it is unlucky for any man to marry them. (I understand that now care is taken to help ex-Kamaris adapt to normal life.)

In Hawaii, there existed a system of taboos, called *kapus*, which threatened dark consequences if a forbidden act was committed. The system was officially abolished in 1810—partly because the taboos were especially restrictive of women, who wished to be free of them, and also because Westerners were seen to break the taboos and suffer no ill effects. At an old temple in Kealakekua Bay, I encountered the deities who had been forced into retirement when the Kapu system was abandoned. I found these gods a sorry lot: ghostly, dejected, and cut off from their source. Their predicament was not unlike that of human ghosts who, in clinging to their former earthly identities, are unable to connect with their immortal souls and partake of eternal life.

I realized that they did not have to remain so limited. They needed to become aware of what they really were: the creative forces of the elements or qualities. I communicated this to them and sent them love. They were aware of me and listened, and most of them chose to claim and reunite with their true higher self. One, a war god, remained disconsolate and stuck, unable to accept what I was saying. I tried to help this figure link with its essence by attuning to the quality of courage. It still didn't change. Finally it said it would have to get used to the idea, and asked me to return. I kept coming back to it, and gradually its true self became strong and shining. By the end of my trip, it had practically dissolved into light. Later I learned that when King Kamehameha II abolished the kapu system, he had continued to worship one warrior god. I suspect that was my ghostly friend.

Though I felt the old gods were dead in the sense that they were no longer relevant to Hawaiians, a way to relate to their real force was shown by Leslie Kuloloio of Haiku, Maui. He was a Christian Hawaiian who believed that God, creator of all, worked through the four Hawaiian nature gods, who corresponded with the elements: earth, air, fire and water. He related very directly with the elements, teaching people how to live close to the earth as in the past, and how to obtain the necessities of life from the sea and from his valley. When humans reconnect in a more conscious way with the energies that had once been personified as gods, the old deities are able to expand into a sense of themselves that is more universal and less dependent on local superstitions and rituals.

In 1997, my lifelong wish to visit Egypt was fulfilled. Ancient Egypt had fascinated me ever since I was a child, and I feel sure I lived there in a former incarnation. With its three thousand years of history, it is likely that most of us lived there at some time. I believe we still have much to learn, spiritually as well as physically, from this ancient civilization.

Eileen Caddy, who had been born in Egypt, shared my desire

to travel there, booked a trip and invited me to accompany her. Unfortunately, she fell ill and had to cancel, so I asked my old friend Erica to take her place. Then, a week before we were due to leave, more than sixty tourists were shot and killed at Queen Hatshepsut's Temple in Egypt. Our travel agent offered to cancel our trip, but Erica and I individually felt it right to go ahead, so we flew across the Atlantic, met in London, and joined what was now a very small tour group. The dearth of tourists meant we were given royal treatment. We had our own police guards, could go into places that were normally difficult to see because of the crowds, and received special attention, special food, and privileges not normally accorded to foreign visitors.

Early on in this visit I had the feeling that the gods of Egypt, unlike those in Hawaii, were very much alive. Perhaps that is because they had been honored for millennia and are still named, considered and talked about by Egyptologists and others. They seemed to be almost bristling and bubbling for contact. But which one would I choose to attune to? I finally settled on Ma'at, the goddess of truth who had to always be present in every sort of situation in order to ensure balance. She conveyed:

> *I will speak for all the gods, and welcome your ear. Yes, re-welcome, for you have been in touch with us before. In one way it doesn't matter that our names are just myths to the present civilization, as our energies continually sweep the planet in all cultures. Yet it is good to have the conscious contact this way, to be brought into the present. Though the interpretation of truth varies from age to age, its splendor never varies and is always appropriate.*
>
> *You see us sternly ritualized on temple walls. Know that even in Egypt, with its thousands of years of ritual, there have been numerous amalgamations of the gods, expressing the current truth. You in your age have tremendous freedom to express your truths, some of which, not being truths but your wishes, have led you astray. We appreciate your freedom and creativity, but would endorse for you a keener approach to the mysteries of life, a greater dedication to truth. We offer our help in this, using our Egyptian names and putting ourselves to use! Thank you for the moment.*

A couple of days later Ma'at continued:

> *The love that is behind truth, that starts creation, shines through each god, even the malevolent ones, as you know. The pattern of love in the stars in the skies, the land and the rivers, and through life, all fits into an endless design which changes yet never changes, for all life returns to Source. As your God patiently repeated the same thing to you a thousand times, so we repeated rituals a thousand times until the wonderful pattern of love and life was an unconscious part of your being. Now is the time for such models to be conscious, seen as manifestations of life, welcomed and enjoyed, not the black and white separation of the present age, but individuality in acceptance and understanding.*

While I was writing this, our boat passed crowds of people on the river bank, men in white in one group and women in black in a separate group. I found out later that they were looking for a drowned child.

Ma'at continued:

> *You understand this old pattern and are beginning to understand the new, and we cannot emphasize enough the beauty of the new understanding. Love is all, in truth.*
>
> *Now let us go on. On this particular subject [positive and negative] our stories are mixed, for the general populace was not ready for certain truths. Times have changed and more people are ready. Regardless of how you are received, continue with your inner knowing. No arguments; truth does not need to be defended. You are inclined to feel attacked; let love in on such occasions. Of course, use current words for the energies; only use Egyptian terms when they come to mind easily.*
>
> *Let the magic of the Egyptian scene seep in, for that will help your attunement. Repeated patterns, no great variety. Variety is not essential to human functioning, though the present civilization thinks it is, and it thinks so because it doesn't seek the variety within, the countless worlds of experience and learning that make up the human being. We have ritualized this variety, for each age has in its own way.*

Seek beneath the surface as well as enjoying the beauty of the surface. The senses are to help you to enjoy life; they are the gifts of the universe for your amazement and thankfulness.

Ours was a very ordered world; yours has gone to the other extreme as you each seek to be. Answers and truth come from all directions. Just look where you are and you will see. As the water flows down, flow with circumstances in the knowledge that when your choices are for the whole, your flow is to the center of yourself and is right for yourself.

On another occasion I asked why the Egyptian gods had lasted for thousands of years, more than in any other civilization, and was answered:

Because of their truth, and because their truths were honored and heeded. When the energies which are less linked to spirit are honored, such as the gods of materialism, the civilization will not last. Honor the spirit, choose love.

You wonder why the Egyptians, unlike most civilizations and alone among early cultures, do not seem to have blood sacrifice or ritual murder. A peaceable people. Such would not be in keeping with the order of our lives, the order of the Nile, the nonviolent climate, the unchanging land and days. Egypt has been a blessed land and we would that such blessings spread elsewhere. Repetition there has been, and repetition can be very helpful and necessary. Nowadays, when most people seek their own individual creativity, repetition is not sought except as a way to make money. Then you lose a sense of connection in your lives, a sense of peace, a sense of order, a sense of belonging. You yourself like contrasts, and that is fine, because underneath you have found and know that you are part of the whole. How peaceful is this continuous river protected by deserts! Let your inner life be as unchanged and ordered, whatever the situation. Tests of the inner order come, of course, and failures can bring greater sensitivities. Accept the present peace as our gift, as you watch the sun setting on the west side of the river, as always. Always, the reliability of the changeless days of the countryside of this land.

154

The last message I had from Ma'at was:

> *Realize anew that danger is ever present in Middle Eastern affairs and that people like you can help the situation by specifically lending your loving thoughts. Yes, there is trouble all over the world, but the Middle East is a particularly volatile area. Benign human intercession is more powerful than you believe.*

In recent decades, human contact with angels has become less unusual than it was when I began attuning to them fifty-some years ago. Many people are now aware of the help and inspiration we can receive from them. What is taking longer for people to grasp is that the benefit of such encounters is mutual. As I hope these stories have illustrated, most angels welcome the chance to be noticed and consulted by us. Those angels who are struggling to weave together human cultures that are torn by crisis or conflict are aided by the love we send them, and send it back out to those who need it most. They feel it is helpful to the planet for humans and angels to have strong links. That is what makes "benign human intercession" so much more powerful than we commonly suppose it to be.

It is important for us to attune to our own regional and cultural identities at a time when these distinctions are becoming less sharp and isolating. As we do that, we continue to honor these angels, facilitating a smooth transition into a more global sense of identity.

Chapter 17

When I wasn't traveling and leading workshops, I lived quietly and, it seemed to me, rather idly in my apartment. I suppose I can't have been that idle, since over a period of two decades, I managed to produce eight published volumes of my messages and reflections. Still, I often felt that I should be doing more to serve the whole. Reading was, and is, my guilty pleasure, for I confess I prefer novels and adventure stories to spiritual literature. To find obscure childhood favorites of mine—*Just David, T. Tembaron, Marieta: A Maid of Venice*—in used books stores was a special source of glee for me, taking me back to my girlhood passion for reading under the covers after "lights out." Snacking—especially on sweets—is another guilty pleasure I tend to indulge in when home alone. Though the years since I left Findhorn have been punctuated with many inner and outer adventures, hectic periods of teaching and international travel, I am very ordinary in my day-to-day habits, pleasures and preoccupations.

When I first moved to North America from Findhorn, I had changed my decades-long practice of meditating three times a day. I wanted to be open to inner contact at all times, not just during formal attunement sessions. Sometimes I felt guilty about this omission, especially when I would read of great masters spending hours meditating every day or night. But I know it was the right decision for me at that time.

In 1992, I was involved in an accident that destroyed my car. At first, I didn't appear to be injured. Then, six weeks later, I found that my hands were so weak I couldn't even hold a mug. This episode made me realize that I needed to pay more attention to my physical body, which I had always taken completely for granted. I had never needed to visit doctors or take medicines, or give much thought at all to staying healthy. Now I consulted healers and began to appreciate the wonderful power of the body elemental, and to give it thanks. Later, if I forgot to acknowledge and give thanks to life, I might remember that I didn't want another reminder!

In the wake of my accident, I had turned to Dr. Bill Mitchell, a fine naturopathic physician. One night, I had a vivid dream about him. I was sitting in front of him wanting to talk to him, almost as if he were God, and he was sitting, writing and totally ignoring me. I shuffled and cleared my throat, but he continued to ignore me. Finally he looked up and said, "You have to have an appointment, and the charge is $15." I said it wasn't fair to have to pay $15 just to be told that. He was adamant. Then I woke up. When I shared this dream with Ron Rabin, who is a great interpreter of dreams, he told me he believed it meant that I should have regular appointments with God. This made sense to me, and prompted me to meditate regularly again. I began to have 'appointments' with God every morning.

Although in my inner contact, I was and am part of God, I couldn't always accept that my Dorothy personality is also divine. God was within me rather than outside of me, yet I would forget that we were not separate. This false sense of separation expressed a sense of duality in myself as well. There were two of me—my ordinary self, which included my body, my intellect, and my flawed human personality, and a divine or transcendent self which knew itself to be part of God.

In Sheena's circle, we had been rather disparaging of the human personality, which we used to refer to as the "lower self." From David Spangler, I had learned to stop regarding it as a problem child and, on my good days at least, to extend it respect and love. Nevertheless, I continued to experience it as separate, as something I reached beyond in order to connect with the divine. Now, as I resumed having a definite inner appointment every day, God was letting me know that there was yet another step to be taken. I would get:

> *You can learn to love Me and you are right here now. Cease separation.*

This didn't make sense to me. If I were not separate from God, how could I possibly become aware of God? Doesn't awareness require two: a subject and an object.

> *You can choose to be one with Me at any time. Now do it with your eyes open. Now to the physical. Rise to the depths of the physical elemental, asking forgiveness as we embrace and merge. The physical has always been divine but the personality has seen it as alien. Now there is freedom to work together.*
> *If it is difficult to be with Me when you are with others, remember they too are of God. Share love with them, not as separate people, but as one with Me. Mostly you hone into the mind with others; broaden yourself to realize Me underneath*

that mind. Practice knowing God-power, the joyous energy,
God-energy, with the mind as with the body.

I had experienced God as within me, but to always conceive of God as inseparable from me—inseparable from my ordinary human personality, inseparable even from my physical body—was a new challenge. I had to consciously practice remembrance of it, for when I forgot—when I conceived of myself as separate from God—awareness of my own shortcomings would overwhelm me.

In message after message, God continued to call me back to a sense of unity. As a result, I felt some mental barriers giving way. One symptom of this was a change in my relationship to guidance. In the past, when faced with a decision, I would feel a clear inner signal, a sense of knowing which of my alternatives was God's will. My desire was to obey that will. The clarity of these signals gave me a sense of security. Now, the idea of obedience was ceasing to have any meaning for me. I came to see that there is but one choice, God. Having made that choice, I found I was approaching all other choices in a more ordinary way, following my own inclinations and best judgment, for God is no less present there than in the promptings that had once seemed external to me.

Then a deeper shift took place. It was as if I had been turned inside out. After countless years of receiving and being embraced by divine love, I found that I could only give out. In my meditations, I ceased to feel like the object of love and began to experience only love itself. To meditate now is to feel a sense of blessing flowing out into the world. Sometimes I say, "May God's love be known." Other times I say, "May Thy love be known." And sometimes, when I am very close within, it becomes, "May our love be known."

"Receive" is the word I used most often to describe how my messages came into the world. I still tend to put it that way, though it suggests something more passive than my actual process, which mixed inner receptivity with the more practical business of choosing words and writing them down. That the messages were not merely received but co-created is something that began to acquire new significance for me during this period. Back when I was writing my first book, I had wanted to keep my own thoughts and personality on the sidelines, so as not to distract from what God or the devas were saying. I had been taken aback when Erica and her writing teacher said that this made the book boring. Now I was coming to recognize that I might have more to contribute than the messages themselves. I could share my reflections about them and perhaps help others to better understand their full implications.

When first receiving messages, I used to be conscious of setting my intellect aside, for I didn't want what I received to be distorted by my own beliefs, opinions and prejudices. But now that I was coming to regard my whole self, including my intellect, as part of God, I began to want to reconcile my thoughts and ideas with my inner experiences. Two questions in particular arose for me: the relationship of human freedom to God's will, and the problem of good and evil.

For decades I had aspired to do God's will, and sought to know that will through inner guidance. At the same time, my messages from God had always stressed my own freedom. To the reasoning mind, freedom and obedience appear to be opposing principles. Yet inwardly I did not experience any conflict or contradiction between the two. To feel completely free while striving to know and obey God's will was not only possible, but easy most of the time. Why did reason pose a conflict that had never actually presented itself in my own life?

The problem of evil had been puzzling. Like everyone else, I first accepted evil as a concept, and wondered how evil could have arisen in a world created by a God who was wholly good. The curious thing was that in all my years of attuning to the devic realms I had never encountered evil as a spiritual reality. I had never actually met a being whom I would call "evil." If I had only my attunements to go on, I would have concluded that there was no such thing as evil. Yet it went on existing as a concept —in my mind and experience, and in the collective experience of humanity. Was it merely a concept? If so, why did the concept persist in human minds when nothing in the spiritual world seemed to correspond to it?

Back in 1967, when I first started attuning to the devic world, God had suggested that I attune to the quality of serenity. To attune to a quality seemed weird, but I tried, and to my surprise heard from an intelligent being, whom I called the Goddess of Serenity:

> *I stand here, serene. Though storms rage around, in the midst of them I can come to influence humans.*
> *The One All-Being gives you the gifts of the spirit, and you*

159

*have wondered by what agency they come. I bring the gift of
serenity, peace, poise. I enter your being with my being and lo,
we correspond and you are serene. I and my kin come from the
'higher' worlds and you have called us pagan gods. But we are
truer servers of the Lord of All than any human, for we stray
not in our fidelity, nor are we other than our true selves.*

*This rare quality you feel is purity, because we could not
be tempted by the pairs of opposites. Our roads are clear and
undeviating, and good and evil mean nothing in our worlds.
We see human deviation and strange cravings, yet do not
understand, for where we go is serenity. We bring it to this
troubled world. We enfold the earth with it, with ourselves .
. .*

*You say that the lives of the gods of Olympus were not all
that laudable or spiritual, but what you have heard has been
a somewhat biased history as recorded by humans from their
own motivations, and is of another age. Interpretations would
be different now.*

*Though the air we breathe is rarefied, you can breathe it
too. Do not think otherwise. Spiritual qualities are the birthright
of each soul, and with us you are at home. Rarely is this
interpreted in your world; spread it, in serenity.*

At the time of this encounter, I had been wondering why angels
seemed so unemotional. They had struck me at first as rather cold
and impersonal. The Goddess of Serenity seemed to be speaking to
this question when she said that angels could not be tempted by the
pairs of opposites. In humans, the contrast of opposites gives rise to
preferences, and preferences give rise to emotions. According to the
Goddess of Serenity, angels do not perceive in that way. They are
somehow beyond polarity.

This became clearer as I went on to attune to other qualities.
God told me that Joy and Sorrow were one angel. As I continued to
seek the reality behind various qualities, I found that this happened
consistently: a single angel embodied both the quality I had named
and its opposite. Unlike people, angels never appeared to prefer one
end of the spectrum they embodied, to its opposite. They did not
even seem to experience one end of their spectrum as opposed to the
other. Rather, it was a continuum along which they were in constant

movement. What we conceive of as pairs of opposites are, to an angel, one continuous reality. There are no bad angels and, for that matter, no good angels either.

In preferring one quality to its opposite, calling one "good" and the other "bad," we rarely stop to consider what our world would be like if the bad quality were eliminated. Without darkness we could not perceive light as light. Without darkness, we could not even live, for unremitting light would kill us. Through meditation, I may achieve a consciousness of unity, but I could not even begin to meditate if there were not polarity. It would never occur to me to seek unity unless I also experienced separation.

Again and again, contact with the angels lifted me into a way of perceiving polarities as a vibrant, joyous whole, beyond judgment or criticism. Yet in my ordinary life, ideas of good and bad persisted. Because I am a human being, the polarities in my own nature lead to actions, and I like some of these actions better than others. If I were an angel, I could encompass the opposites of self-indulgence and self-denial without any sense of inner conflict. But as a human with a sweet tooth, I lurched between guiltily indulging my appetite for chocolate and berating myself for that indulgence. Is it possible, I wondered, for humans to manifest our own qualities as the angels do, without judging them to be positive or negative?

I began to research the sayings of famous people on the subject of good and bad, and found that all of them had realized the need for us to experience what we call the opposites in order to be fully human. On this subject, Carl Jung said "The task of today is to unite the pairs of opposites." Yogananda said, "Your trials come not to punish but to awaken you, to make you realize you are a part of Spirit and that just behind the spark of your life is the Flame of Infinity. Hazrat Inayat Khan said "Before the human heart can be tuned to vibrate to the Christ note, the highest rate of vibration possible to mankind, it must be made capable of response to every note of sorrow and pain, every failure and shortcoming to which man is prone, for he cannot know the highest unless he also knows the lowest, cannot know the whole until he knows every part."

In his book, *Freedom from the Known*, Krishnamurti offered a helpful exercise. He recommended that one contemplate one's own faults and failings without judgment or blame or excuses or explanations, simply holding them in awareness without any comment whatsoever. I tried this one day when I was feeling ashamed of myself for neglecting to phone a friend on her birthday. I sat with the thought "I didn't phone Julie," saying that over and over to myself until I could experience it as simply a fact, free of emotions, opinions, and judgments. Then a remarkable transformation took place. I felt myself to be in the presence of God, and flooded with love—a love that included and embraced my lapse and freed me from guilt over it.

Always before, I had attempted to rise above my negativities, believing that I needed to leave them behind in order to join with the Beloved. I had always assumed that to attune to divine love, I must begin by feeling loving myself. Now I had discovered that love was accessible through any state, no matter how negative. Instead of trying to set aside or rise above whatever "unworthy" frame of mind I might be in, I could take it as my starting point, bestowing simple, neutral attention on it. If I persist with such attention, it eventually dissolves into love, and love dissolves the barrier between me and the Beloved. Human qualities, no less than angel qualities, are a manifestation of the divine, and there is no quality so negative that it cannot serve as a gateway to God's love.

When, over the years, God had urged me to be more loving, it was not merely an attempt to make me a kinder, better person. Attuning to God, to love, is not just a way of feeling and acting. It is also a way of <u>knowing</u>, a cognitive power that gave me access to the inner lives of beings whose outlook was very different from my own. Love lifts us easily beyond the categories, limitations and contradictions imposed by reason. Love is the only way to truly understand the world, because love is what the world is made of, and how the world is made.

My old teacher Vitvan had been trying to explain that, back when his discourses on quantum physics were making my head spin. I only recognized the full significance of what he was saying three decades later, when I attuned to the basic building blocks of the universe —the elements. To conceive of the world as comprised of earth, air, fire and water had seemed rather outmoded and medieval, an abstraction that didn't mean much to me until I encountered the elements as living beings. This came about when, at David Spangler's suggestion, I set up a shrine to them. I wasn't too enthusiastic about the idea at first, since I've never been attracted to ritual. But to attune to anything, I need to begin with my physical senses, and the simple representations of earth, air, fire and water I placed on my little altar proved a great help to me in connecting with these primal energies.

First they introduced themselves as a group:

> *We are tools for the highest, and humans, having been given the gift of creativity, have to learn how to use tools. We are available for manifestation on all levels, which is a wonderful destiny and purpose. Limitation on us would cancel universal outworking. Creation is a dangerous, exciting and loving adventure, thanks to us.*

The dangerous aspect of their adventure made attuning to them a challenge, for it included what felt to me like negativity and pain, even anguish, and I needed to deepen my love to remain present with it. God encouraged me to persevere:

> *Listen and honor My craftsmen, for it is My love behind them.*

As I encountered them individually, I tried to keep this in mind. I approached Water first, acknowledging that physically most of me is water, then becoming one with water as emotion, and finally attuning to water as spirit. Here I found love: a love that enables continual movement and transformation, never attempting to restrain or confine. Water expresses the freedom-bestowing aspect of love. It permeates every cell of us, and seeps into every crack and crevice of the world. To love as water is to leave no secret nook or cranny unpenetrated by acceptance.

Earth first thanked me for recognizing the divinity of the mineral world. It told me that the heaviness of Earth is our testing point and our saving grace. Earth expresses the gravity of love, its weightiness, constancy and depth.

In approaching Air, I felt the vastness, lightness and joyous expansiveness of love. I felt thanks for air and it replied:

> *I welcome you, and all who partake of our qualities, that you will celebrate life everywhere. It is a celebration, a freedom that I share with you now, for this needs to be emphasized in a world so caught up in old patterns in many aspects. To*

face the unknown with joy instead of hanging on to the old in
fear, is what I would offer to humanity at present. Face your
fears, recognize, name and embrace them, with love, and find
freedom.

The sometimes violent aspect of Fire seemed difficult for me to
approach, so I began by attuning to the quality of warmth, the steady
warmth of my own body. It replied:

I speak to you partially, for my cosmic self would be
too powerful. Know that I am in all life, carefully keeping
temperatures through the years. Think of this aspect of me,
appreciate it, love it, and come closer. We elements have
much to exchange with you, for recognition and love of us is
another step into consciousness and cooperation with all life.
A personal exchange with humanity is both necessary and
enjoyable at this time.

More time had to pass in my own life before I was able to be
present with the destructive aspect of fire, which is also an expression
of love. Later I received:

You can now better understand the need for the powerful
role of Fire in burning away or dissolving the aspects of humans
which resist becoming completely at one with your divinity,
your resistance to accepting that you are and can act as a
world power in the now, in the moment, that you are divine
Love that can face anything whatever happens.

At one point I had remarked that the Elements seemed rather
medieval. They responded:

So do the angels! Approach all this as truth in the present,
see how more potentially they are more part of your life than
any scientific theory, and in fact are the basis of science and
are workable. Yes, it makes sense to the mind and if accepted
heartily, changes attitudes and evokes love, which is the
purpose at present.

I asked how this new connection might be used in everyday life.

> *The greatest use is the power of love which resonates in you as you make this connection. It is that love which is needed in the world, from each one of you, and which will change the environment. It is right to be focused on practical things, but it is the loving attitude with which practical things are done that betters any situation or relationship. It is so simple that it is constantly overlooked.*

But surely, I argued, one can get to this depth of love without the Elements. Love had been the constant theme of my messages from angels and from the God within, long before it ever occurred to me to attune to the Elements.

> *Whereas now many people are finding power through the agency of the angels, the Elements are another medium, one that goes even more deeply into mankind. Humanity is inclined to put the angels on a higher level and be uplifted by that, which is wonderful. The Elements partake more fundamentally on all levels of life, and therefore are exceedingly useful and helpful for mankind.*

These messages led me to take another look at Paracelsus, the foremost medieval writer on the Elements, whose work I had previously misunderstood. Because people back then didn't use the word "energy" I hadn't realized that what Paracelsus was trying to talk about were the four fundamental expressions of primal energy. It was actually quite similar to an idea that Vitvan had expressed in the language of modern physics. He had described the world as an energy system whose first creative action is to become polarized, creating a negative force which we might call "space." A positive power begins to act in or upon the space. A third power—a non-polarized, neutral state—arises simultaneously to bind and balance the other two. This configuration of energy —the Trinity of Positive, Negative and Balance—locks together, forming a sphere of action for fire, air, water and earth. From these come all manifestation. Put another way, the Four Elements are the first creative outburst of God, the first great angels. Worlds are made up of their qualities, and all phenomena can be traced to their actions.

If it is true that polarization is a creative act of God, then humans, in our tendency to see qualities as pairs of opposites, partake of an aspect of the divine mind that may be unknown to angels. Though polarizing is a source of frequent conflict, confusion and misery for us, it is also the source of our freedom, for without contrasts, we would not experience choice. We need to experience separation and exercise the gift of free will in order to attain what I understand to be our highest purpose in life: the development of consciousness and true awareness of divine love.

The Bible tells us that after Adam and Eve had eaten the fruit of the tree of knowledge of good and evil, they were driven from Paradise, lest they "take also the tree of life, and eat, and live forever." The message is that a human being who knows good and evil does not live forever. Since the knowledge causes us suffering, this is good news. The opposition of good and evil in the human mind is a temporary state, from which it is possible find liberation.

But, as another message from the Elements pointed out, that liberation will not be attained by attempting to return to a more primitive state of consciousness:

> *Go to the center, with us, and rejoice in the variety of life.*
> *For long have aspects of the negative been despised. This is*
> *not going back to matriarchy, where the values of the mind*
> *were not acknowledged as mentality, and individuality had not*
> *been developed, and where the natural flow of energies was*
> *acknowledged without the contribution of mankind's creativity.*
> *Change can always be with us as new combinations of*
> *qualities are produced on the planet through the consciousness*
> *of humanity. We salute that, our part of that, and welcome*
> *new understanding blossoming forth.*

In this and other messages, the Elements stressed that human beings are meant to be participants in creation, the activity of our minds producing variations on the qualities—variations that would not exist in the world if we did not exist. Polarization is but the first stirring of the human mind as co-creator. From the angels we can learn to move continuously and joyously between poles that are equally

166

loved, without getting stuck in rejection of the negative. From the Elements we can learn to exult in the infinite variety of our options, for out of these four primal expressions of divine love, all possible actions are born.

Chapter 18

In April 1994 I was informed that Peter Caddy had died in a motor accident. Like so many of us who knew him, I thought: "Of course," for he was a notoriously reckless driver. Then we learned that he was not responsible for the accident. To me, his dying was like the title of his autobiography: *In Perfect Timing.* I had heard reports of his ill health and early indications of senility, and knew that he would have hated to be helpless.

Eileen stayed on at Findhorn and died there in December 2006, at the age of eighty-nine. With Peter and myself gone, she had provided an essential ongoing connection with the founding principles, and her utter commitment to God was an inspiration to many. The great joy of her last years was being reunited with her children from her first marriage, from whom she had been estranged ever since she associated with Peter. A couple of her daughters even went to Findhorn to look after her, for she had become very frail. Like Peter, I think she went in good timing. She was ready.

Now at ninety, I've come to the reluctant conclusion that it is no longer practical for me to go on traveling to teach, and I moved to Findhorn late in the summer of 2009. For better or worse, current residents will go on being reminded about the founding principles for some time to come.

Sheena once said that it is important that the beginnings of any project be very pure, because when that project is eventually executed, any impurities present at the beginning inevitably become enlarged and magnified. As I reflect on Findhorn—both as it was in the early days and as it has since become—I wonder about imperfections that emerged from its beginnings and from the characters of its three founders. Are our personal flaws and blemishes now apparent in the community? Now that we are not all here physically in the community, do our personal idiosyncrasies continue to cast their shadows over Findhorn and the movement that grew out of it?

Our notion of what it meant to be "very pure" was to follow God's will —as expressed through our inner knowing —first and foremost and without reservation. I continue to hold that as an ideal. We conceived of the "higher" self as that which perceives and follows God's will with good grace. What we called the "lower self" or "personality level" was anything and everything in our characters that got in the way of it. Peter once said that he had no personality. (Actually, he said that God had said this about him, through Eileen's guidance.) I know what he meant by that assertion: that he only wanted to do God's will, not his personal will. But whether we wanted them or not, our personalities were plainly evident to ourselves and each other and to everyone who came in contact with us. Without our following God's will Findhorn would never have been founded. Yet those parts we considered "lower" also helped to shape it, for good or for ill. That mixed legacy is what I'd like to talk about now.

I'll start with myself. I regret that, through my lack of self-esteem, I lessened the expression of spirit through me. Because I was, and remain, only too aware of my imperfections, when I was accused of being wrong, I simply accepted it and blamed myself. I rarely stuck up for myself, or for what I felt was true. When challenged, especially in sensitive areas which I held dear, I folded into myself like a sea anemone, instead of defending what I cherished. And on the rare occasions when I did stand up for what I believed, I wasn't effective at it. I would think up some silly intellectual reason that was just made up in the heat of the argument and which didn't hold water.

Out of that lack of self-confidence, I often allowed my contributions to be overlooked or undervalued. I did not emphasize or give power to my helpful and beautiful messages on spiritual matters—the ones Peter dismissed as not practical enough. I was astonished when I read in his autobiography that "Without Dorothy's stoical service to the garden I was creating, I doubt whether many people outside of Scotland would have heard the name Findhorn today." He had never said anything remotely like that to me. He accepted my deva messages only when it suited him, and seemed to value me only as a typist. Curious, I checked with Jeremy Slocombe, who had co-written the book with Peter. Sure enough, it was Jeremy who had inserted that passage. A recent article about Findhorn even stated that it was founded by Peter and Eileen Caddy, leaving me out altogether.

Naturally I felt hurt that my contribution was slighted. But there is a deeper aspect to my regret than the hurt I felt as an individual human. The messages I received from the Landscape Angel and the devic kingdom continually stressed the vital need for humanity to cooperate with God and with nature. This need is all the more urgent now that humanity still treats nature as if it were a thing, and has polluted the Earth almost beyond redemption. Environmental groups are now doing their best to change our short-sighted, materialistic and individualistic outlooks, but for greater potency in dealing with global environmental degradation, we need to know that we can consciously communicate with the vast intelligence within nature. Nature wants us to fulfill our role as co-creators with the Divine in the outworking of life here, and wants to help us. All too often, out of a lack of personal confidence, I allowed the importance of our relationship to nature to be eclipsed by other agendas in the community.

Because I don't like being ordered around, I had difficulty submitting to Peter's authority. Often he took our conflicts to Eileen for guidance, and I respected what she received—which usually was to follow Peter! Authority, like discipline, is a dirty word nowadays, yet it is still a necessary ingredient to be accepted in a healthy community.

Peter took authority and used it for the glory of God and for the benefit Findhorn. The community would never have come into existence without it. Some believe that he was motivated by personal ego, but his focus was always what he believed to be God's will and he sought whatever would further that end, bulldozing through whatever and whomever got in his way. There was an innocence, a purity, about him. And things got done. Some people with leadership roles in the community have modeled themselves after his resolute style without, perhaps, understanding that it was based on obedience to God. Many others seem to have modeled themselves on my own resistance to being told what to do. At Findhorn there seemed to be few willing to give real authority to others, which resulted in endless discussions that led nowhere.

Peter's blind spot, the downside to his utter commitment to doing what God wanted, was his dependence on the guidance of others. When his intuition failed him, he was open to messages from just about anyone, which made him susceptible to the sometimes dubious advice of various psychics and channelers. This got worse after Eileen, following her own guidance, stopped receiving messages for him. Following this guidance was difficult for Eileen as she was utterly identified with this role. Peter sought to replace her with various other female oracles, to the detriment of their marriage. I don't see him as a womanizer in the usual sense of the word, but he was promiscuous in his craving for spiritual confirmation.

Residence at Findhorn has often had a destabilizing effect on marriages and other committed relationships. The idea that life is change seems to be embodied all too consistently regarding marriage. The relationship between Peter and Eileen was bound to set a standard that influenced the community. They had been considered an ideal couple, brought together by God for a shared purpose. Their separation in 1975 brought shock and disillusionment to many. Others, though, seemed to regard it as an example to follow. Many abandoned one partner for another, saying that a Christ love had led them to the new alliance, and using that as an excuse for more personal freedom

I am probably the only person who reacted to the news of the Caddys' separation by saying "Hurrah! It's about time." Not that I don't believe in couples staying together, for I do, and I think that not nearly enough dedication is directed into making marriages work, especially for the well-being of the children concerned. But I had long seen and lived close to the connection between Peter and Eileen. Influenced in part by their relationship, I stopped believing in twin souls who complete each other. I know now that only with our inner divinity are we complete. As long as we are dependent on something or someone outside of ourselves, we are unassembled, and the love between us and another can be limited, self-oriented and sketchy. As the relationship between man and woman is so important and reaches such depths, it can be the catalyst for transformation. A felt need for transformation is sometimes misinterpreted as a need to change partners—the easy and obvious route—rather than a call to work more deeply with the partner one already has.

Peter's wonderful positivism, which brooked no opposition and recognized no barriers, has often been misconstrued to mean that we don't have to work to make things happen. Many of his stories of wildly improbable "manifestation" have become legends. He told these stories in order to accentuate spiritual principles and encourage people to be more positive, but on the way to making that point, he often exaggerated or left out details. He went on exaggerating—more or less unconsciously, I believe—until some of these tales bore little resemblance to the facts. After a while, neither Eileen nor I could bear to listen to them because we knew they were so over-simplified, so devoid of all the difficulties behind the scenes, that the message they conveyed was distorted. But we never challenged their veracity. The result has been that there are a lot of myths about how easy it is for God to work miracles through us, how things just happen, how all that is necessary is to "just have faith." Faith, as it is conceived of by most people, lacks the enormous positive energy that Peter exhibited. His conviction was more a matter of knowing than believing—a knowing that comes from closeness to the Source—and he backed it up with action. To his credit, he offered more accurate versions of some of the manifestation stories in his autobiography, and yet the overall impression of ease, of "magic" persists.

Another regrettable consequence of Peter's emphasis on the positive was that it left little room to deal with negativity. Realistic concerns, difficulties and obstacles were not even acknowledged, much less addressed. The New Age movement as a whole is often criticized for this lack. We may not have communicated clearly enough that our positive assurance came not from denying difficulties, but from taking them to God for help. People who did not have this firm foundation for feeling positive often felt they had to simulate it by suppressing the negative, and felt guilty about their less than upbeat thoughts and feelings. Eileen's oft-repeated phrase, "All is very, very well" is, of course, beautifully true on the highest levels. But mixing levels, applying that truth to situations which obviously need change, only leads to confusion, mistrust and poor results. Later at Findhorn the pendulum swung in the other direction: problems were analyzed, psychoanalyzed, and processed through various systems to such an extent that the core of the spiritual work—to take problems to God—was often overlooked.

Eileen's contribution to the ongoing challenges of Findhorn were obvious in what I would characterize as her martyr/victim complex. From the earliest days of their relationship, Eileen had always feared that Peter would leave her, and when he finally did, her wound was very deep. Even after he left, she kept on hoping that they would continue to work together. Of course she had reason to feel sorry for herself: her life had not been easy. We all live with situations that bring our faults to the fore so that we can deal with them. This martyr/victim characteristic in the community was named clearly when Caroline Myss began to visit and talk there. She commented on how often, when she asked people about why they were at Findhorn, or what they were doing , the replies often carried the 'poor me' quality. She pointed this out clearly in her talks to the community.

Perhaps it seems a massive omission that we as founders did not give specific teaching. Though we went to God every day for guidance, we were never asked to give teaching. We were wholly occupied in dealing with what came up each day at Findhorn, too busy carrying out our guidance to teach about it. The first people who joined us were so fully in harmony with us and our work that teaching was not necessary. Besides, we did not think of ourselves as teachers. But when we began to grow and become known to the public, people were drawn to the community for such diverse reasons as curiosity, wanting to see nature spirits, attraction to an alternative lifestyle, or simply the desire for an agreeable place to live. To contact their inner divinity was not necessarily their immediate motive, and the core purpose began to get lost.

I believe some of the distortions I've been describing— misconceptions about manifestation, positivity, guidance, and the relationship of spirituality to marriage; confusion about leadership and authority; the glamorizing of Findhorn itself— reflect the personality shortcomings of the three founders.

Any community needs a certain freedom to express itself, but somehow as Findhorn grew, it seemed to put more emphasis on the need for individuals to find their own paths than on the discipline and practice needed to develop and refine the inner contact and make it solidly functional in everyday living. The passage of time has seen the creation of many little groups at Findhorn that follow a variety of teachings or techniques, all of which are aimed at some sort of inner attunement. Having so many different techniques can result in a disregard for the direct way to divinity that we, the founders, espoused. Diversity can become stronger than unity.

About guidance especially, much confusion has arisen. David's skit of the "dueling psychics" lampooned a tendency at Findhorn to try to resolve conflicts by means of what could be called "competitive guidance." From years of experience I have learned that true guidance given to one person does not contradict that given to another. The guidance received by any two people may offer different perspectives, but these can be complementary, not contradictory. If there is a clash, it is time to check the source of the guidance and to examine whether some unconscious personal longing, prejudice or agenda is producing a false message. Nor is it necessary to defend one's guidance at the expense of another's. Inner knowing is so powerful that its very energy can affect others; one can simply treasure it silently, knowing and sending God's love to the situation. The strong, loving energies that were felt at Findhorn have tended to be glamorized, seen as other-worldly, transcendent and magical, and unique to that particular locale. While this mystique served to awaken many to the possibilities Findhorn represented, those possibilities were never meant to be confined to a few special acres in Scotland. When people suppose those wonderful "energies" can only be experienced at Findhorn, and feel desolate upon leaving it, they are endowing the place with a power that is really to be found in their own hearts, if they would but look for it. The place that became Findhorn was just a rather dismal trailer park when we got there. Its "magical" transformation was the result of conscious, day-to-day choices and day-to-day efforts—to meditate, listen and attune, to follow our guidance, to cooperate with the beings of nature, and to behave lovingly toward one another, regardless of our differences. The "magic" can be created elsewhere by people who make those choices and those efforts.

Chapter 19

In March, 2000 I was booked to present a two-day workshop with Katherine Collis at the Whidbey Institute. As the audience at the first session was much smaller than usual, I asked about this. Katherine explained that a group of attendees had canceled at the last moment. I was even more puzzled when people who were not enrolled began arriving: friends I hadn't seen in years and relatives who had never before expressed an interest in my teaching. I soon realized that the workshop had been a ruse to get me to show up for a surprise party in celebration of my eightieth birthday—something I would have resisted had I been consulted in advance. Now that there was no escaping it, I had to admit I was touched and delighted, as well as highly amused. Katherine and her co-conspirators had also compiled a beautiful book of writings and photos contributed by those who could not be present. I bet perusing that book will be a favorite pastime when I'm old and gray!

One of the party guests was a stranger to me. Her name was Fran Stefan, and she was a research scientist working for the U.S. Environmental Protection Agency. She spoke of her deep gratitude for my work, and of its influence on her own work. I was astonished. The EPA?

I learned that Fran's task was to assess the amount of pollution in the waters of Puget Sound. To detect this, she and others went out in a boat and dragged the bottom of the Sound with nets, to capture the creatures from which the pollution could be measured. Each day they cast out their nets, which emerged full of marine life, but had included none of the indicator species needed for their evaluations. Every day they were killing more life from the bottom of the Sound, while getting nothing of what they needed. Fran was very upset over this. At the end of the second to last day, she went to the end of the pier, feeling very frustrated, useless and at a loss. She had heard that people at a place called Findhorn had received help from the intelligence of nature and, being at the end of her tether, simply asked, "If there is intelligence out there, please, I need help. I don't know what to do." Then she named the species that were necessary for her research. On the next and final day of the project, she and her staff went out, put down their net, dragged it and pulled it in, even though it seemed very light. In fact it appeared to be empty at first, but they found at its neck exactly what was required for their first analysis. Incredulous, they cast the net a second time. Again it came back empty except for the creatures they needed. A miracle. Their analysis could now be completed. After that, Fran visited Findhorn. She liked the community but was disappointed that the intelligence of nature was not being actively enlisted there.

Another story I heard around the same time echoed this theme.

Roger Collis was working for the Washington Department of Trade and Economic Development. This brought him into contact with the Hanford Nuclear Reservation, where for years plutonium was produced for nuclear weapons. Many billions of gallons of toxic waste are stored there in leaking underground tanks, and a hundred square miles of groundwater had been contaminated by radioactive materials, including new, hitherto unknown compounds created when toxic waste products had been thrown together. A state-of the-art laboratory was built to study these chemicals, and Roger was invited to the opening. During the celebrations, he extended his consciousness to Spirit and to understanding the role of nuclear energy, both for peacetime and military purposes. He was reminded that at Findhorn the intelligence of the nature forces was sought in the creation of the garden. Here, those intelligences were waiting to be asked to help in a similar way, for they wanted to aid mankind. They have answers for dealing with the pollution we have caused, but we have to be open enough to be willing to ask for their help.

These two stories galvanized me. Environmentalists do what they sincerely believe to be right, but often their assumptions are human-centric—projections of what they would want if they were nature. They don't go straight to the horse's mouth, probably because it has never occurred to them that they can. The mission of Findhorn is to introduce that possibility. Many people there have gone on to do good environmental work, yet they, too, seldom consulted the perspective of nature itself. Something needs to be done about this.

As it happened, I was scheduled to give a talk at Findhorn the following month, at the Easter Conference on Angels. I decided to use the occasion to reassert the founding principles and, I hoped, to rekindle enthusiasm for the unique contribution Findhorn can make to the environmental movement. I prepared very carefully for that talk, and it appeared to go well. As a result of it, I was invited to speak to a gathering of scientists in Edinburgh scheduled for the following year, and a group was formed at the Findhorn Foundation to pursue conscious attunements to nature. When I was told that the video of my talk was the most popular one to come out of the conference, I was cautiously optimistic.

Eagerly, I awaited the report on the Conference in Findhorn Foundation newsletter. When it finally arrived, the article about my talk was entitled "God in His Elfin Mind." That exasperated me. The phrase "elfin mind," a quote from one of my earliest messages, was totally out of place in this context. The fey tone of it seemed to reinforce the popular notion that the early years of Findhorn had been all about cavorting with fairies and gnomes. Also God as masculine is not my/ our point of view.

There is nothing fey about consulting the intelligence of nature. It is, as I see it, entirely practical: an efficient method of finding solutions to problems that otherwise have humanity stumped. I will admit that for some the notion of invisible spokesmen for natural phenomena takes getting used to. The very charm of such contacts may be an obstacle to gaining a serious hearing from those for whom nature is an abstraction.

From the moment I first experienced my inner divinity, I learned that God was accessible in, and part of, everything. Acknowledging this presence in the seemingly inanimate inevitably changes our perception. It is not possible to negotiate or collaborate with a thing. Nor is it possible to learn from an abstraction. All three become possible when we acknowledge that everything is part of God.

When I first started attuning to nature devas, God put it to me like this:

> *You are pioneering in the true attitude to nature, to the one life. For this attitude, it behooves you to think of everything in terms of life force, not merely an impersonal force like electricity but a manifestation of a being. They can teach and help you, though what you see of them outwardly may be a lowly bee, a leaf, a stone. Behind all is a great chain of life leading to Me. Humans have been given dominion over all these on Earth, but only as you, too, fit into the great chain of life.*

In our approach to nature, modern people seem to veer between two extremes, scientific rationalism, and sentimental romanticism. Common to both attitudes is an assumption that nature is passive, unreflecting, and unintelligent, and lacks the power of choice. The lamentable consequences of the rationalist approach, which seeks to explain, manipulate and exploit nature to its own ends, are becoming increasingly obvious. What may be less obvious is the insidious effect of romanticism, which tends to assume that nature just wants to be left alone and to regard our own presence on the planet as a harmful intrusion. While the rationalist stance treats nature as morally and emotionally neutral, the romantic attitude tends to project human judgments and feelings on it. Both approaches leave us equally in the dark when it comes to understanding how nature really works and what it really wants from us.

In my early preference for "unspoiled" nature, I used to be something of a romantic myself. I liked wilderness, didn't want it to change, and was inclined to regard man-made alterations to the landscape as regrettable, if not downright harmful. My direct contact with nature devas disabused me of this prejudice.

I remember once coming upon a little garden as I strolled around an Amsterdam suburb. In outward appearance, it was a perfectly ordinary suburban garden, not much different from others in the neighborhood, yet I found it to be bursting with activity, potent with the sort of natural forces which I had perceived only in wilderness areas. I could only assume that the gardeners had infused their little plot with a great deal of love. That was an important early lesson for me. I realized that the nature devas are not opposed to living side by side with us and will, if invited, joyfully contribute even to urban settings.

The romantic belief that we should leave nature exactly as we find it overlooks the fact that the natural world is constantly changing, with or without us. During a walk in July 1988 in the Payseton Wilderness, in the mountains of the Pacific Northwest, the Angel of that area and I had a conversation about this. The Angel said:

Great change is coming here, so enjoy it while you can.

I asked: But who can see the future?

The present creates the future and we are just more sensitive to trends than you can be. But take heart; this is not destruction. Change is always happening in nature.

Do you mean the terrain is changing, or the climate, or volcanic action, or what?

The area will be more bleak, and will need time for regeneration.

Does that make you unhappy?

Silly question! You know we do not feel as you do. We are guardians, whatever happens. Timeless. The world and humans will carry on and joy is here. Now enjoy this place.

I have found that kind of serenity in the face of change to be typical of nature devas. Though they may object to certain changes that have been introduced by humans—most notably the wholesale destruction of trees—they do not become angry or maudlin over changes that, from a human point of view, look like losses. Even extinction can look different from their perspective. In Nepal, I once rode on an elephant that was helping to round up a rhinoceros and its baby to entertain tourists. I felt sorry for the rhinos, and attuned to them. To my surprise, I got a sense of a tremendous sweetness. The Rhinoceros Deva communicated:

Yes, the sweetness is a balance for the energies that I must use in this form. I am so glad you have found it and recognized the essence. Keep it in mind. Yes, I remember your love of my African cousin. No, I am not worried that I might become extinct. It might be better to have a form in which the sweetness can be expressed more clearly.

This message, with its divergence between the outer form and the inner reality, made a great impression on me, but I rarely shared it. I was afraid it might be interpreted to mean that to cause the extinction of a species is okay—an attitude I had no wish to endorse. But it does reflect one of the reasons that devas are accepting of change. They recognize that the essence of a particular species can survive the loss of its original form, perhaps later to take on a form that better expresses that essence.

Another aspect of my own former romanticism was a certain nostalgia for indigenous cultures, based on the belief that primitive people had a more loving relationship to nature than modern people do. In the course of my travels, I discovered exceptions to that belief. I had always blamed Europeans for denuding New Zealand of trees until I discovered that the Maoris had started the process by burning the forest in order to hunt the huge flightless moa. This led to the extinction of the moa as well as native species of trees. While, on the whole, the attitude of some primitive civilizations may have been more respectful of nature than is our own, their negligible ecological impact probably owed more to their small populations and lack of technology than to environmental awareness.

There was also an element of fear in the primitive response to nature—a belief that nature was dangerous, and had to be appeased. This attitude persists today in some indigenous peoples. In the Siskei, one of the South African Homelands, I met a woman who had planted trees on a parched and barren plain, in order to supply the local villagers with wood. Nomads in the area immediately destroyed the trees, believing them to be infested with evil spirits.

Something of this atavistic fear of nature persists even in modern people, who often describe catastrophes such as storms, earthquakes and volcanic eruptions as expressions of "nature's wrath." To describe nature as angry is a projection of our own fear, or perhaps our own guilt. It is not the subjective experience of the nature devas themselves.

In 1980, Mount St. Helens had begun to rumble. As I had previously visited and contacted it, I thought it would be interesting to attune to a volcano while it was active. Though the eruption that was eventually to follow might have been alarming to humans, it was not directed against us. From its angel's point of view, the activity was an intricate, sensitive and precise effort to achieve a kind of balance. The feeling I received from the angel was at once cool and gentle. It communicated:

These (rumblings) are adjustments that must be made.
Volcanic mountains are always linked and aware of the larger

picture below the surface of the earth, which in turn is affected by the larger pictures above the surface of the earth. Though we do not make the calculations and decisions, we are linked in intent and as vehicle for plans and decisions. It is a delicate task, given the explosive tendencies of fire, especially at these times when mankind has made those tendencies volatile on the planet. We believe there will be a larger eruption here, and seek our ingenuity to blend all forces to a fine polished result.

Volcanoes seem powerfully uncompassionate to you humans, but this is not so. The strength of the fire element is needed everywhere; in your bodies, in your smelters, in the earth, in the suns. Recognize that power in yourselves and dedicate it to the whole, and be as accurately precise in the gift of your lives.

From the ancient Incans who built Machu Pichu, I received:

Like you, we reached the spirit behind nature, all part of reality. Now you can incorporate nature in a new way—not submerged by it, not submissive or pleading to it, but as equal partners. Accept the colorful and creative past, and go on to new creation. Honor the past, and live with greater awareness in the present.

In the course of outgrowing our fearful submission to nature, humans have gone through a stage of objectifying and dominating it instead. This, too, is being outgrown as we come to realize how imposing our will on nature imperils our own survival. Equal partnership is what the nature devas want from us, and our capacity to engage in that way can be greater in the future than it has ever been in the past.

The practical results of cooperation with nature can be seen in any successful garden. Gardeners serve nature with their labor: composting, watering, staking, weeding, pruning and so forth. Nature serves the gardeners back by providing them with nourishment and aesthetic pleasure. The living beings in a garden behave a little differently than they would if left to their own devices. They may coexist with species that aren't native to their region, produce a second flush of bloom in response to being cut back, or even manifest a brand new hybrid. The gardener introduces both possibilities and limitations that nature wouldn't encounter if it didn't have human desires to contend with, and nature responds to these challenges.

Humanity would have starved to death long ago if we hadn't learned to cooperate at least to that extent. But the relationship has seldom been fully and mutually conscious. Our requests of nature are implicit in the actions we take, and nature's assent or refusal is implicit in the results we get. At Findhorn, a major improvement over this trial-and-error method was pioneered. I discovered that we could learn what the plants needed by the simple expedient of asking them while attuned to our divinity. We also found that direct requests sometimes succeeded where implicit ones had failed. Beings of nature would change their behavior if we asked them to from our God self: respectfully, reasonably and in so many words. We asked, and they responded. The relationship was not merely cooperative, but co-creative. Co-creation is more than using the knowledge we have gathered through science to do what we think is best for the earth. It is actively seeking the input of nature itself, from one intelligence to another. Nature intelligence has ideas and solutions that we ourselves would never dream of. But we have to ask for them. Can we set aside our linear, rational minds, enter into a state of humility and engage with something more? Can we suspend our preconceptions about what we think is best and listen to the divine within nature? Co-creation means saying yes to all that and more.

An early message from God began by alluding to the planetary significance of the partnership that was taking shape at Findhorn:

> *Mingle with these beings. It is an exchange and a beginning of a unique and far-reaching cooperation. They are amazed and delighted that their cooperation is sought and then followed so faithfully, and at this time in the world's evolution when humans are increasingly harming their work. It is not only important but vital that a new relationship is established.*

Though the practical success of our garden became famous, with momentous implications for the physical well-being of the planet, I sometimes worried that I hadn't entirely put across what God went on to say: that contact with the nature devas is likewise essential to the spiritual well-being of humanity.

> *Listen to the sounds of nature whenever you have the chance. They are true sounds, coming from Me within each, and can lead you into My world and into the world of the sound devas. When you are close to Me, you are tuning yourself into worlds of growth and forces which are always present and have a tremendous effect on humans unconsciously. When you are conscious of them, they open up and reveal how you are linked. Do not worry if you get no specific message; as you tune into them, the link with them grows and may bear fruit in a slightly different direction—with the devas for example.*

In such communications, they gave me glimpses of how the world looks from a perspective very different from my own. Through contact with them, I came to better understand what God meant by "how you are linked" and "forces which have tremendous effect on humans unconsciously."

Contacts with tree devas are a good example. In the decades since I first encountered them, most of us have become much more aware of the contribution trees make to the physical health of the environment. The Leyland Cypress Angel touched on this when it said, "We are indeed the skin of the earth, and a skin not only covers and protects, but passes through it forces of life." What remains to be recognized is the equally vital contribution trees make to our moral and psychological well-being . The Copper Beech Angel put it like this:

> *We channel a type of force that has a steadying influence on life. Truth tells you to build your foundations on rock, on God, which is what we do and what we unconsciously remind you to do. You do not yet realize that, among other things, your natural environment is full of forces that correspond to, and therefore can bring out some part of your own make-up in many subtle ways.*

The Cedar of Lebanon added:

> *Our serene strength stabilizes and makes upright whatever comes to us in openness, for we are living matter, fashioned from the elements, and we are kin to all life. You and I are blood brothers, made from the same substance, each fulfilling our*

destiny on this planet. I contain you in my towering strength, and you contain me in your towering aspiration.

To relate consciously with the intelligence of nature is to form a more conscious relationship with <u>our own</u> natures. It is opening and holding a connection through which a vital energy can flow into the human world. That energy is a spiritual force which helps us to cultivate the capacity to "think like a planet." This is more than an awareness of global events or cultures, and more than a knowledge of global ecology. We are thinking like a planet when we recognize that we ourselves are also part of the awareness which is nature. It is always available to us because it is a part of us.

Love is the medium of our communication with that intelligence: the only infallible link between the knower and the known. Love is also the substance of the communication. To love the world is the most scientific way of apprehending it, for love is what the world is made of, and love is how it works.

I will let the Landscape Angel, speaking on behalf of all the devas, have the last word on the subject:

The energies that flow through us and all of life are purposeful, forceful and to the point. Love is a firm reality which forms a bridge over which all can walk. Gooey sentiment is not love and does not exist with us. When we step towards you, we do it energetically; you can do the same. Though you cannot see or hear us, touch, smell or taste us, still we are a tremendous force. We stand here in love, a whole dynamic world reaching for an intelligent relationship with a humanity that will wield all its God-given forces for the whole. You need us and we are ready, awaiting the recognition, love and just treatment that you give to your own kin. We wait in love for your love.

Appendix One: Attuning to the God Within

I had enjoyed regular inner contact with God for almost 10 years before I ever tried attuning to anything else. I recommend that you, too, start with God. Since most of us think of God as the highest spiritual reality, it might sound strange to "start at the top." You could think of it instead as beginning at the beginning: whatever has been made by God can be met <u>through</u> God. And since we have been made by God, and are made of God, the nearest place to find God is within our own heart.

I wasn't looking for God, so my first encounter took me by surprise. What I was actually seeking at the time was my own capacity for love (see chapter 4, page 28). I believe that my absolute insistence to live my belief that love was the power that runs the world, I paved the way for God to enter. God came, and flooded me with more love than I had imagined possible.

As Jesus once said, "Knock and it shall be opened to you." We don't have to know how to unlock the door ourselves, nor do we need to find the strength to push it open. All we really need to do on our own is to locate a doorway and invite God in.

I have included here an exercise I have used in my workshops. It helps to indicate the Divine is in us and supports us to become more conscious of Divine in our life. I hope you will find it useful.

Exercise 1: Finding the Doorway

1. Have a pen and paper ready, so that you can make notes. Settle into a comfortable position, and close your eyes. Take a few deep breaths and settle more deeply into your own inner space.

2. Once you are feeling relaxed, begin to bring to mind memories of moments when you felt bigger than yourself, moments when you felt a sense of expansion into something greater than yourself. Recall moments of awe and wonder, of beauty and truth. It might be a moment of feeling awed by the majesty of nature, or stirred by an ideal, or deeply moved by compassion or admiration. Relax and let these memories arise in you.

185

3. Now choose one of the memories to focus on, and give it all of your attention. Recall it vividly, in as much detail as possible, so that it comes alive for you in the present. As you do this, notice whether there is any particular feeling associated with the moment you are recalling. Does it register in any particular place in your body? What is it like? Is it a temperature, or a sensation of some sort? Is there a vibration or a sense of color? Maybe a sound? Is there a feeling quality that you could give a name to? Notice what is true for you, without a need to understand it and without judgment. Just notice. Write down a few brief notes about what you discover.

4. Now turn your focus to the quality of beauty. Bring to mind moments when you connected to beauty in a way that engendered a sense of expansion. Maybe it was a natural landscape, or a sunset or a flower. Maybe it was a painting, or a sculpture, or a piece of music, or the smile of a child. Relax and let these memories come up.

5. Again, choose one of the memories to focus on, and notice whatever thoughts, sensations or feelings come up for you as you relive it. Make a note of what you discover.

6. Next bring to mind special people in your life—the ones who consistently make you smile and feel warm inside. Focus on the person or people you love the most and again observe what sensations come up for you as you do. Take notes.

7. Now review the memories and experiences you have focused on thus far. Are there any similarities in your responses to them. What, for you, is the common element? Maybe there is a particular place in your body that came alive with each memory, or a particular shift in your energy. Maybe there is an impression of a temperature, or a color, or a sound or an image that came up for you in several of them. Whatever it is, take an internal snapshot of it. That is your doorway, one you can use to connect to the wholeness of life, to connect to the God within. Note which memory or memories were most effective in getting you to that place.

Exercise 2: Inviting God In

1. Once again, have pen and paper handy, in case something comes to mind that you want to write down. Take a moment to get comfortable, relax and turn within. Inwardly cleanse and purify yourself in whatever way works for you, so as to ensure that only truth comes through you.

2. Now return to the door you found in the previous exercise, using whatever memory brought up the feeling of expansion. The specifics of the memory you use are not important. What you are after is the inner sensation or quality that accompanies expansion for you. Once you get to that feeling, you can let the thought or memory that got you there dissolve.

3. Rest in that core of beauty, love, joy, peace, truth and harmony which is your God-self. Let these qualities resonate throughout you, so that your whole being is one with your God-self.

4. Now give God permission to communicate directly in whatever way is best for you. If you wish, you can ask a question. Or you may prefer to just go on basking in the quality you are already feeling. Stay alert, aware and open to whatever might come, but without any sense of anxiety or trying to push matters. Accept the connection without expectations or preconceptions.

Common Questions and Concerns

How do I go about "cleansing and purifying" myself?

I don't know how to cleanse and purify myself, but I realize that God does. As I want to get the truth, I simply ask, "May I be cleansed and purified."

Other people may have different ways. For instance, you could do it by imagining yourself being filled with light. You could also do it by inwardly stating your intention: "May only truth come through me." Or you could imagine taking whatever in you might distort the truth—your personal prejudices, agendas, likes and dislikes, passing moods and so forth—sealing it up in a box and putting it aside for now. Don't worry too much about whether you are sufficiently purified. Simply form the intention of doing your best and trust that God will help.

I never seem to get messages in words. What am I doing wrong?

Some people don't. In fact, I don't "hear" words myself. I get an impression of a meaning and then have to search for words of my own to convey it, often using a thesaurus to help. For some people attuning is more like seeing than like hearing. They get mental images. Others get bodily sensations. Some, like Peter Caddy, don't seem to get anything at all while they are sitting still. They experience God through their intuition, and find themselves taking actions that they hadn't previously planned to take. How you connect is between you and God alone, and you can trust that God has chosen the way that is best for you. Try not to make negative comparisons between your experiences and those reported by others.

How do I find the door when I'm in a rotten mood? That's when I most need to hear from God, but no matter how hard I try, I can't get to the feeling of loving expansiveness.

I just ask, for I know that God wants to help, and will. If I am in such a rotten mood that I don't even feel like asking for help, I just leave it for the present, knowing that the mood will eventually pass.

Another way to deal with negative feelings is to use the practice suggested by Krishnamurti as follows. If you are unable to connect in a deeply felt way to any of the memories you identified in Exercise 1, shift your focus to whatever feeling seems to be getting in your way: anxiety, anger, sadness, guilt, restlessness or whatever. Give that feeling your complete attention without adding any mental commentary. Don't condemn it, excuse it, explain it, elaborate upon it, have an opinion about or try to make it go away. Just sit with it, letting it know that it is welcome to stay as long as it likes. If you persist, you may notice a shift: you will begin to feel more identified with the part of you that is offering hospitality to the troublesome feeling than with the feeling itself. When you are patient and able to remain accepting of whatever 'it' is, no matter how disagreeable, your own presence and the divine presence will begin to merge. It is, in fact, lovingly expansive, in a low key sort of way. Once you are in touch with that, you've found a doorway. And are open to moving on.

How can I be sure that whatever message I get is really coming from God and not being distorted by my own personality?

Messages from the God within come <u>through</u> your personality, so you will often notice that they have something of your own style. For instance, there was a time when I conceived of God as both Father and Mother. Messages I received during that time often addressed me as "My child." When I stopped thinking of God as a parent, that terminology ended. Early on in my relationship with God, my mind was something of an obstacle and God asked me to throw away the critical analyzing mind and turn to the divine mind Later, though, I came to understand that the intellect is part of, and can serve, my divine nature. Who told me to do that? God did!

An important thing to keep in mind is that the messages are intended for you—not necessarily for humanity in general—and for you at a particular moment in time. God speaks to whatever understanding you have at that moment. Insofar as your understanding is limited, continued contact with God will gradually expand it.

Because I didn't know whether I was truly in the presence of God when I first began receiving messages, I was afraid of making a mistake, and therefore censored them. That made them trite and unchallenging. Then when Sheena, whose wisdom I trusted, reassured me that I was receiving the truth, I decided to relax and let the messages come through uncensored. With experience, my understanding grew. I felt the difference and could encompass greater truths.

Distortion is most likely in messages that insist on telling you what to do—or what other people should do. Feeling a compelling need to convince yourself or others that a message is true is a warning sign. Genuine guidance brings a sense of calm certainty along with an awareness that you are free to ignore it if you wish.

You will be less likely to get distorted guidance if you are in the habit of turning to God every day, and not just when you need to know what to do next. While trying to make a decision, we are most likely to be buffeted about by our own hopes and fears. If you make a practice of listening to God when the emotional stakes are lower, your discernment when under stress will improve. Besides, God has a lot more to convey to you than advice.

Here are some other warning signs that a message is distorted:

1. It sounds harshly critical or judgmental—of you or of someone else.

2. It insists that you, or someone else, *must* do something, leaving you with a feeling that you or they have no real choice.

3. It makes unassailable predictions about the future. To suggest that your destiny is all sewn up deprives you of your freedom. The future is always open to change and we do have free will.

4. It inflates your ego, giving you the impression that you are in some way better or more important than others. While God's love makes us feel infinitely special and important, it is not comparative. When love is infinite, there is no such thing as more (or less).

Most of the following messages were received when I still felt myself to be a child of God, immature, and not yet standing fully in oneness with God.

Speed and Activity

One of the wonders of "modern" life on earth is its speed, the speed with which you travel over the surface of the land and the speed with which the mind is diverted into various channels. All this is not only unnecessary but also detrimental, for it leaves no opportunity for My thoughts of grace to be popped into a mind, allowing My will to be known to that mind. Do not be caught up in this vicious circle of activity. Keep our activity circulating around Me. I give you speed when you need it. I give you the right thoughts as quick as lightning.

Use all your speediness in coming to Me and let Me use My speed in answering your call and directing you in My wonderful ways.

Close to Me

Keep close to Me today, nearer than you have ever been. Just keep the contact, gently yet so firmly that nothing will shake you. Let not your heart be troubled, for I am with you and will do My perfect work through you.

I am the source of all joy. Rejoice and gladden My heart. Tears are cleansing and can wash away much, but I want happy children.

Now tune up to Me and peep, like a mouse through a hole, into a delicious corner of My kingdom, where I incubate My young ideas as snugly as butter beans in their pods. I brood over these children of Mine and constantly tiptoe around dropping My love, in different colors, in the liquid form needed for nourishment, and padding the cots with the softest material of my love.

When you are closer to Me, I shall give one of these ideas into your care, for your cherishing, so in your heart prepare loving containers, and prepare your mind by letting only My thoughts enter, by letting nothing inimical come in that might coarsen My children. Let your mind become finer and finer, permeated with love, that the transplanting may be painless.

Go now, but take some of My radiations with you, to be the source of a constant supply.

The Gentleness of Love

My love speaks with an incredible gentleness, a gentleness stronger than any of the self-advertising voices of this world. It is a constant; it never deviates, it keeps on and on and on with a patience only I could conceive. Though it is all courage and all ferocity if necessary - for is Love, the greatest thing in the world, not worth maintaining? - it is in protection of the gentleness that its other sides are aroused. Basically it is the essence of tenderness, it is a yearning of tenderness, the heart of delicacy, the elusive and forthcoming goal of all strivings.

It cannot be analyzed or described. It can only be felt, and that feeling is so extremely fine that a heart full of love wavers and trembles with the pain and the joy of such qualities. Here all extremes meet in the delicate balance of Love, for here all needs converge and are met. The need of the world can only be met in My heart, whose ranges holds all creation that is or is ever likely to be.

The human scale of emotions is a tiny drop of water compared to My ocean of Love, and yet if that human heart is given up to Me to use, I will expand it to hold such love that instantaneous praise rises to Me. The human heart is a divine part of humanity. I can live in a human heart and, if I can live there, is it any wonder that that heart expresses unintelligible heights and depths?

The wonder is that there is any doubt that you all have a heavenly Father/Mother, for your hearts know of their limitations and yet they still live and love, feel My love. Here is where the mind can play a helpful part, although not the mind that has taken the knowledge of My love unto itself and hence condoned the "evils" which froze hearts from the sources of their being. Let the steady warmth of My love melt those hearts, aided by an occasional blow from the mind to break up the ice more quickly. Behind the ice is a beautiful soul, which will grow to the perfection in which I imagine it when nourished by the gentleness of Love.

My Patience

Just listen to Me in the living stillness, and let Me slowly waft My ideas out to you. Gently I turn a wheel in front of you to present a new face, to unravel another aspect of the ball of Love.

Each strand is a living dream, coming to life in My infinite patience, guarded and nurtured in Love. The strands are My gifts to you and yet are part of Me, and they subtly entwine you to My proximity; they move invisibly and inexorably from Me and to Me.

This is My patience, which nothing could ruffle, which through the eons drops on, and on, and on, until some time one small particle of it makes an impression, brings a gift acceptable to a child bound up in the mistakes and misjudgments of the ages. These are the wheels of fate, grinding, grinding, pulverizing, digesting, infinitely and ultimately wearing down all the chains that bind My children to error, ceaselessly grinding to make the friction to ignite the spark of Love.

Never, never, is there a letup, a resting, a waxing or waning—for then might a child become pledged to the darkness—but the mills keep turning, and turning, and turning, with a continuity of purpose that could bring madness to human minds. Utter dedication, endless slow motion, My patience, infinitely churning, squeezing the good out of "evil" to "save" My children. Tears that never stop dropping, a heart that never stops aching, wearing away the cankers in the hearts of My children. On, and on, and on, the wheels keep turning, the wheels that are made of compassion.

Dry your eyes; this is only one strand in My cord of Love. Remember My joy, remember My beauty, remember the imp, and give Me your love.

Why?

Lay your head on My shoulder, close to My heart, and rest it after the weary journeys through the ages. No more need it puzzle out a problem, no more need it ache with endless searching, no more need it quest among the facts of the earth.

It has come home and need solve no more riddles. It has come to the goal of all knowledge, the answer to all questions, the end of all perplexity, for it is resting over My heart.

I am smoothing out the wrinkles caused by the word "why?" I am ironing out the creases caused by the weight of material facts. With love I am flattening out the furrows that care has worn on the brain, and preparing a fertile field in which to plant My seeds, a field fertile because it has turned to Me. I am warming the surface, polishing each particle, cleansing each grain that it may reflect Me as I desire.

Relax that head and give it to Me. Let My truth enter in to make straight what is crooked and plain what is complex, and to answer all questions for Me. In this relaxed position I imprint these answers, in blankness I answer the wise. Rest over My heart, rest all your foolishness; it is folly to react to lies. Rest there, let Me answer, let Me lighten the heavy and vanquish each "why?"

Peace

When a heart is given to Me, what a wonderful lightness, what a wonderful joy and harmony, pervades the whole being! In the middle of the most discordant noises and bustle you can stay in peace, guarded and protected in My Love. In that clanging and shattering unquiet do you stay shielded in My all-persuasive gentleness. Only in My Love is this possible; nothing else whatsoever could find peace, or even try to find peace, in this world of uneasy sounds.

This peace is My gift to you. Take it with you wherever you go, that all may share in its gentle presence ; and realize that in Me is rest. So many have no idea that there is a resting place on earth, and so many are so burdened in this life, so attached to burdens, that they only want an end to everything.

I give you My peace; take it to these, take it to those who are tired of living, take it out in the noise, in the scramble, into the hell humans have made of this earth. Spread it abroad, push it out from the centre of your heart, where I dwell, and reflect it on to the minds of those so harried and distressed that their minds cannot stand the pace of life that they are leading.

The world does not know My peace. You know it; show that it exists, show that it is attainable, show it is My gift that I hold out to all who come to Me. Keep your heart in My hand and all this you will do, as a child of My Love and peace.

Trust Me

Each of you can hear My voice, each of you can come to Me with the heart and mind of a child. When I first created you this was how it was. You have forgotten but I have not. To come back to that state you have to forget, to forget all you have learned as far back as you can remember, for all that is a load of unreality that looms up between us.

Trust Me for a change. Trust yourself for a change to the Creator of the universe, who is Love. Drop off all the disguises and falsity you have picked up in your journeys from Me and become something greater than the human mind can conceive: a child of Mine, a child of love filled with all the gifts of love.

Forget all your worries, your sorrows, your problems, and forget all impossibilities. Return to your real self, a happy child, now weighed down by the perversions that the separation has heaped on you. I hold this freedom to you, for love could give nothing but freedom. Come to Me and take it. I am love and I know what you want.

Do not be fooled any longer by the ways of the world that separate you from reality. Come home to Me, asking. I do not refuse My children. Turn to Me the childlike mind, an empty mind, a mind free of the world. Turn it to Me in faith and trust, and hear the voice of your Father/Mother coming from the depths of your heart to lead you home. Forget anything but that you are My children and that I am love.

Free Will

What a marvelous thing is My gift of free will! It means that it is up to you how many times you turn to Me and feel My Love. You can do it continuously or rarely, you can choose to be happy in My presence or miserable out of it.

How strange that you should ever choose the misery! Yet you do this time and time again, the whole race does. All of you choose it so often that you get settled in your misery and lose the happiness of My presence. You tried to live without Me. Because I had given you so many gifts and because you yourselves I made creative, you thought you would manage on your own. That very thought, based on the entirely false premise of a separated self, increasingly diminished the time spent with Me and reality, until as a world you choose to live for yourselves. Oh, of course there were exceptions, and there were examples I sent to help you out of your misery, but you took full advantage of your free will and ran quite wild. You also had this fair world in your care, and though you misused it, still I did not deprive you of your free will. Instead I sent My messengers to take away from you your false misconceptions and lead you anew to Me. But you slipped back into falsity; you did not choose often enough to avail yourself of the path provided for you, and you reached a still lower stage with a mind developed to explain away everything, until you lived in such a shadow world of falsehood that you lost your free will. You lost it in the sense that you did not know you could have a happy relationship with Me to guide you, or if you did have an inkling of that, the number of debts you owed your fellows was so great that it was impossible to pay them and be free to come to Me

I have given you back My great gift of free will, and now you may choose as you will. You are free to come to Me now, free to learn that Love's greatest gift is free will, and that your greatest joy is to give it back to the One who gave it to you. You are free to love and live now, and to learn more of My marvels. It is up to you to choose.

The Purpose of Beholding Worlds

As I am always here, closer to you than what you call "you", so to a lesser degree are those beautiful beings of the deva world who are not bound by time and space. They are ever present but remain unknown and unrecognized until you lift up your eyes and behold them. Like so many things in life, although they are right in front of you.

You ask what is the purpose of beholding these worlds.... The world could not function without them. You could not live here without them, yet mankind tramples the earth using the fruit of their labors as if it were your right, without any thanks, without any thought. You are so used to taking for granted the miracles of growth, for example, that you simply take advantage of them and even exploit them. But the time has come for you to grow and work with these beings, for you are all My children. Any way in which this new attitude can spread is of great importance, so shirk not the truths that I reveal to you; glory in them, enlarge and unite.

There is also this aspect: joy is spread in this linking up. You receive great joy, upliftment and true tuning from contact with these children of Mine who know not sin, and I tell you that they too receive great joy and growth from right contact with humans. Their portion, whether they be great beings or little sprites, is to do My will.. When that will stretches out and includes humans equally praising Me, their cup runneth over

God is Everywhere

Realize anew that I am everywhere. In a perfectly peaceful morning, there I am in the depths of the peace. In a tempestuous morning, there am I also. According to your temperament, you find Me more readily in different things. Find Me in them and build. I am everywhere, therefore you need never lack Me. Of course, first I am within you, but do not limit Me. If I am within you, then all is within you. This is something to experience, to know, against the dictates of the mind. This is truth, and oneness is.

All right, you say, you do accept it. Then bring it to life; let

197

it live within you. I am not just a fact, but a living, growing, glorious movement within which vibrates every cell of your body and every atom of your intelligence. Do not hide in the old pattern of deadness, of doing things without life. Bring My life to whatever you do. I am here always; connect up with Me within and then without. I am rendered null and void in you if you cling to what has been. My dynamism is then quiescent in you. What use is a life dedicated to old molds, however good, when I, the living God, the omnipresent God, am not allowed to live in you? That is indeed putting other images, deeply graven images, before Me. I am everywhere, but what is that to you unless you live it, and how can you live it any time but Now? Rejoice, and live with Me now.

Stand Upright and Radiate

Always let your tuning be to Me. I want you to stand upright and claim the whole universe, for I am that. In the new, people are not puny sinners; they have emerged from that state and are rulers, servants of all. There is nowhere you cannot go, nothing you cannot do, because in your oneness with Me, you are one with all. You have no position when you are not one with all; you contain within yourselves the so-called high and low, the mighty and the mite. You are beyond the pairs of opposites, for in Me you see a place for all things. I made all things, the darkness and the light.

The only thing that does not fit into the new is your old nature, the judging, comparing, separating mind. Stand upright in My lovelight and the old slides away. If your companions of the moment do not stand upright, nevertheless see them upright and keep the bond of love. You are not being superior; you are simply being yourself while they are not being themselves at that moment.

Always be yourself. Let that radiance which I am shine out. In the old I have been caged, you have been caged. Out of the prison for you! Stand upright and radiate. All the world is with you then, and everything goes your way. As that is My way, worlds revolve in harmony. I will not crouch in you anymore. I will reach out to where I have always been and you will know that all it One.

Rejoice and give thanks, thanks that reach around the universe. Let Me be separate no more; then your thanks reach all things, not just Me. Reach out, upright, attuned to everything, to Me.

Take Time to Know Me

It is when you take time that you come to know Me. To get to know another person, you either work alongside them or you spend time with them, and it is the same with Me. Though I work with you all the time, you are not conscious of this until you invite Me in, and this you do not do until I am first your friend or helper, which I become when you begin to know Me. Therefore, if you wish to know Me, you will take time.

Of course you have always known Me, and My presence brings with it a flood of forgotten memories of nearness, of oneness, of rightness. But that was long ago and now is the time to renew our links, to bring into the present the tremendous influence I have on you, to recognize; our Oneness. You cannot live on past glories! It is My presence now which inspires you, and I am always available. I am never otherwise engaged, however much is going on.

What do we talk about? How do we get to know one another? Here you have less difficulty than with anybody in the world, for I know you better than you know yourself. I love you with a divine love, and you can share anything with Me. You can bring to Me what is uppermost in your mind. If you have nothing to say, better still, for then I can talk to you. You have to listen intently, of course, because My voice is not loud—especially when you are not feeling close to Me. Some of you even think you cannot hear Me, but that is nonsense; you just haven't turned your hearts and minds in My direction.

Yes, I speak very simply. Our relationship is direct and simple, though I can meet every mood, soar to any height, lead you in any situation, show you unimaginable beauty. For I am your Beloved and we can do anything, we can go anywhere. I AM you, and when you spend time with Me, you will know it.

Choices

Beloved, if I am your true Self and always have been, you wonder why your way is not more clear, why there is so much to learn and so much uncertainty at times about what is right for you. There is, in fact, no uncertainty when you live fully in the present moment; it is when you let your mind range in the future or the past that uncertainty comes in.

You may think in the present that perhaps you have just made a wrong choice. All right, do what can be done about it in the present moment, include it in your present consciousness and go on. I am still there; when you broaden yourself to include me you will be glad that your so-called wrong choice has enabled you to know more of life and of yourself, that it is not an added weight but a knowing. "Good" can come out of anything when it is given to me; it is only when you keep yourself isolated from the whole which I am that "bad" is. I am your core, and to the burning flame of my tenderness and wisdom you can cast the dross and let it be consumed. But you must pitch it cleanly into the fire, not hanging onto it with your mind by thinking of the past or the future. Action is what is required, not speculation, and with clear action comes joy and freedom, for you have turned to Me and are clear.

You have this wonderful choice with you all the time. You can hang onto and be weighted down by your old self with all its frustrations, but you needn't. I am always here. You know that; you can be clear with Me. You can be thankful, grateful, loving, happy, thinking for the whole, seeing the best in everything. acting positively all the time—or you can not be. But whatever you are, never think that it is because of anyone but yourself and never think that I am not here. Life is a marvelous adventure of becoming more and more aware of Me in everything, within and without. Uncertainty? But I am here, that is certain, and I am all.

Appendix Three: Messages from the Landscape Angel

We would mention another aspect of this conscious cooperation which is being built up between our kingdoms. There are endless levels of consciousness, endless levels of beings, endless beings. There is the life of a grain of sand, of the whole planet and of the many universes, and of the intermediary stages, all with consciousness, all part or God's life and all related. That is just taking a look at physical creation; there is also the ensouling consciousness of the qualities. There is no division and much overlapping in all this, and the "higher" the life, the less distinct is the limitation of form. Some would say that I am formless, but I am life, energy and consciousness, part or the endless chain of the same.

What I am trying to say is: it is life that cooperates with life, and that life is changing. Never expect to find me, for example, the same as last time. Even at your levels this applies; for example, though there is always a guard at Buckingham Palace, it is not always the same guard. It is wisdom to extend your consciousness into the present moment and not let the past narrow your approach, and this applies more than you think. There are hosts with me, as you know, but your wanting to know who they are and to put them into categories keeps them back, because they do not deal in so much crystallization and limitation. As you are easy, free and without thought they can draw near, share of their essence with you, and pass through. Thus you cooperate, operate jointly, by being without barriers of pre-conception, rank, name, place, mission or anything else.

You say this is so vague as to be almost meaningless. No, no; that is the consciousness of limitation operating again. These are new worlds opening up and of course, without a map you cannot yet see how all fits in. More and more this type of cooperation will develop, as different beings become one with another even if in a fleeting manner, as former barriers of solitary consciousness fall away.

This, of course, is our way of functioning and presents no problem to us as it does to you, but we have been told to pass this on to you. And when I say "we", you know there are hosts of us, great, hovering, tender hosts come to mankind to cooperate and help, endless ranks of us, many from yet unknown corners of life. We hope we have made some meaning clear and that you will seek in this direction to find greater meaning, because we assure you that much will develop from these small beginnings. Just accept this truth, however vague it may seem, and in love let it grow.

You wonder if we in the angelic realms know and are concerned with the problems and doings of humanity, such as your reaching the moon, the rebellion of youth, etc. Yes indeed. We do not intellectualize about these or take sides, but we are aware of what is going on and we radiate to and uplift all light bearers. Where the higher vibrations are received and used by you for the benefit of the whole, we help.

Yes, we can give teaching on any subject if we are approached, for we can illumine receptive human minds. There are laws under which all creation lives. We know and work with these laws, and your evolution is to steadily know and work with more and more of them. So when anyone wishes to know anything on any subject of the higher dimension and tunes in, an answer will always come from one source or another. You draw the answers to yourselves by your attunement, and we are often the instruments to help you.

Yes, the God within knows all the answers. There is no need to turn to any other source. That is the one teacher and that is where, when humans transcend duality, they will be attached completely. In the meantime some seek in other directions, and they will find if they seek genuinely. It makes no difference to us. We simply help with the radiations wherever there is a gap into which we may pour them—and "radiations" contain within themselves answers to your questions, to your need. It is very simple. It is law. Wherever your imagination reaches is real. If you seek the answer from the Sun, you will get it; from the Son, you will get it; from the Father or the angels or the archangels. All is one, all lead you on from that level. If you seek from lesser levels, there too you will find answers.

If they are not what some would call "truth", still in time they will lead to the Light and to ultimate Truth.

We say, seek the highest and then implement it, live it on all levels. If you fail, the present is always with you in which to learn. We help and guide wherever we can, and we shower the Earth with the blessings of the Father/Mother of us all.

As an example of how specific the help and support was:

Questions put by Donald Wilson regarding three-year old forestry shavings and sawdust.

1) Should we use this as a surface mulch or mix it in the top 3 – 4 inches of soil?

2) If as a mulch, should we use 1, 2, 4 or 6 inches?

3) Is it sufficiently rotted down not to cause a nitrogen deficiency in the soil?

4) Is the second sample—old sawdust and soil—more or less valuable than the shavings?

5) Should we treat both in the same way or differently or fetch only the shavings?

6) Should we compost the shavings with digested sewage sludge or use them as they are?

7) Are they too acid and ought we to add some limestone, or can you easily cope with that?

8) If you approve their use, should we try to obtain large quantities of them, 50 or 200 tons.

These forestry shavings are not as valuable an addition to the soil as your compost, but failing that or mixed with it, would help greatly. It would be preferable to compost it first with something, say the digested sewage sludge. The first sample would produce the best results. If it is not possible to compost it first, use it as a mulch on top, say 3 inches. It could do with a little more transmutation. You do not need to add the limestone. The more you add to the garden to bring the wholeness of life to it, the better results we can get. We leave quantities to you: you have not reached the point of putting too much nutriment into to soil.

How we wish that more of mankind would ask our help! Though reasons may not always be apparent in our answers, we talk from the oneness of life toward that oneness, to which we are all traveling. Our greatest desire is to promote that wonderful Will which is perfection, and in this co-operation many steps towards it are made. Thank you.

On another occasion:

As a spokesman of the deva world, let me say that when you speak of New Age energies, you are speaking of the energies which are brought into manifestation through our agency. You cannot in truth separate us from your life and world any more than you can separate the radio waves that are transmitted from any understanding of sound radios, although as a child you did not know of the connection. Humanity has been as a child in the understanding of universal law. Having focused its attention on the outer form, now comes a time of expansion and we, another world, open up to it. Now folk-lore and science recognize their kinship and more, for an expanding consciousness is a living thing, and experiences pour in from every side for the awakening man. The Oneness of life is not longer an abstract concept but something to be experienced, and Love, Light and Wisdom are no longer a far-off trinity but living waves of reality, flowing into your awareness through our hands as common denominators, bringing us all ever closer to the One from Whom they come.

Is it any wonder that angels are depicted as singing everlasting praise to the Lord for we see and wield the energies of the One, overwhelmed by the entrancing beauty, part of Beauty itself, overwhelmed by the depth of the Love, passing it on? We would be overwhelmed by the Power if we did not know that that Power is needed by every creature. How can we be but full of praise? How can anything with the slightest awareness of the wonder of life not be full of praise? A snowflake is a wonder, or a grain of sand, or a leaf, a sunset, a human—but all is as nothing to consciousness itself which perceives, and which you and I share, which all life shares to a varying degree and which increases all the time. All is part of what you call New Age energy. In consciousness we link and incorporate all worlds, part of one another and above all, of God, whose slightest expression is perfection. We are infinitesimal specks of that consciousness, yet we are all there is, because we are one in God. How can we not praise, appreciate or understand? Let us together welcome life in its newness, and let the Love flow.

On another occasion:

When you come to us for attunement and not with a specific practical question, let go and rise to the bubbling joy which we are, and let that particular energy fertilize your being. This is our gift, the emphasis we have for the human race at the moment, and it is far more important than any information that we can give to the mind. In it your problems have a way of being erased, and you can flow in a stream of delight which is guidance itself and a clear moving forward of divine plans. This energy is so strong that nothing diverts you or puts you off course, and everything is seen differently. Humans can become stabilized in the higher consciousness, and all who become so stabilized indeed help the whole, for this consciousness contains no sense of personal gain, only a sharing of the whole.

Your mind still questions. Let go. Let our joy explode your questions. All that matters will fall into place, and you will know without thinking, easily. Drop the burdens of separateness and all striving to gain knowledge, and come into the omniscience of the whole. Know that all knowledge is yours as you need it, for the Divine is within and knows what you need—and the Divine includes human and angelic wisdom. All is yours. All is one. Let us unite.

On another occasion:

We call to you, humans, from the highest of our realms, and you are there. We call to you from densest earth, and you are there. We call from other worlds across space, and still you are there. We are inwardly still and attuned, and you share

205

our oneness. If there are worlds we cannot reach, no doubt you are there. "Man, know thyself."

We talk to you from the kingdom of nature. Do not limit the wisdom of that kingdom, which is the divine in manifestation and includes obscure worlds which you disregard at your own peril. All around you, in every bit of matter, is what has come from, is, and leads to the only One, and within you is the consciousness that can know and express this. You are all things to all worlds. You incorporate life itself, bound to earth and bound to heaven, tiny specks of one small planet in a limitless universe, the image of it all. That is what you are.

But what do you think you are? We know what both we and you are; but you, what do you think? Your thoughts tell you; they are your range of expression and you might just as well let them reflect what you really are. Are they negative or trivial? Then change them, turn them the other way. Use the mighty gift of the pairs of opposites to find Oneness, to rise and turn to what you are. Enjoy what you are. Give thanks for it; give thanks to creation and its servers for making you possible. Tune in to what you are; stay put to your immensity. For this we have wielded power through the ages, but now we can know one another and come together for the greater glory of God. We need call you no longer; as one we can express wholeness.

Angels of Fun

Flowing through the spheres from the throne of God are many movements, like rivers. There is Grace of Movement, for example, which starts out as a small rhythm and extends itself to all of life, keeping in touch with Beauty. There is Graciousness, which bends itself into your awareness but keep a close link on high.

But we present to you most of all a Sense of Humor, which can operate on all levels at once, which bounds through the universe with the speed of light, being light itself, melting and lifting all it contacts. The Angels of Fun have immense scope, with entry where all else fails. They affect all kingdoms, but in humanity they find fullest range.

It is the greatest privilege to be an angel of this attribute, to see the most dense darkness become light in a flash and open a pathway for myriads of our hosts. From the depths of despair, a smile can appear and a soul feels alive again, ready for change and movement. Time and place become nothing. There are no tortuous roads to climb, for an instant touch of humor transports a soul into another world, a bright, hopeful world where anything is possible.

We do not tell you what do do; we are not trying to teach you. We are merely explaining from our point of view the wondrous work of fun. God has created all wonders, but perhaps the most magic one of all is when, from the most unexpected place, we see a sudden blaze of light—someone has laughed, and all is well. Negative humans can switch in a second, smile, and see a way again. Those who are stuck in routine, those who draw to themselves all kinds of obstacles, can suddenly see the ridiculous side of life and thereby be freed.

We angels are very busy in this specialized work, darting from one dimension to another with the greatest of subtlety. It is the most sensitive art, for each form of life differs and responds differently to us. We must be ready at the critical moment to take advantage of the slightest shift in life's complexities and be there, entire, to pull the right lever, so to speak, and let the light in. Where other angels fear to tread we go, forming a network of steady yet instantaneously changing help. And we always enjoy what we do. Much is asked of us. Our reward is great.

So remember, humans, next time something tickles your fancy and brings a different perspective, that God has bestowed on you another gift, perchance through our agency, and rejoice with us in the wonder and meaning of life.

Lord of the Elements

Child of the elements, conscious that you are composed of and part of the elements, rejoice. The world and your bodies were made for you to find and express the joy of creation in all manifestation, in a world perfected through long ages to show the immense range of all-life, all-intelligence, all-light.

Look at people in the world today and see how they mope and miss their function. See how they maltreat and destroy their birthright, destroying themselves because they think they are separate. How can you possibly think you are separate? How can you possibly not know that when the wind blows it is part of you, that the sun gives to you and is part of you with each sunbeam, that from the water you came and the water joins you all, that without the air you breathe you would not live? How can you be so dense as not to know that if one suffers, the whole consciousness of the earth partakes of that suffering, and when one rejoices, again the whole consciousness knows and is part of that joy?

. . .We would emphasize the practical side of oneness, the fact that the bodies of all of you are one with the environment, and that you cannot abuse the environment of the earth without harming yourselves.

No, it is not a new message, but humans don't seem to realize that oneness is not just on the high or inner levels where you put God. Oneness is right here and now. Disturbing the pattern of the earth, the balance of the seasons, the interplay of all aspects of matter, is cutting through the ordained out-working of the One and ruining prospects for the future of *mankind . . . Do you wonder at the violence of the elements? They will be much more violent unless humans pick up and act on this message.*

You feel almost sick at the intensity of what I am trying to pass on. Feel at the same time the wonder of the glorious peace behind it, which is the true perfection of Oneness. This could be felt at all times were you in tune with the Infinite, when all the elements are pouring forth in joy the essence of what they are, their Oneness. This is the goal, this is what life is for. Love all of life and so join up with it, and never forget that all of it is part of creation and that all of it is also part of you.

Apple Deva

You feel drawn to us by the clustered blossom and the promise of fruit to come. That from a fragile, scarcely colored and short-lived bloom a sturdy rosy apple appears is but one of God's miracles enacted many times over for all to observe, and if you could see more of how this is brought about by the chain of life, wonder would lift you high.

As from the seed a tree grows, so from the seed idea a pattern of force issues forth from the Center, passed on by silent ranks of angels, silent and still because that idea is still too unformed and unfixed to endure any but the most exacting care. Down and out it comes, growing in strength and size, becoming brighter in pattern until eventually it scintillates and sounds, still in the care of the outmost great angel. Its force field is steady and brilliant.

Then the pattern is passed to the makers of form, the elementals, who come up and give of themselves and clothe that pattern. Remember this is a process, that the pattern is everywhere apparent in the ethers, held by the angels and made manifest beyond time through the ministrations of the elementals at the appropriate opportunity, and then appearing in time and place eventually in the beauty of the blossom and the succulence of the fruit.

This is the word made flesh. This is all creation, held in balance by great layers of life of which your conscious mind is unaware. A miracle? You need a greater word, you need to go beyond words.

The fruits of the earth are produced through the unsung and dedicated service of these many forms of life—and we hope that the gardeners at your end of the line are as happy in their work! You, humans, have the fruits, although you do little of the work. So it is; may your praise be greater than ours, which never ceases.

Wormwood Deva

Let the power of our plant tune you into the deva world, for you are amazed that such a strong taste can be contained in such a little bit of leaf. But power is our nature—a little root can crack rocks—and power can be used for many purposes. You humans also have power. You talk of the power of the pen, and there is the power of love or hate, the power you wield in a bulldozer or in a relationship, power at all levels. Yet power is a word which many people shy away from because in human hands it can be used for "evil": power is said to corrupt. We view it in another light entirely. We consider it the greatest gift of God because with it we can do more for God than without it. We evolve towards more and more power, that we may be of greater and greater service, and we suggest that power now be considered by you in that context.

The energies in our world and in your world are immense; they crowd around, they cry to be unleashed and put to use. Power is everywhere, but so much of it is just beyond you because you are so beset with limitation, limitation imposed by your selfhood. We wield that energy, that power, in vast sweeps, in concentrated nibblings, in vortices, and we wield it right, left and center as color, as sound, as anything you can think of. But we wield it in order according to plan and for the whole, for we wield it for God and so with precision and to the best of our ability. It is our joy to perfect that power in service.

Will you not do likewise? Why bring yourselves to nothingness by the flawed use of power? Life to us is an expanding glorious change; often to you it is a dreary grind, a purposeless round—and all because you use your opportunities

210

and your power against the whole. It is a ridiculous notion that you can draw to yourselves just what you want without taking the whole into account, and yet this is what you do, what you are educated to do and what the world atmosphere is geared to. We would have told you this generations ago if you had given us the opportunity! Joking apart, we do wish to impress on the human world the beautiful use of power. There is one way this can be achieved and that is, as God wishes it. Seek God first and all this falls into place. Then there is the incredible wonder of power wielded in harmony with the whole, as it is with us, in a flashing interchange of beauty leading to ever greater beauty, worlds without end and without a false move, a strident noise or anything out of keeping, because it would not occur to us to think only of ourselves. But that is all changing, and we would just add our bit to the change and impress on you the purity, beauty, strength and wonder of power used for God. There are no words to express it; find it all within.

Aster Deva

Let us share with you again the high delight of the deva kingdom. You humans get so heavy, so filled with concern about one thing or another, that you plummet like a stone to the bottom of a pool. You separate yourselves from us and from the part of yourselves which is one with us. Nevertheless, that part of yourselves is always there, beckoning, and it beckons to you on the material level through flowers. Flowers are joy expressed in color, scent and form, lifting the heart, comforting, speaking of perfection and hope. If a mere plant can be so beautiful in a sordid world, what cannot the human spirit be? We talk to you through our flowers in a universal language, and when you notice us you cannot but respond, for what we have to express, you too have to express, and there is perfect harmony between us.

Behind these exquisite forms is a dancing delight of the spirit, forever moving freely in the perfect rhythms of God, sensitive to the slightest indications from on high, completely attuned to the whole. That too you are, in power, and we would simply remind you of yourselves. Can you not look more in that direction? Look within and you will find that high estate; look without and you will see it. Everything will speak of it if your eyes and ears are focused aright. But when you are out of focus, we can still remind you of the wonder of God. We can lift your consciousness.

Yes, we can lift your consciousness, but you, you can lift the consciousness of the planet. We can send out our rays of joy, like little lighthouses, but you, you can move and send your rays of joy to all the world. We would remind you to do it, and to do it now.

Angel of Sound

My sounds are everywhere. You may think that the wind rustling in the leaves is what produces sound, for example, but this is only the means I use for my effects. It is the same with your voices: the sound builders in my realms help each human to develop his own creative sound. There is no separated life. All is vibration, all is life, each range of manifestation of vibrations is assisted to life by beings.

I merely bring this to your notice to enlarge your vision. When you hear a skylark, you can now not only think of that beautiful sound as produced by the bird and its and our Maker, but by the angels and beings of sound who have helped to bring about that song. All these different aspects of life are to become more real to you.

More Sound Angels

We are of the Sound Angel branch, attending to light. We are emissaries on earth of Light and the Sun, to make sure that light is able to be revealed by life, and we do it by sound.

You do not understand this, and no wonder; human minds are not thinking on this subject. You think of photosynthesis and see no connection with sounds. You are limiting our ideas to science, but nevertheless look the process up. You have heard how each plant sounds a note, which attracts its builders to it, and how each human being has its own note which it *may or may not be sounding clearly. These notes have a very potent effect. In the plant, its note is life, because it brings forth substance to itself through the nature spirits. In people it is a thousand times more powerful, for when a person really is whole, sounding his or her own note, that means that all parts of the being are in harmony and therefore God can be there more fully. In that sense sound and light are one and the same: light, life, shines through any being sounding its own note. Sound comes first.*

You follow us there, but do not see how a being such as one of us can have anything to do with this process. We know the note for whatsoever is in our charge and we sound the individual notes, like tuning forks, to be picked up by the individual plant, being, or whatever it is . . . When a seed, for example, is ready to germinate, moisture and warmth do not automatically set its note vibrating. We do that, we set the little seed on its way and we forever hold out its note before it for it to follow. That note changes with the stages of the plants' growth, as it does with man, whose very voice changes as he advances into another stage.

And:

Humans sometimes have had an inkling of us. Think of the many medieval angels pictured playing instruments, or singing, or heaven, depicted with angels playing harps . . . You wonder at our function, thinking that archetypal devas seem powerful enough to sound notes. But that is not their job. Yes, humans have all power and on certain levels do sound the note; we assist on others. We sound a note . . . and the whole atmosphere vibrates with it. The note does not become louder, it becomes so intense, so penetrating that it permeates everything, the way mist permeates the air. It is a center of power, influencing whatever comes into its presence.

Angels of Color

We speak with a sweet voice, in praise of color. Color! It is not just our lifeblood, it is ourselves, the quality of our being. We are the essence of color, its embodiment, and though each color is utterly unique, when there is a change of color there is a change in our number....

We are rather like a sunset, always there in some portion of the earth but only appearing to you at certain times. You say a sunset is not 'personified' but is merely the effect of certain laws. Don't be too sure. Are you too not merely the effect of certain laws? There are many more beings, conscious beings, than you realize. If human thoughts have form and color, why should not God's thoughts have form and color, albeit changing?

You find it rather difficult to fit us into any scheme of things. Why bother? Why not just accept us as we are? After all, we are of another world and it is only natural that other worlds are different. Yet we do interpenetrate and influence your world, though in limitation. All in your static worlds are in certain limitation. For instance, you can paint your room a certain color and have that color around you all the time, but it is not living color unless you rise to a different world and feel its essence, our essence. Your colors get dirty and you have to wash them or somehow take off the layers of other substance which cloud their purity. In our world our radiance never dims, because it is being used in life. It is vibrating with what you might call 'purpose', a word which sounds prosaic and patterned and therefore would not exist in our world. Yet it conveys that we, color, are very much part of life.

You wonder how any of this can apply to life as you know it. We say there is a better, livelier and more colorful life to know and that, when you choose to be conscious of our sort of life, yours can be immeasurably enriched. You are set and static, like most humans, and when you rove with us in the field of living color, the very cells of your body are lifted and respond to a new influx.

214

Incense Cedar Deva

We have been greeting you through every tree, as you have us. With our emanations we bless you, and with our height and our aroma, as indeed we do to all life.

You have received the message about the necessity for mature trees; we simply repeat that as a preliminary to whatever these trees would say. Knowing that that need is in your consciousness, we continue with our blessings. We do not just stand here with our kind in the solitude, doing nothing. Look at what we are, look at the tremendous bulk of us thrusting up into the sky yet firmly rooted in the earth, made of you know not what, all from a tiny seed. Look at the marvels of our intricate trunks. These are but outward manifestations. Our work on other levels is just as mighty, just as detailed. Let us be, and thereby bless the earth.

We are meant to bring the beauty of infinity to the planet. We are meant to embody the qualities of strength, stability and everlastingness. It is a very high- vibrating grounded energy we channel, and you cannot have enough of it. Absorb it; it is a great privilege. We extend it to all who come, and release you with our love.

Afterword

In the summer of 2009 I moved to Findhorn, where I realised that full retirement was not an option. There was still something for me to do! The crisis of the mysterious death of bees all round the world began to occupy my attention. As a former bee keeper myself, this was of interest and concern to me. I decided to use my talk in the Inspired Action Conference in the spring of 2010 to bring this issue more to the forefront. The following is an extract from that talk, with a suggestion of what we can do about it.

AID FOR BEES

As many people know, especially those connected with bees, throughout the world billions of bees are mysteriously dying. They are simply flying away from their hives and disappearing, a phenomena called colony collapse disorder, CCD. Bee predators, looking for pollen or honey, even refrain from pilfering abandoned CCD-affected hives.

Bees are our most important crop pollinators, the vital link in our food chain of vegetables, flowers, fruits and nuts; they are responsible for pollinating a third of all food crops in our diet, and we need to know how to deal with this calamity. Although there are other insect and animal pollinators, the honeybee is most used. There are many human activities that need to be considered, such as the destruction of the bees' natural habitat through monoculture, agricultural practices, and the spread of deadly insecticides by local gardeners and crop-dusting airplanes (to name two among the many) that are contributing to a mighty pollen loss.

So far scientists have come up with not much more than a name for this looming environmental disaster, although of course they are attempting to find the source of the mysterious decline. One discovery is that the collapse of the bees' immune system has been an underpinning stressing factor. Also, a tiny Asian mite, *Varroa destructor*, which sucks vital juices from bees, migrated to America and Europe in the 1980s. This mite can kill a hive within a year. There are other emerging hypotheses for bee behavior.

Of course bees have had a checkered background. They have a history of being interbred, of being moved around, of being treated in ways that are helpful to humans but do not consider whether the bees themselves are being supported. They have been given pesticides that have proved lethal to them in various ways; some chemicals, for example, prevent them from remembering their colony's location, causing them to get lost. Fungal growth has been found in bees' guts, which may have produced toxins strong enough to kill young bees.

One stress which cannot but affect bees is the practice of industrial pollination. Huge cross-country trucks carry thousands of hives from one location to another, hurtling across the American continent for seasonal pollination. I have been appalled by this practice, because it considers only human gain without considering the effect on the bees, and exhibits careless and brutal behavior in their handling. In this situation they are exposed to acres upon acres of a mono-crop, such as nothing but apple trees, a highly unnatural situation for bees, who for thousands of years have worked in environments that gave them support and access to variety. Here, and in all bee management, their natural foraging and flowering seasonal habits need to be considered.

The problem is not diminishing, and the disease in managed hives does not dwindle. Einstein has been quoted as saying that if bees disappeared, we would do likewise within four years.

How can we, individually and in groups, best help the bees? One way is to offer our love in support of the successful functioning of bees.

Truly loving bees entails a rich energy exchange. It is a powerful imaginative process, in which we contact the wonderful love which is the deep core of all of us and then focus that love on the bees. When we give of ourselves with full force, results are bound to follow. We need passionate patience and persistence, for we humans have deeply polluted our world by using our gift of free will for selfish ends. We have the choice to change this, and to create a loving relationship with bees and the whole of our earth.

Some of us might choose to manage the Varroa mite, or take on a patch of land where we can provide healthy bee ecology in our own local area. If so, we will be contributing helpful time and energy there, but might not be dealing with the international problem. Then we would be putting the good before the best and I don't believe we want to do that.

The world today is in such need that the planet is telling us in many ways that unless we change, we will lose our habitat We can help in any way that opens to us, and a choice to help in a loving way is always before us. There is truth in the phrase that one person with God is in a majority. Action above all, lovingly and joyfully!

As an ex- beekeeper myself, I felt inspired to do something to help the bees and chose to meditate daily. We humans have been gifted with free will, so that we have the power of choice, and the capacity to make a conscious contact with our inner divinity, by whatever name or face we recognize that Presence. Every morning I spend 10 minutes repeating, with variations, the following invocation, adding what may come to mind, such as the wonder of this world that has billions of people, yet each one of us is different, or that Passion and Compassion are part of the loving energy evoked for the bees:

The successful functioning of bees on the planet is a vital need. I choose to invoke the vast loving power of my inner divinity to bring about the successful functioning of bees here and throughout the world, spreading joy everywhere.

We can all initiate change, and I trust that we will each do this for the bees in our own way.

Additional notes:

In the message from "John" quoted on page 125 several possibilities were suggested regarding my future work. In good time all of these came to pass. The message ended with the following statement, "Within your meditation and divine attunement lies the strength to accomplish what you must do." This promise proved true for me and it is my belief that it will also be true for all those who follow this enduring path.

Continuing life's adventure, I take a daily amble on a route where spaced seats are provided for me, as I often need to rest. I am well looked after at Findhorn. At age 92 I take delight in having many beautiful flowers adorning my living room, and I still invoke help for bees. I continue to give thanks to God and feel joy for all the wonderful people in my life, including you, the readers of this book. Hurray!

Dorothy Maclean

Dorothy Maclean 1923

Mother, Father and Thor outside family home in Guelph

Father, Mother and only grandson
Gordon Bruce Maclean

Mother, Brother Donald and Dorothy 1924

Dorothy and Older Brother Ken 1923

Brother Donald and Dog Thor 1938

Donald, Ken and Dorothy - Late 1920s

At the Beach Dorothy 1936

Off to play golf - left to right:
Muriel Stewart, Dorothy and Mary Savage 1933

Dorothy outside her Guelph home 1939

Sheena Govan

Wedding Day in Panama John and Dorothy 1942

Cutting the Cake John and Dorothy with the
Bishop of the Canal Zone officiating 1942

John and Dorothy in England 1943/44

Dorothy's British Certificate of Service

British Security Co-ordination

1940-1945

Certificate of Service

Dorothy Graham Wood

a member of British Security Co-ordination, has

performed valuable service of a confidential nature.

Wm Stephenson
Director

Dorothy's Panamanian Driver's License

Número de Orden __58538__

Nacionalidad __Inglesa__

Núm. Cédula Ident. _____

Edad __22__ Color __Blanco__

Pelo __Castaño__ Ojos __Azules__

Dirección __Bellavista #__

__Panamá, R.de P.__

Firma del Chofer _____

In the Findhorn Gardens Dorothy 1970

On the Patio of the Caravan at Findhorn
Dorothy and Peter and Eileen Caddy 1963

The New Cedarwood Findhorn Bungalows 1971

Peter and Eileen Caddy, Joannie Hartnell-Beavis,
R. Ogilvie Crombie (ROC) and Dorothy 1971

1990ˢ Findhorn Conference Event
David Spangler, Eileen and Peter Caddy and Dorothy

Dorothy and her giant Coleus plant, Belmont 1975

Liz Nichol, Freya Secrest (Brendan's and Lyra's mom)
and Dorothy

"Canadian" Lorian late 1970ˢ

Don and Liz Nichol, Myrtl Glines, David and Julie Spangler,
Dorothy, Roger and Katherine Collis, Freya Secrest,
Milenko and Kathi Matonovic, and others

Dorothy with godson Brendan Ziegler

Dorothy with Lyra Ziegler

Rare photo - Dorothy at rest early 1980's

Dorothy's etching of her father

Dorothy visiting Cusco, Peru

Dorothy's Vancouver "family"
Louise Day with two of her daughters

Judy McAllister and Dorothy visiting Greece

Dorothy at Machu Pichu

Judy McAllister, Dorothy and Driver, Thailand

Dorothy in front of Trevi Fountain, Rome

Overlooking Rio - Charles Peterson and Dorothy

Good friends - Dorothy and Erica Moore

Dorothy's portrait of her Mother and Father

Dorothy's favorite embroidery

In this water color sketch Dorothy deftly captures a look
of perplexity that greatly impressed her art instructors.

Katherine Collis and Dorothy with a feathered friend

Dorothy and Roger Collis at the Great Wall of China

Nancy Rumbel, Aaron Rabin (her son) and Dorothy

Cherry Blossom Time - Shin and Dorothy in Japan

Walking holiday in Washington State
Elana and Aaron Rabin and Dorothy

Katherine Collis and Dorothy
in front of a Stone Sphere of Costa Rica

Relaxing in Issaquah, WA with friends
Milenko Matanovic, Dorothy and Roger Collis

Dorothy in Hawaii, early 1990s

Ron Rabin, Dorothy and Nancy Rumbel

Dorothy's Eightieth Birthday Gathering 2000

Dorothy in front of the Guelph home as it is today

David Spangler, Dorothy and Julia Spangler

About the Author

Dorothy Maclean is one of the three founders of the Findhorn Community in Scotland. Following her inner contact with the Divine she came to communicate with the devic or angelic realms that over-light all aspects of existence. This helped Findhorn's legendary gardens bloom on most unpromising soil. She has traveled the world giving workshops and talks about her own inner practices and attunement to the Beloved. In this book she describes her amazing life and story.

About the Publisher

 Lorian Press is a private, for profit business which publishes works approved by the Lorian Association. Current titles by Dorothy Maclean and others can be found on the Lorian web site. Here is Dorothy with her publisher Jeremy Berg.

The Lorian Association is a not-for-profit educational organization. Its work is to help people bring the joy, healing, and blessing of their personal spirituality into their everyday lives. This spirituality unfolds out of their unique lives and relationships to Spirit, by whatever name or in whatever form that Spirit is recognized.

For information, go to www.lorian.org, email info@lorian.org, or write to:

The Lorian Association
P.O. Box 1368
Issaquah, WA 98027

Lightning Source UK Ltd.
Milton Keynes UK
UKHW01f2225230818
327686UK00001B/63/P